Indigenous Knowledges

Critical New Literacies

THE PRAXIS OF ENGLISH LANGUAGE TEACHING
AND LEARNING (PELT)

Series Editors

Tarquam McKenna (*Deakin University, Australia*)
Mark Vicars (*Victoria University, Australia*)

VOLUME 11

The titles published in this series are listed at *brill.com/cnli*

Indigenous Knowledges

Privileging Our Voices

Edited by

Tarquam McKenna, Donna Moodie and Pat Onesta

BRILL
SENSE

LEIDEN | BOSTON

Cover illustration: *Cultural Tree of Knowledge* by Deanne Gilson, a Wadawurrung woman graduated from NIKERI Institute. The image is about celebrating culture and traditional practices of Aboriginal and Torres Strait Islander Peoples.

All chapters in this book have undergone peer review.

The Library of Congress Cataloging-in-Publication Data is available online at http://catalog.loc.gov

Typeface for the Latin, Greek, and Cyrillic scripts: "Brill". See and download: brill.com/brill-typeface.

ISSN 2542-9396
ISBN 978-90-04-46163-5 (paperback)
ISBN 978-90-04-46162-8 (hardback)
ISBN 978-90-04-46164-2 (e-book)

Copyright 2021 by Tarquam McKenna, Donna Moodie and Pat Onesta. Published by Koninklijke Brill NV, Leiden, The Netherlands.
Koninklijke Brill NV incorporates the imprints Brill, Brill Hes & De Graaf, Brill Nijhoff, Brill Rodopi, Brill Sense, Hotei Publishing, mentis Verlag, Verlag Ferdinand Schöningh and Wilhelm Fink Verlag.
Koninklijke Brill NV reserves the right to protect this publication against unauthorized use. Requests for re-use and/or translations must be addressed to Koninklijke Brill NV via brill.com or copyright.com.

This book is printed on acid-free paper and produced in a sustainable manner.

Contents

Notes on Contributors   VII

1   Introduction   1
    Tarquam McKenna, Donna Moodie and Pat Onesta

2   Articulating 'Country' in Aboriginal and Torres Strait Islander Land Management: The Story of One Australian Post-Graduate Course   10
    Sue Nunn

3   Indigenous Knowledges and Global Knowledge Systems: Co-Actioning Thresholds in Australian Science Curricula and Initial Teacher Education   32
    Gabrielle Fletcher and Kate Chealuck

4   Passing Time   54
    Kelly Menzel

5   Where the Rivers Meet   68
    Jodie Satour, Naomi Nirupa David, Rosemarie Garner and Gracie Scala Adamson

6   Thought Ritual: An Indigenous Data Analysis Method for Research   87
    Tyson Yunkaporta and Donna Moodie

7   The Value of an Integrated Relational and Culturally Responsive Pedagogy in Teaching Aboriginal and Torres Strait Islander Teacher Education Students   97
    Lisa Bell and Kate Chealuck

8   A Meeting of Freshwater and Saltwater: Opening the Dialogue of Aboriginal Concepts of Culture within an Academic Space   117
    Kelly Menzel and Liz Cameron

9   Critical Social Work from Indigenous Perspectives   147
    William Abur

10 Conclusion   162
    Tarquam McKenna

Notes on Contributors

Editors

Tarquam McKenna
is a Professor and Chair of Indigenous Knowledge (Research) at Deakin University, Melbourne, Australia. He has been active as an arts psychotherapist for thirty-five years and is past president and honorary life member of the Australian, New Zealand and Asian Creative Arts Therapies Association (ANZACATA, formerly ANZATA). He is keenly interested in qualitative research methods and especially their applicability to Indigenous social and emotional health using 'the arts'. Tarquam has taught, researched and supervised widely in the area of the arts, gender and education. His praxis continues to examine social justice and the legacies of Paulo Freire in particular, and how colonisation has impacted on multiple lives around the world.

Donna Moodie
(Goomeri/Gamilraay) is a Lecturer in the School of Education, Faculty of Humanities, Arts, Social Sciences and Education (HASSE) at the University of New England (UNE), Armidale, New South Wales. Previously, she was a Senior Lecturer with the Institute of Koorie Education (IKE), Deakin University, Waurn Ponds campus, Geelong. She now teaches in both undergraduate and postgraduate units in Contextual Studies at UNE. Donna is due to submit her PhD thesis in 2021. Her thesis explores better engagement processes between Indigenous and non-Indigenous people and organisations. She is also a practising artist and enjoys painting; her preferred medium is acrylic on canvas.

Pat Onesta
hails from the United States. He has worked in Hawai'i with a number of Native Hawaiian communities and organisations in the community development field as a Community Planner. Prior to this, Pat spent a number of years working in banking and financial services in New York. He is currently the Higher Degree by Research and Research Assistant at the National Indigenous Knowledges, Education, Research and Innovation (NIKERI) Institute at Deakin University.

Authors

William Abur
is a Lecturer in social work at the National Indigenous Knowledges, Education, Research and Innovation (NIKERI) Institute, Faculty of Arts and Education,

Deakin University. He has worked and conducted research in the areas of social work, mental health, refugee settlement and participation in employment and sport.

Gracie Scala Adamson
is the seventh daughter of an Italian migrant family, raised in Melbourne and now residing in Geelong. Gracie's cultural upbringing enabled her to appreciate that there are many different ways of perceiving and understanding the world. Primarily working in early childhood education, as a kindergarten teacher, Gracie's continued studies have now brought her to teaching in higher education, at the Bachelor of Education (Early Years) at the National Indigenous Knowledges, Research and Innovation Institute (formerly the Institute of Koorie Education) at Deakin University.

Lisa Bell
has more than 35 years of teaching experience in primary and tertiary settings in Victoria and the Northern Territory. She is currently a Lecturer at the NIKERI Institute, Deakin University, where she has worked since 2011 in the Bachelor of Education (Primary).

Liz Cameron
(Dharug) is a Professor and Chair of Indigenous Research at Deakin University. Her role involves forming collaborative partnerships within an Indigenous framework within the creative arts, land, and sea traditional practices and Health. Liz is also a practicing artist and uses visual dialogues to enhance learning experiences.

Kate Chealuck
is a Lecturer of Education in the School of Education and the National Indigenous Knowledges, Research and Innovation Institute (formerly the Institute of Koorie Education) at Deakin University. She is a P-12 science teacher and currently teaches science education, and design and digital technology education, to primary and early childhood pre-service teachers in both undergraduate and postgraduate degrees. Her research interests include building teacher confidence in teaching science in primary schools and early childhood settings; teacher interactions with science in online environments; and co-actioning Indigenous Knowledges with western science teaching and learning.

Naomi Nirupa David
is a Lecturer of Education (Early Childhood) at the School of Education and the National Indigenous Knowledges, Research and Innovation Institute (formerly

the Institute of Koorie Education) at Deakin University. She is currently completing Doctoral Studies that focus on children's identities and family curriculum. Having worked internationally and in Australia in both kindergarten and community-based projects, she has an interest in the field of advocacy and early childhood education. Her research looks closely at identity-making in transnational families.

Gabrielle Fletcher
(Gundungurra) is a Traditional Custodian from the Blue Mountains of New South Wales. She is an Associate Professor and Director of the National Indigenous Knowledges, Education, Research and Innovation (NIKERI) Institute, Deakin University. She has previously worked within Indigenous spaces at the University of Newcastle, Macquarie University and Curtin University, and has a background in Critical and Cultural Studies, Indigenous Studies and Creative Writing. Her work examines Indigenous authenticity in post-colonial spaces, mobilising ficto-criticism and creative non-fiction as strategies of encounter. She is increasingly interested in post-humanism and narrativity. Gabrielle is grounded by her experience in Indigenous community and the responsibilities of remembering.

Rosemarie Garner
has been teaching for more than 20 years in both the UK and Australia spanning pre-school, primary and tertiary settings. Since 2010 she has worked as a Lecturer in the Bachelor of Education (Early Years) at the National Indigenous Knowledges, Research and Innovation Institute (formerly the Institute of Koorie Education) at Deakin University.

Kelly Menzel
is a proud (Ngadjuri) woman from the Adelaide Hills in South Australia. She is the youngest and only girl in her in her family, a child of teachers and a nurse by trade. Kelly is a healer, teacher and learner. She is a holder of her ancestral knowledge and still has very much to learn. She has been in adult education for 20 years and is a Senior Lecturer in an Indigenous learning space.

Sue Nunn
has been a lecturer at NIKERI for over 20 years. Her early graduate teaching experience was gained in a newly independent Zimbabwe and then in the southern regions of Sudan. During this time, she learned the value of contextual and creative teaching. She has built up her experience through learning from her students and designing context-based curriculum design in natural and cultural resource management and, now, Land and Sea Country Management.

Suzanne was part of a review of the experiences of people working in the arena of Joint Management in Victoria in 2018 and is currently designing a digital resource that can be used to inform university students about the management of Land and Sea Country in Australia. Other interests include the use of film as a way to bring Country into course design and teaching.

Jodie Satour

is an (Eastern Arrernte) woman and Senior Social Work academic from Alice Springs, in the Northern Territory. Her teaching is situated in transformative pedagogy by changing the environmental landscape and learning for First Nations Peoples whose voices have been excluded and marginalised within society.

Tyson Yunkaporta

(Wik) is an academic, an arts critic, and a researcher who belongs to the Apalech Clan in far north Queensland. He carves traditional tools and weapons and also works as a Senior Lecturer in Indigenous Knowledges at Deakin University.

CHAPTER 1

Introduction

Tarquam McKenna, Donna Moodie and Pat Onesta

For 65,000 years, the First Peoples of Australia have consistently passed on their Indigenous ways of knowing through law, lore and knowledge systems acquired through millennia of experience and oral (historical) anecdotes. This knowledge, passed on through rituals and practise, embraces the centrality of story to the identity of people. In Chapter 6 of this volume, Donna Moodie and Tyson Yunkaporta elaborate on the oracy of knowing, stating that the act of shared understanding is the "... hybridisation of ancient oral culture practice and contemporary thought experiment, grounded in Aboriginal protocols of communal knowledge production".

This edition in the *Critical New Literacies Series* examines how, and indeed *if*, education in 21st century Australia, with its various levels of complexity and with significance, can keep the First Peoples of Australia's culture and collective memories alive. In Chapter 2, the reader is reminded by Sue Nunn (citing Carter, 1993) of the capacity of story "becoming a humanistic way to communicate to a range of audiences the personalised, intimate, idiosyncratic way in which educators practice their craft in institutional settings". These stories are critical in their capacity to impact on what Gabrielle Fletcher and Kate Chealuck note in Chapter 3 as an imperative: that we must 're-cast' the "embedding of meaningful Indigenous content in our work". They propose a framework based on efficacy, and consider Indigenous Knowledges as a 'threshold concept'. This concept takes into account the subjectivities, epistemologies and context of such systems, and provides relevance and inclusion for Aboriginal and Torres Strait Islander People in the university context. The subjectivities are the stories presented in the next eight chapters – what Fletcher and Chealuck would refer to as eight "bearer[s] of agency".

The reader is asked to critique the knowledge presented here and whether the work can be considered a threshold concept. How do we read this work without manifesting 'white dominance' (Land, 2015, p. 146)? As a reader, you are asked to 'wander around' these stories and 'build trust' in these tales from the field. Land (2015), referring to the pre-eminent scholar Linda Tuhiwai Smith, reminds us that "an indigenizing project ... works to disconnect many of the cultural ties between the settler society and its metropolitan highland". As readers of this book, you must re-centre the "landscapes, images, languages, themes and stories" in the Indigenous world (Smith, 1999, p. 146). The primacy of Country is such a core issue to learning and engaged relational learning. The fact that sapient and sentient beings are a reality – albeit metaphysical for doubters – is a reality not always understood. Country has a strong presence in these readings.

In Chapter 5, Naomi Nirupa David, Jodie Satour, Rosemarie Garner and Gracie Adamson address how 'rivers meet' and ask that we see the conceptions of community landscapes, teaching and learning, power and agency as intersecting thematically in their teaching delivery. Identity, power and agency are at the heart of this collection of writings. Specifically, David and her colleagues set out to address identity, authority and Country especially by questioning the academy's taken-for-granted actions and thinking about who they could be and should be as teaching professionals in this special space. This unique space is the interface between Indigenous and non-Indigenous staff working together at Deakin University. This 'space of confluence' attends to the 'recentering' narrative as noted earlier, but it is also space where counter-narrative is "evident when students weave" their own journeys with the cultural knowledge and find a place where intersections can "enable their identity to be recognised and thrive". All these chapters are ultimately paying attention to delivering a space of belonging.

This volume of work contextualises and contributes to the issues of appropriate and inappropriate use and understanding of Indigenous knowing among non-First Peoples (white) of Australia. These chapters do not explicitly bring to the fore the fact that sacredness is central to all of the First Peoples of Australia's educational and lifeworld processes. But the work of profound meaning is woven around relationships, connecting, disclosure and intimacies of encounter. This is expressed by Aboriginal and Torres Strait Islander or First Nation's own epistemological and ontological understanding of the lifeworld of this unique group of people. This is not without challenge. Liz Cameron and Kelly Menzel remind us in Chapter 8:

> a consequence of colonisation, structural inequalities, different cultural norms and worldview, different ways of speaking have emerged among Indigenous and non-Indigenous lines. Because Australia's dominant culture is white and patriarchal, white patriarchy has become deeply embedded as standard, neutral and legitimate. Therefore, it is requisite for Indigenous people to code-switch, to adapt to the dominant culture to improve our prospects. This requires work on the part of the 'switcher' and places no onus on the listener. It is incredibly difficult, marginalising, disempowering and a form of assimilation.

As authors, we wonder why and how the matter of Indigenous Knowledge got lost in the forced structural inequalities noted throughout this work; or how a dominant white and patriarchal society took it away. We wonder why, while Australia expands, the issues of representation, power, and control are only occasionally critiqued from the perspective of Australia's First Peoples. How can we disrupt the white 'normal, neutral and legitimate' marginalising prospects? This quietness or so-called lack of critique, or maybe amnesia, is not because Australia's First Peoples have failed to comment on the performance of those who have authority; it is the performance of those with authority that has clearly enforced silences. This book disrupts these silences, giving voice to the ignored and suppressed. Only those who have always listened and are prepared to continue to hear the comments of these fourteen authors ultimately matter in this conversation.

An objective of this book is to bring the voices of the First Peoples of Australia to a broader audience by yarning loud and clear around education at Deakin University and especially at its National Indigenous Knowledges Education, Research and Innovation (NIKERI) Institute (formerly the Institute of Koorie Education [IKE]).[1] This is where the authors all worked at the time of writing. We hope the book gives power to the voices of Australia's First Peoples, with compelling descriptions and engagement around our learning and teaching.

Many cultural misunderstandings still prevail for both non-First Peoples and First Peoples of Australia on considering the knowledge systems and the needs of the latter. This collection of work emphasises the need for cultural appropriateness in education in a way that, in the past, may not have respectfully acknowledged Australia's First Peoples' capacity to engage with the academy. There is a sense of engagement here, with the authors attending to the spiritual, physical and educational needs of individuals, their families and especially their communities. The place of community cannot be emphasised enough and while, in the past, holistic, collaborative and community educational practices may have been seen as 'less valid', these writings now serve to acknowledge the practices of the educational workplace.

Whilst education can and should be used to address Indigenous cultural, familial and social issues, we are called to not "pass"; a call that is relevant to all scholars. Passing is an adaptation to oppression when the concealment of identity is experienced. In Chapter 4, Kelly Menzel states she will not pass and her work is a provocation to others not to pass or collude with the practice of passing. Kelly demonstrates her "Indigeneity by refusing to be white". She calls this race refusal her refusal to be white and draws on the scholarship of Kowal and Paradies (2017, p. 108), noting "assimilation, white sociality and everyday racialization" are interrupted when whiteness is refused. Her chapter closes with this loud comment:

> My refusal of whiteness is my way of challenging systemic racist practices and policy that were established when Australia was invaded and colonised. It is also about exhibiting hope. I hope to be part of a regenerative conversation that challenges stereotypes and sows the seeds of transformation.

Australia's First Peoples are utilising a unique epistemology within their communities from individual and localised contexts. At the time of the first contact between the First Peoples of Australia and the colonisers, differences in views and values arose, with ontological clashes emerging from differing epistemologies centred on the ongoing spirituality and philosophies of existence.

The ontologies and epistemologies that the First Peoples of Australia use begin in and with the Dreamtime. In their models of knowing, Ancestral Beings created the world and Country of each group of First Peoples. Dreaming might be seen through the translation of the word alcheringa from Arunta/Aranda (Stanner, 2009, p. 57, cited in Martin, 2010), a Central Australian language. In these writings, we acknowledge that Australia's First Peoples share concepts that are similar but slightly different in specific translation. For example, alcheringa is more commonly known than bulurru, the Far North Queensland Djabugay word, which translates into Story-time – the time of the world's making (Bottoms, 1999, p. 1). Another example is the translation from Pitjantjatjara and Yankunytjatjara of tjukurpa (Eickelkamp, 1999, p. 88) into the Dreaming. This is enlivened through the retelling of stories where ceremony is essential as both a process of reflection and a series of lessons for the First Nations People's lives.

Again in Chapter 6, Tyson Yunkaporta and Donna Moodie attend to the knowledge system of the story with a data analysis approach that is unique to their research. This chapter generated from their experiences as Aboriginal and Torres Strait Islander individuals in their respective communities. They recognise and privilege other ways of being and knowing. These two authors attest that their model of inquiry and research practices honours "a world of many worlds, worlds including sentient beings usually regarded as inanimate, reinstating their knowledges and healing Country through interaction" with multiple sites. In many ways, the space of Dreaming is central to their chapter as well as the more familiar term, synchronicity, which is used to consider the quality of encounter that is kin to the notion of Dreaming. 'Thought ritual' as a way of knowing is, in their words:

experienced as a startling moment of synchronicity and convergence in the researcher's lived reality, whether on Country or in cyberspace or a workspace. It may emerge as an unexpected or unexplainable synchronicity within the data itself.

Donaldo Macedo (1999) writes of the need to understand "that a global comprehension of Indigenous Knowledge (IK) cannot be achieved through the reductionist binarism of Western versus Indigenous knowledge", and "the essence of IK is found in the experience of the colonised". Semali and Kincheloe (1999, p. xi) offer the following understanding:

> the study of indigenous knowledge injects a dramatic dynamic into the analysis of knowledge production and the rules of scholarship. Such a dynamic opens a new discussion in not only the discipline of education, but in a variety of scholarly fields including philosophy, cultural studies, agriculture, health, nutrition, music and religion.

So the knowledge in this book can be situated as shown in Table 1.1.

TABLE 1.1   Knowledge in this book

Our knowledge	Western knowledge
Ways of valuing	Axiology
Ways of knowing	Epistemology
Ways of doing	Methodology
Ways of being	Ontology

Understanding the place of Indigenous Knowledge in the academy creates a compelling case for change. How do we translate this to practice with knowledge, philosophy, application and support? We all need to 'buy-in' through our personal philosophy, informing our professional practice and our professional orientation. We all need to understand the part we continue to play in the colonising process and indeed the decolonising process. Indigenous Knowledge is no longer concealed by processes of colonisation and will not be further silenced. It exists, always has done and always will. It is uncovered, not hidden. Whilst Indigenous Knowledge was concealed, another signifier of colonialism has been the silencing of Australia's First Peoples' voices (Nabobo-Baba, 2004, p. 17; Ashcroft, Griffiths, & Tiffin, 1998, p. 175; Stanner, 2009, p. 182, cited in Martin, 2010) and language – "the political condition of colonised people is bound up with language" (Ashcroft, Griffiths, & Tiffin, 1998, p. 83). The taking of "Aboriginal languages away from Aboriginal peoples in the name of a process toward a universal English language [being] the initial step" (Battiste, 2000, p. 264), when accompanied by restrictions on access to the learning of English, produced silence.

As already stated, a goal of this collection of writings is the interruption of silence. We have set out to attend to that which cannot be constricted. We have re-covered, re-vealed and un-covered to disrupt the hiding of the important realities of Indigenous ways of knowing. In so doing, we are bringing back the peripheral realities of Indigenous Knowledge – bringing this knowledge back to the centre.

In Chapter 9, William Abur recalls that history

> … tells us that institutions played and are still playing a big role by continuously pushing Indigenous communities to the edge of services which causes those communities to be viewed as fringe-dwellers. At the same time, these institutions have viewed Indigenous peoples as having 'extreme need of social services, education, housing and child protection services' (Green & Baldry, 2008, p. 390). Well, indigenous communities have been victims of brutal policies from the government since the beginning of colonisation and that victimisation is continuing in some institutions today, such as hospitals, community health centres, education and police departments. This continuous pushing and practices are problematic and also exist in higher education fields.

Education and training require that we see the embodied encounter through the yarn as a way of threading together the de-colonised lives of the First Peoples of Australia, to redress their silences and the notion of these women and men as 'problematic'. We are reminded that by following the threads woven in the yarn, the unseen and unheard stories of Stolen Generations and their descendants as the First Peoples of Australia can now be heard. The loss they have suffered is not just physical or psychological but has impacted on the sense of Country. The fabric of the lives of these multifarious peoples is complex, and it is clear that the intersection of stories expounded here is more than the warp and the weft; there is a tangled web of interactions beyond mere thematic analysis. The consciousness of the First Peoples of Australia permeates the work of this education.

In Chapter 7, Lisa Bell and Kate Chealuck instil the belief that "the integration of a relational and culturally responsive pedagogical approach is effective for our students within their teacher education degree as it centralises relationships as the key to nourishing student engagement, achievement and wellbeing". They are also positioned by the historical notion that Aboriginality in Australia, and the diverse reflections of identity, will require us to hold to an acceptance that the First Peoples of Australia are engaged in "social and political activity as well as a psychological one ... embedded in a cultural and historical context" (Boud, Keogh, & Walker, 1988, p. 17).

Through in-depth, thoughtful reflection on significant life experiences, education incorporates knowledge of Australia's social, cultural and political movements at times of momentous life-making events. As Liz Cameron recalls in Chapter 8:

> Reflecting on historical, cultural ignorance and misconceptions based on flawed assumptions produce(s) feelings of despair as many of these notions remain prevalent today. I argue that cultural knowledges and practices continue to be ignored and/or undermined and are 'weakened to the extent that they fail in their capacity to imbue individual existence with meaning and value' (Halloran, 2004, p. 4). I wonder today who has read my thesis or does it sit on a dusty shelf.

The educational encounters described in this book are negative and positive for the individual and community alike. The encounters presented help us deliberate on the impact of moments in time and cultural and historical 'movements' on the lives of the First Peoples of Australia. The authors mirror these movements, as these too are physical, philosophical and psychological for the women and men who contributed to this volume. The lives of those written about in these chapters are within the 'bigger' yarn. But without their small yarns, there is no big story.

The First Peoples of Australia are still the most disadvantaged population group in Australia, perhaps in the world. Education should help to close the 17-year life expectancy gap between First Peoples and non-First Peoples of Australia. Has the western world failed to honour the notions of knowledge of many First Peoples? The process of education as elucidated here would ideally create community and build trust. These values commit us to caring, if we care we can build trust. This is the basis of relationships. We hold to the idea that education, with the use of traditional knowledge systems alongside mainstream education services, can and should be envisioned. In closing, it is because of obligation to give back to the community that we must bring these complex experiences to the academy. In so doing, we connect, co-create and disrupt the perception of only the white way of doing and being.

Note

1 In 2020, the Institute of Koorie Education (IKE) was renamed the National Indigenous Knowledges, Education, Research and Innovation (NIKERI) Institute. The Institute grew out of work that began in 1986 when two programs for Aboriginal and Torres Strait Islander people were offered through Deakin University's Faculty of Education. The Koorie Teacher Education Program (KTEP), a Victorian community-based program in teacher training for mature-aged Koories, began to address the need for Indigenous teachers in Australian schools. From these early beginnings, the Institute currently offers courses in Arts, Psychology, Health and Medicine, Social Work, Law, Nursing, Public Health, Indigenous post-graduate research and Land and Sea Country Management.

References

Aboriginal Pedagogy. (n.d.). Homepage. https://www.8ways.online/about

Ashcroft, B., Griffiths, G., & Tiffin, H. (1998). *Key concepts in post-colonial studies*. Routledge.

Battiste, M. (Ed.). (2000). *Reclaiming Indigenous voice and vision*. UBC Press.

Bottoms, T. (1999). *Djabugay country: An Aboriginal history of tropical North Queensland*. Allen and Unwin.

Boud, D., Keogh, R., & Walker, D. (1988). What is reflection in learning? In D. Boud, R. Keogh, & D. Walker (Eds.), *Reflection: Turning experience into learning* (pp. 7–17). Kogan Page.

Carter, J. (1993). The place of story in the study of teaching and teacher education. *Educational Researcher, 1*, 5–18.

Eickelkamp, U. (1999). *'Don't ask for stories ...': The women from Ernabella and their art*. Aboriginal Studies Press.

Green, S., & Baldry, E. (2008). Building Indigenous Australian social work. *Australian Social Work, 61*(4), 389–402.

Halloran, M. (2004). *Cultural maintenance and trauma in Indigenous Australia*. Paper presented at the 23rd Annual Australian and New Zealand Law and Historical Society Conference, Perth.

Kowal, E., & Paradies, Y. (2017) Indigeneity and the refusal of whiteness. *Postcolonial Studies, 20*(1), 101–117.

Land, C. (2015). *Decolonizing solidarity: Dilemmas and directions for supporters of Indigenous struggles*. Zed Books Ltd.

Lawlor, R. (1991). *Voices of the first day: Awakening in the Aboriginal dreamtime*. Inner Traditions.

Martin, J. H. (2010). W. E. H. Stanner: The dreaming and other essays [Book review]. *Australian Aboriginal Studies, 1*, 124.

Macedo, D. (1999). Decolonizing Indigenous knowledge. In L. M. Semali & J. L. Kincheloe (Eds.), *What is Indigenous knowledge? Voices from the academy* (p. ix). Garland Publishing.

Nabobo-Baba, U. (2004). *Talanoa and Indigenous Pacific research: Some reflections.* Paper presented at the Second Pacific Graduates Symposium, Fale Pasifika, The University of Auckland.

Semali, L., & Kincheloe, L. J. (1999). *What is Indigenous knowledge? Voices from the academy.* Falmer Press.

Smith, L. T. (1999). *Decolonizing methodologies: Research and Indigenous peoples.* Zed Books.

Stanner, W. E. H. (2011). *The dreaming & other essays.* Black Inc.

Steering Committee for the Review of Government Service Provision. (2007). *Overcoming Indigenous disadvantage: Key indicators report.* Productivity Commission.

CHAPTER 2

Articulating 'Country' in Aboriginal and Torres Strait Islander Land Management: The Story of One Australian Post-Graduate Course

Sue Nunn

Abstract

The inclusion of Indigenous Knowledges and the articulation of culturally guided land management values and practices within post-graduate curriculum design is rare in Australia. Currently, there is one course in the country that includes the words 'Country' and 'land and sea' in its title. This consciously assumes that all Australia is Aboriginal and Torres Strait Islander land and is worked upon and managed as a cultural landscape.

This chapter traces the history of one enduring post-graduate course as it has morphed and changed over a 25-year period whilst responding to land justice issues as prioritised by Aboriginal and Torres Strait Islander land managers and their Communities. One of the features of the course is the expression of Aboriginal and Torres Strait Islander cultural agency to drive priorities and goals to institute land-justice projects and programs on Country. For the duration of their study, students apply Aboriginal and Torres Strait Island cultural perspectives to create new and innovative approaches that will transfer knowledge and skills into land management practices leading not only to the intensification of cultural practices but also the education of government land management agencies.

By examining, reflecting and writing the story of the course's history, a rich and compelling argument emerges that supports the reality that academia can not only be a site for social change and student mobilisation but also a place where the inclusion of Indigenous Knowledges can support future curricula design based on a distinctive land justice framework.

Keywords

Indigenous Knowledges – Australia – curriculum design – land justice – Aboriginal and Torres Strait Islander

1   Introduction

In 2019, I attended a three-day Recognised Aboriginal Party (RAP)[1] Forum that brought together approximately 30 participants who actively work in the land management sector in Victoria. This included Aboriginal Elders, CEOs, cultural heritage officers, archaeologists, Traditional Owners, Aboriginal Heritage Council representatives and local council members. The aim of the RAP is to safeguard Country, Aboriginal stories, cultural practices and cultural landscapes. Because of their composition and importance, bi-annual RAP forums are serious get-togethers.

One of the guest speakers – the CEO of the Gunditj Mirring Traditional Owner Aboriginal Corporation – announced that the Budj Bim Cultural Landscape nomination had been accepted by the World Heritage United Nations Educational, Scientific and Cultural Organization (UNESCO)[2] panel and its declaration would most likely be announced in Azerbaijan in the coming months. As was predicted, Budj Bim was declared Australia's first Aboriginal Cultural landscape and is now recognised as one of the world's oldest and most extensive aquaculture systems, conveying knowledge retained through oral history and the continuity of cultural practice for thousands of years. It is now considered a landmark in Australian heritage history (UNESCO, 2019).

As I listened to the speakers discussing cultural heritage matters, I started to wonder why this RAP Forum felt so significant to me. After some time reflecting, I came to realise there were at least six people in the room who had either been associated with, graduated from, or were studying the course I have been involved with for the last 20 years. Now called the Graduate Diploma of Land and Sea Country Management, the course has been offered at the Institute of Koorie Education (IKE)[3] for 25 years. Aboriginal and Torres Strait Islander students from all over Australia come to the Institute to study the management of Country in all its facets.

The associations gathered in the room that day stirred me to consider what particular contribution this course has made towards increasing the presence of Aboriginal and Torres Strait Islander men and women working in the arena of Indigenous land management throughout the state of Victoria and Australia. In a rather modest way, this chapter tells the story of the course and documents its history. In doing so, it relays how important a post-graduate university course can be in contributing to the inclusion of Aboriginal and Torres Strait voices in the representation and management of Australia's cultural landscape. I write as a non-indigenous woman who has worked in the field of higher education and community engagement for 30 years and acknowledges the Wadawurrung Country in which she lives and works.

More and more, the telling of stories is becoming a humanistic way to communicate to a range of audiences the personalised, intimate, idiosyncratic way in which educators practice their craft in institutional settings. Scholarly research is also more commonly inspired by personal experience, which can then be used to direct the analysis of teachers' knowledge (Carter, 1993). In this case, writing about this course as a form of personal narrative gives the course a voice and presents to the reader the nuances, stuff of life and dynamic nature of its delivery (Clandinin & Connelly, 1987, p. 499). It also contributes to explaining the impacts and consequences of particular institutional practices, such as those expressed at a post-graduate university level, which have the power to either transform or, in some cases, underwhelm (Elbaz, 1991). It is a story that documents the course origins, and the features that underpin the course design, content and delivery. Finally, it offers reflections and insights that are anchored in my experience of developing course materials and teaching into the course.

To place the course in context today, contemporary land management in Australia is conducted within a complex partnering matrix between Traditional Owner groups, government agencies, Elders, Community, not-for-profit sectors, corporations and a wide-ranging combination of scientific environmental restoration strategies. Traditional Indigenous Knowledges are now, however, widely recognised as a valuable and indeed necessary component of that 'scientific' mix. This is having the effect of transforming agency relationships and partnerships in a largely positive way (Altman, Buchanan, & Larson, 2007; Barbour & Schlesinger, 2012). This course in particular has been designed to include and enhance Indigenous Knowledges as well as enhance transferable skills for Aboriginal and Torres Strait Islander practitioners working in this quite broad arena. In many ways, the course has walked alongside this transformation and now sees graduates working in the fields of land and sea Country management throughout Australia.

2 Conversation with the Curriculum: The Lived Experience

Whilst researching for this chapter and now looking back, it became clear that a significant process began 27 years ago between the local Aboriginal Community and Deakin University. Victorian Elders created a partnership that would ultimately lead to the re-imagining of a course that could offer a career-pathway and, most importantly, prompt a change in the way cultural heritage was managed and represented in Victoria. To support this process, Deakin University was granted $100,000 from the National (Priority) Reserve Fund to design a course that would offer the skills, capacity and qualifications to inject a number of new cultural heritage officers into strategic positions at National Parks, Aboriginal cultural heritage organisations, Keeping Places[4] and Aboriginal Cooperatives. The idea was to develop and deliver an innovative equity program that would respond to the expressed needs of the Victorian Aboriginal Community to establish a post-graduate course that would recognise "Koorie[5] cultural and natural resources Management, Knowledge and Perspectives" (Deakin University, 1995, p. 1).

In essence, the course would be called upon to produce post-graduates who would clearly articulate their voice and bring Aboriginal Knowledges into workplaces and organisations. This would provide the management skills necessary to actively re-orientate the cultural heritage industry in Victoria. As part of the project, incoming students also informed the development of a new unit called Koorie Perspectives. This was aimed at non-Indigenous Deakin students who would be able to self-reflect in their future roles as heritage consultants, consciously locating Aboriginal perspectives at the forefront of Aboriginal cultural heritage interpretation. For Aboriginal Elders at the time, the prominent issues around cultural heritage that were glaringly obvious were: insufficient protective powers of state cultural heritage legislation; the inadequate number of Aboriginal archaeologists working in the field; limited access to policy-making decisions and a lack of understanding of localised place-based Aboriginal Knowledge and history. It aimed to instigate a new, fresher and comprehensive course more relevant to Aboriginal people who see Country, history, and environment as a cultural landscape and who want to practice culturally-informed management of land and heritage. It would also be a course that assumed custodial responsibility as a priority for all students who took up a place in the course. In hindsight, it could be said that what it ultimately achieved was to plant the seed for Deakin University to recognise that tertiary education could also serve as a conduit for the long drive towards land justice.

After focussed consultation, it was decided the best way to get a course up and running in the timeframe required, was to modify an existing course, characterised as a 'museum and curatorial course'. This was targeted largely at international and Australian practitioners who worked with museums, collections, cultural heritage conservation and protection. It was decided that existing course guidelines could be updated to become more inclusive of Aboriginal Knowledges and actively respond to Aboriginal needs. The course would be delivered at the IKE which, eight years beforehand, had started to offer Bachelor courses in a Community Based Delivery (CBD)[6] method of study, solely for Aboriginal and Torres Strait Islander students from various communities around Australia.

To have a course offered in the Faculty of Science and Technology was particularly important to the Community Elders. The consultation committee argued this requirement would put Indigenous Knowledge on an equal footing with the 'scientific knowledge' that had historically dominated environmental science and the accompanying assumptions that underpinned common research methodologies. The new approach would concentrate on two-way knowledge and learning, with the reciprocal exchange of knowledge and perspectives leading the way. A new critical conversation, particularly with archaeologists, was evident and, as such, the Community required skilled and confident graduates who would enter the on-site working space of cultural heritage protection. At that time in Victoria, there was a recognised need for Koori Cultural Officers to undertake formal professional qualifications to increase their access and say in the arena of cultural heritage protection, with the aim of gaining more control over the representation of Aboriginal history and culture. A common objective was to reinterpret the existing static 'museum' representation of media signage, and transform it into a 'living tradition', more representative and relevant to contemporary Aboriginal life.

The course content, entry point, teaching pedagogy and assessment task requirements also became points of difference that ushered in new and innovative approaches. The inclusion of cultural knowledges and Aboriginal perspectives were to become key components. This motivated assessment task design that would guide students to articulate their own connection to Country and so use localised projects that would be of more relevance to themselves and their communities. The context in which students would situate their tasks were to become more relevant and detailed. Big picture issues were also to be examined with a greater focus on real-world discussion. This would include recommendations for policy changes in cultural heritage legislation, new avenues to become part of decision-making processes, and the inclusion of local Aboriginal language in interpretative media. Additionally, of critical consideration in preparation for future course enrolments was the course entry requirements. Community Elders wanted an alternative entry point that would recognise an equivalence of Aboriginal people's extensive cultural experience. This would ensure that appropriately aged and experienced applicants could gain entry.

Recruitment of the first course cohort was completed in 1994, after extensive consultation with Elders who were asked to provide a recommendation from their local Aboriginal Community. The applicants were chosen by a panel of both Aboriginal Elders and university teaching staff. Thirteen Aboriginal Elders were admitted into the course, which, at this stage was called the Graduate Certificate in Environment and Heritage Interpretation.

Over the next year, the newly enrolled students would become the co-producers of a process that would develop into a unique post-graduate course. Whilst conventional course design practices are normally determined by university staff, a new re-framing of the course content and approach took place through a more collaborative process. The early preparation of the course direction and re-writing of course materials was informed largely by the students as Elders. A number of significant fieldtrips were established as 'fact finding missions', taking students to key organisations where Aboriginal cultural artefacts and history were curated and represented. These spaces included museums, Keeping Places, cultural centres, art galleries and, what was then called, Aboriginal Affairs Victoria (AAV). These visits focussed attention on questions such as: 'Who owns the past?', 'How are interpretative displays designed?' and 'How is the custodianship of material culture managed?' Along the way, the whole 'language' of the heritage industry and its core business was interrogated. Staff and students concluded that interpretative signage, or the absence of it, could actually be described as a tool of subjugation, marginalisation and oppression. What the students learned from their own research during the course was taken home to families and Communities and became the stimulus for suggesting change.

Other on-Country fieldtrips included visiting the Tindale collection[7] in South Australia. This was followed up with a Community visit to Camp Coorong and the Point McLeay Aboriginal Station sites of a former mission, and other specialist collection libraries. During these visits, the issues of control and representation formed part of the conversations with Community Elders. The Dayna Centre on Yorta Yorta Country was visited. This is a Community Cultural Centre designed to house Yorta Yorta stories and culture, often viewed as the epicentre for Yorta Yorta self-determination and their struggle for land justice. The main issue discussed on Yorta Yorta Country revolved around the intense historical exploitation of the bush and the tensions between the enjoyment of traditional foods and the economics of timber production. Who managed traditional lands and the rather exclusive management techniques used were also critiqued (Deakin University, 1994).

During these preparatory fieldtrips, conversations between students also sparked a reinvigoration of cultural priorities. These priorities included a renewed focus on local Community history research and writing through personal story and autobiography; greater articulation of Aboriginal values and knowledges that could transform interpretative displays; and a strengthening of the skills required to develop oral interpretations for place-based cultural education and tourism. Other priorities included advocating a greater focus on critical analysis and the identification of any inappropriate displays of cultural artefacts. The aim of this was to re-interpret media to include Aboriginal views on nature and culture. This resulted in an assessment task, still used 25 years later, which asks students to document the meaning of their own cultural landscape viewed through the lens of their own personal biography. Conversations during these fieldtrips also led to future longer-term changes. For example, as a result of a visit to the South Australian Museum, arrangements began with Melbourne Museum to repatriate skeletal remains back to Victoria.

On reflection, at the time of these fieldtrips, the privileging of western perspectives on cultural heritage safeguarding, interpretation, and the management of environmental conservation on Country were still dominant within agencies and heritage organisations (Barbour & Schlesinger, 2012). The re-framing of this course acted to position the students as Elders and leaders in their community. They could actively guide the course foundations with content that would defend students' interests, as well as favour widening participation and equal opportunity to secure a strong continuing voice in curriculum design. The student Elders indeed initiated a 'conversation with the curriculum', which has continued to this day.

This curriculum-design approach supports what Trowler (1998) observed as a move away from a top-down approach, dominated by rationalist underpinnings, to a more flexible approach that attempts to "situate an understanding of education policy in the context of cultural and ideological struggles, in which they are located" (p. 158). Whilst the course was a re-imagination of an existing course, the impetus for its evolution, I believe, was an expression of collective invention and 'imaginative academic activism', which could be described as an 'institutionally embedded activism' (Morris & Hjort, 2012, p. 1). This was driven by incoming students with the support of an enlightened Community.

In 1995, one year after the course re-design took place, nine students attended the graduation ceremony to accept their awards. They wore newly designed Koorie colour stoles, introduced as a direct result of student discussions with the Protocol Office at Deakin University. In recognition of the university's collaborative process working with Koorie and non-Koorie knowledge systems, a stole was presented to then Vice Chancellor. This has since been worn by all Vice Chancellors during graduation ceremonies and, as a consequence of the ground-breaking work set in motion by these Community Elders as students, all IKE (now NIKERI) graduates wear the stoles for graduation ceremonies. The Winter 1995 edition of the Deakin University *Alumni News* reported the nine graduating students as "one of the biggest groups of Koorie students to ever graduate from a single course in any Victorian University" (Deakin University, 1995, p. 6). Early graduates from this course now work and research in a multitude of areas, including state government agencies, Native Title organisations, Aboriginal-based organisations and corporations, not-for-profit organisations and universities throughout Australia.

Since 1995, the course has attracted enrolments from all Australian states and territories, and more than 120 students have graduated. There have been three major course reviews and a number of course title changes[8] that have been directly related to the changing lexicon and nature of land management in Australia. The most recent name change occurred in 2017, with the course now called the Graduate Diploma of Land and Sea Country Management. This is the first time the word 'Country' has been included in a course name at any university in Australia. It has attracted several state government scholarships and the Institute has partnered with at least two local Aboriginal Community land management organisations. The course is still going strong and has gained a reputation with families and Communities as a course that specialises in career advancement in the sector of Land and Sea Country management. The unofficial alumni group is still a source of networking, two-way engagement, conversation, advice-giving and reciprocal invitations to Community and agency workshops and conferences.

3   Continuing the Conversation: Bringing Country in the Classroom

When I joined the course 20 years ago, students were enrolling from all different states and territories in Australia. Asking why they wanted to study the course, the message was clear: 'I want a seat at the table' and 'I want my cultural knowledge to be acknowledged'. To me, the course's application was always very obvious – to effect a noticeable change in the way government agencies and their staff Australia-wide viewed the knowledge and needs of Aboriginal and Torres Strait Islander communities. Further to this, it would initiate new ways of 'seeing' the Australian landscape as cultural rather than simply 'the environment'. From this recognition, the Aboriginal and Torres Strait Islander spiritual and cultural connection to Country could begin to be articulated and understood more clearly. As was the case with the reframing of the course five years previously, it was very important and necessary to continue the 'conversation with the curriculum' and maintain the original aims and purpose.

With these early foundations firmly embedded in the course, what became glaringly obvious was that the already established two-way exchange of learning would continue to inform course delivery. To safeguard this, the then Director of IKE ensured the course team was mentored by an Aboriginal Elder – Aunty

Dawn, a graduate of the course – who would guide and educate us in the protocols and ways of teaching in this space. Working with Aunty Dawn became pivotal to shaping and enriching my teaching pedagogy, which became based on the principles of listening, respecting and maintaining a positive standpoint.

Whilst I did not really know it at the time, I later began to understand the purpose of this collegial, as well as cultural, way of learning and I accepted it wholeheartedly with gratitude. Aunty taught me to listen, learn Aboriginal family names and come to understand what the age-old connection to Country meant. To learn and understand we went out on Country with students and listened to and met with Community members and Traditional Owners.

We drove long distances, talked about family, life experiences and the history of Victoria seen from an Aboriginal Elder's eyes. I came to realise that these early experiences, or my time of learning, were gifted to me to ensure the wellbeing of the course and the assurance of a continuing commitment. Listening to the students also ensured they would remain the key knowledge holders, keeping the course content fresh and relevant. Their continued input into the course heightened not only the students' interest but also their commitment to study and maintain a relationship with the course. As a result, this has become an attribute of the course, often expressed by continuing communication and conversations between staff and graduates year after year.

What I learned to do was not only to listen to students discussing the key issues, but also acknowledge their concerns and then stimulate group dialogue that could advance change. This was an early form of problem-solving, which has now become a prominent feature of working with complex land management projects (Zurba et al., 2012). Ensuring that everyone in the group had their say also created a nurturing of the idea of 'communities of learning'. This feature now reflects a new style of relationship and cooperation between land managers, Indigenous ways of knowing, academics and the scientists in contemporary land management practice (Robson et al., 2009). I considered myself an enabler, rather than an instructor. My role became one of facilitator, often acting as a conduit or broker between what the students considered relevant and the course materials that would stimulate their reading. The whole idea was that students would bring their own cultural knowledge and identity to the table and then interact with the course materials and address the assessment tasks as they related to various Community needs and circumstances. Students could live on or off Country; work for Aboriginal and Torres Strait Islander organisations or government agencies; or be new to the arena of caring for Country. It did not matter, as long as the student had a place or organisation through which assessment tasks could be based on the needs of Country.

4 The Graduate Diploma of Land and Sea Country Management in a Digital Age

Since 2017, the latest iteration of the course title and learning outcomes have incorporated the articulation of Aboriginal and Torres Strait Islander cultural perspectives, interests, and practices even more explicitly. Changing the title from the Graduate Diploma of Natural and Cultural Resource Management to Land and Sea Country Management, was a bold but conscious decision. Introducing this new term – land and sea Country – into the land management lexicon was motived by the desire to 'lead the way' in re-defining how the Australian cultural landscape is managed.

Course learning outcomes also gradually changed. Currently these include more explicit outcomes such as: 'articulate Aboriginal and Torres Strait Islander cultural knowledge and its underlying custodial ethic'; 'co-engage Aboriginal and Torres Strait Islander cultural perspectives to re-shape and impact policy'; transform information and experiences into a narrative'; 'evaluate practices in order to mitigate negative outcomes for natural and cultural heritage and resource environments'; 'privilege Aboriginal and Torres Strait Islander cultural perspectives, knowledges and frameworks'; and 'protect, maintain and respect the diversity of Aboriginal and Torres Strait Islander cultural perspectives'. These outcomes require an explicit focus on Aboriginal and Torres Strait Islander perspectives, positive transformative actions and critical evaluation, as well as maintaining a diversity of cultural perspectives. They create what Fogarty has called bringing Country into the classroom (2012). This is expressed in two ways.

Firstly, through attendance in intensives – or one-week residential teaching blocks – where students come together as a community to steer the inclusion of relevant topics into group discussion in an active and collaborative way. Students, as representatives of Country, physically bring Country into the actual classroom. With them come place-based concerns, local environmental issues, cultural priorities and potential project briefs.

Secondly, Country in the Classroom is supported by a wide range of course materials and resources, including digital resources such as film, YouTube videos, podcasts, interviews and links to Aboriginal community websites. The course also has features that underpin a well-formed mode of collaborative two-way learning and assessment task design. Particular features include yarning circles, relationship building, and dynamic networking. Each of these is discussed in more detail below.

4.1 *Yarning Circles*

Initially, these get-togethers were established as a simple way to bring all students together at the start of a one-week intensive. This would help re-familiarise and reconnect them, as well as create an opportunity to plan the week ahead and report back on how assessment tasks were linking to workplace or Community-based projects. The discussions usually lasted for about three hours. Down the track, this activity came to be known as a yarning circle, becoming a permanent feature of the intensive timetable. It has now become a time when the course team can write down issues and matters that require following up for future course content. Students relay the latest news from their Community, often related to news on Native Title determinations, project development, emerging or continuing environmental problems, policy changes or, most importantly, opportunities for project development that students could follow up.

These yarning circles tend to adhere to self-regulating etiquette and cultural protocols, providing a time and space where individual students can voice their positions on matters in a safe and united space. As the yarning circles bring together both new and returning students, the returning students provide a huge amount of new information, advice and support to those just beginning the course. During the yarning circles, new terminology, language, concepts and flashpoints or issues are raised and discussed. For example, in the early 2000s, the concept of cultural water values was beginning to gain currency in land and water management circles. It was also a time when the concept began to affect new water management terminology.

Final discussion at the end of the intensive summarises the circulation of knowledge and plans for the next intensive. As such, this becomes a practice that provides a wrap-up and the time to plan for study when away from the university. The students, through their study, as well as the knowledge and ideas they bring with them to the course, continually enrich the course content organically, thus instilling relevance and cultural priority. This, in turn, prepares students for the further implementation and introduction of these cutting-edge terms in workplaces, policy-making workshops and board rooms: the places where decisions are made and influence is felt.

4.2 *Relationship Building*

Another very important feature of the course revolves around building and maintaining relationships with and between students. This all-important feature is nourished in a number of ways, just like it has been from early course development. Visits on Country to gain an understanding of how projects are implemented are a critical feature and during these fieldtrips course team/student relationships strengthen. Over the years, we have visited some key Indigenous land management events that have contributed to gradual changes in the way land in Australia is managed. Staff and students have jointly attended all the Indigenous Land and Sea Management Conferences that have occurred in

Australia, including Ross River, Cardwell, Broken Hill and Darwin for the World Indigenous Networking Conference. This brought together Aboriginal Rangers from all across Australia and the world to showcase their project outcomes, discuss future strategies and network. Participating in these conferences has placed students right at the heart of the land and sea Country movement since the 1990s and, as a consequence, they have become a key part of some significant conversations.

4.3   *Dynamic Networking*

From its very beginning, a key feature of the course has been the inclusion of Aboriginal and Torres Strait Islander guest speakers and past graduates. Speakers, whether representatives of one of the various land management agencies or past graduate Elders, are invited to present on subject matter they believe will be of interest to students. The inclusion of such guest speakers is designed to ensure current information is shared with students in a real-world context rather than in an abstract manner. Allowing the speaker to choose the content and issues on which to focus creates a more collaborative and spontaneous conversation. This can set the stage for student-led questioning and analysis. It also provides a time and space where current issues can be brought to the attention of the whole class. The guest speakers have a two-way conversation with the students and with this, can gain access to the perspectives of Aboriginal and Torres Strait Islander people from different state-wide workplaces. The information coming from these guest speakers can then be incorporated into course content and applied through assessment tasks. This dynamic networking is considered a key attribute of the course.

5   Linda Tuhiwai Smith – Using 25 Indigenous Projects as a Framework

In the early 2000s, Linda Tuhiwai Smith's seminal text *Decolonizing methodologies: Research and Indigenous peoples* (1999) became an important resource for the course. In particular, the chapter 'Twenty-five Indigenous projects'[9] struck a chord. It helped embed a relevant framework in which to contextualise assessment tasks to connect to real-world situations in the students' workplace or Community. After reading the chapter, I realised the 25 projects 'spoke to' the students on an intellectual level, arousing passion and deep thought. I also observed that Smith's suggested research areas generated an even greater motivation for students to work with their assessment tasks. The empowering projects she referred to seemed to provoke or energise students to embark on their own form of reclaiming, affirming or investigation. This culturally relevant methodology aligns with the idea that students become researchers as provocateurs (Mertens, 2010); their critical interrogation of dominant discourse can then challenge common assumptions or positions.

In the course, the majority of assessment tasks invite students to centre themselves and their concerns from within their own family and community. They can then document these concerns and design projects that can be acted upon in the future to address them. By doing this, the priority for the student is to plan and write creatively about projects or programs that can address land or social justice matters actively in a way that can improve or transform. The latter is particularly important. This planning by the student is commenced right at the beginning of the course. The course outcomes are predicated on the student articulating their own Country issues – whether they be environmental and/or cultural – and then address these concerns through offering suggestions or recommendations considered to them to be transformative. After reading Linda Tuhiwai Smith's 25 projects chapter, students find a context and extra motivation for undertaking the task. In particular, claiming or re-claiming, storytelling, intervening, remembering and re-framing have become powerful stimuli for students to undertake in-depth research for assessment tasks. Each of these is discussed in my detail as follows.

5.1   *Claiming and Re-Claiming*

During the conversations and discussions that lead up to a research activity, a motivating force can be to re-tell or re-interpret place or event histories that have been misinterpreted, underreported or remained invisible. Re-telling the history of a family or Community is also a way to celebrate strength amidst family adversity. Writing these histories then becomes a communicative means of informing extended families and, in turn, Community. One example of this can be found in Patsy Cameron and Linn Miller's research on Tasmanian stories, *Reclaiming history for Aboriginal governance: Tasmanian stories* (2011). The authors found that whilst the story of contact and relations on the Tasmanian colonial frontier had been extensively researched, the stories of colonial incursions researched and written by Tasmanian Aboriginal people are of "vital and immediate concern for Aboriginal people themselves" (p. 32). Responding to a similar need and their own 'immediate concern', after completing the course, several graduates have gone on to complete post-graduate study centred on family stories in the context of Australian history and society. In this sense, assessment tasks can stimulate a desire and provide the skills to continue the researching of family histories and piece together unconnected threads, as well as reclaim and celebrate family lineages and stories.

5.2 Storytelling

Each individual story is powerful and enlightening and, as Linda Tuhiwai Smith states (1999, p. 144), "these new stories contribute to a collective story in which each Indigenous person has a place". Storytelling examines past interpretations and can play the role of addressing contested histories. This is where the stories that have been generated from this course become such a great storehouse of memory. These stories can then sow the seed for further research as a community shares its stories. Documenting the story also prompts students to ask questions, find photographs, have cups of tea, meet, and go to family events. Tertiary education can often be a legitimating way to find out more. Education is usually highly regarded and the desire to 'find out' is often met with respect and assistance and can act as a validation of the course and its reputation in Aboriginal Communities.

5.3 Intervening

This is very much a part of what students are asked to think about and participate in actively during their course of study over two years. Project aims are defined; strategic planning is directed to include the needs of the local Aboriginal and Torres Strait Islander communities; and interpretation of Country becomes a matter for Communities themselves. Intervening can work, for example, when local Community government-based relationships include Aboriginal voices in committees or council conversations. Institutional change becomes a priority that can be implemented successfully by having a 'seat at the table'. During yarning circles, ways of intervening and changing 'business as usual' are often tackled with strategies offered by fellow students. I recall one graduate who came to realise that the local shire he was situated in was not actively collaborating, inviting an Aboriginal voice or requesting representation on council matters. On thinking about this, one assessment task was dedicated to outlining the strategies used to change this relationship. This one task ultimately instilled the confidence to continue to develop a new relationship for the benefit of his Community.

5.4 Remembering

This is a means for Elders in particular to reveal painful stories through the use of researching, revealing discrepancies and discovering misinformation. The act of researching into massacres that have occurred in students' home Communities is an example of this. Having the time, space and determination to seek out the truth is a strong motivation for this research activity. The rewriting of a version of events, taking the time and effort to get the story right, can evoke powerful healing not just for the student, but for close community members who may not have the tools or time to access or interpret past documentation.

5.5 *Re-Framing*

In 2015 the book *Dark Emu Black Seeds: Agriculture or accident?* (Pascoe, 2014) was introduced as a set text within the course. This book became a powerful addition, highlighting the assumptions the course has always been based on: Aboriginal and Torres Strait Islander people have been managing the land and its resources for literally thousands of generations. Every student had to read the book and draw examples from the text to assist them in designing their own local place-based research. In many ways, making this a set text simply reconfirmed the 1994 're-framing' of the original course outline.

6 Post-Graduate Study: What's in a Qualification?

One of the most important aims of the course goes right back to its 1994 origins: to continually increase the number of Aboriginal and Torres Strait Islander graduates who can represent their own Community interests and cultural priorities on Country. These graduates have now become part of a growing Aboriginal and Torres Strait Islander workforce and network, employed as CEOs, Stolen Generation archivists, researchers, academics, partnerships coordinators, advisory board members, park rangers, interpretation specialists, cultural water officers, catchment management project coordinators, Caring for Country facilitators and heritage consultants.

In the future, we will conduct research on student experiences of the course and graduate employability, but for now, a number of testimonies provide some insight. For example, when asked to highlight the positive aspects of the course, one graduate stated:

> I researched the history of one Reserve I know at Killalea State Park and found a man named … who was removed from his family at the age of 2 years and had never met his sisters and passed away in 1992. I searched the cemetery for days until I found him, and I continue to visit him on a monthly basis. I contacted the family who he was living with and they provided me with little info at the time. I emailed LinkUp and I never heard back until two years later on July the 14th, 2016 … foster parents at the time stood at my doorstep with … This was one of the best days of my life! (Deakin University, 2016)

Responding to how the course contributed to his career, another graduate outlined the activities he had participated in, including:

> Submissions and inputs into Acts of parliament; strategies in government agencies to prioritise the safeguarding of cultural heritage; policy writing; partnerships and liaison; invitations to Aboriginal Heritage Committees; able to use the language of politics and management to proactively put forward community concerns and priorities. (Deakin University, 2016)

International connections. with other Indigenous communities have also been nurtured. One graduate arranged a cultural exchange visit with Community members to convene with local North American Indian Elders. This activity was inspired by the networking that took place at the World Indigenous Networking Conference he had attended in Darwin years before. Further testimony included:

> Since I graduated from the NCRM [Natural and Cultural Resource Management] course I have created a business that will see our people become financially self-sufficient without handouts but with hand ups. I have found myself being invited onto the State Aboriginal Heritage Committee to give advice to the Minister of Aboriginal Affairs on all things heritage. I have participated with the tools learnt at IKE in meetings with government and mining to keep them honest and more importantly, I have shared my knowledge with Community, so they too are empowered. (Deakin University, 2016)

Over the years, conversations with students who keep in touch with the team continually echo the sentiments offered in the above testimonies. Graduates keep sending Community and workplace colleagues to the course, which has helped grow and maintain a community of practice for 25 years.

7 Maintaining Community Relationships

Continued connections with graduates throughout the life of the course have created relationships that have initiated invitations to collaborate with Victorian Aboriginal Communities. The course team has remained in partnership with the Lake Condah Sustainable Development project, initiated by Traditional Owners and their Community, which spearheaded the eventual World

Heritage declaration at Budj Bim, as mentioned at the beginning of this story. The course team has been invited to hold workshops on the design of interpretation narratives for future tourist interpretation to accommodate World Heritage visitation.

In 2015, as a recommendation from a past graduate, the course team were commissioned by Parks Victoria to conduct an experiential review of Joint Management in Victoria (Nunn & Sutton, 2016). The review concluded that 'relationships are everything' and a greater emphasis on cross-cultural adaptive land management will be the key to the successful management of land between the State and local Aboriginal Communities (Nunn & Sutton, 2016, p. 93). Additionally, the study and graduation of one student in 2008 led to a fruitful project relationship on Wathaurong Country, working on the Wurdi Youang property to develop a proposal for the declaration of an Indigenous Protected Area (IPA). Activities that evolved from the project included cultural heritage research and protection for a significant stone arrangement and a reinvigoration of cultural connection and Wathaurong land management practices on Country. A collection of Kangaroo Grass seed has taken place to create seed banks and customary burning has recently resumed after a long recess. An intellectual property agreement was developed along with the recruitment of Indigenous Rangers to work on Country.

Currently, a new digital knowledge platform is currently under design to provide digital resources to the Faculty of Science and Built Environment. This will provide knowledge and information on Indigenous Science for staff and students. These digital resources include links to Aboriginal and Torres Strait Islander land management corporations, video clips of County, Aboriginal and Torres Strait Islander authored texts, and literature on topical cultural and environmental issues. The objective is to ensure that all Deakin University graduates have interacted and engaged with Aboriginal and Torres Strait Islander perspectives around contemporary land justice issues.

8 Reflexivity and the Teacher

Teaching over a long period of time requires not only constant reflective practice but also a consistent interrogation of teaching practice. It has been vital for me to continually check and move with the needs of students and their Communities to ensure a meaningful and fruitful relationship with the students I work with. I use the term 'work with' because this is largely what I see myself doing in my daily facilitation and teaching practice. This also applies to course design. Course content requires constant updating as policy and environments

keep changing in response to the complex and ongoing issues that confront our planet. Below is a summary of reflections that characterise the course:
- The course content and topics under discussion must consider the constantly changing nature of on-ground projects delivery. It is also essential to regularly 'gauge' the environmental policy landscape, both politically and culturally.
- It is important to discuss contemporary policy, asking students to respond with their own unique recommendations as a way of improving their own community's outcomes, while placing this in a land justice framework.
- All resources must be vetted for relevance, currency and quality, with a high ratio of Indigenous authors.
- Fieldtrips and bringing Country into the classroom are integral components of the course delivery, acting to ground students in real-world situations as well as nourish the relationship between the course and the broader Community.
- Assessment tasks much be contextualised, considered relevant and designed to enable the implementation of projects in the future. This increases the veracity and value of assessment tasks as they relate to real-world solutions.
- The best knowledge and ideas come from the students themselves and is considered trusted information.
- Relationship-building between the students is vital. This involves students in a process of trust-building that can lead to the future exchange of ideas and job opportunities. Allowing students to work together in groups is vital during the one-week intensives. As a result, the course inspires and mobilises sentiment through strong relationship building between the course team and students.
- Course developers have institutional agency and the ability to update information regularly and in a systematic way.
- Reaching out to anyone who asks for support or assistance relating to the skills and tools for studying is an absolute imperative for success. If students find it difficult to work with the tools they need, it can delay effective and enjoyable study.

9 Continuing the Conversation

Nakata and Maddison (2019, p. 408) have stated in their detailed exploration of Australia's "settler state", that creativity and resistance are necessary "to reorder relationships" in this country. They also cogently remind teachers, facilitators and the academy that: "The fracturing of the hegemony of Western/settler knowledge is underway" and the current course design acknowledges this. The course honours the skills and sensibilities that equip graduates to work within the framework of the settler-state's order of relationships, characterised as largely a negative historic relationship from the beginning of colonisation. The course's offerings also support Uncle Lester-Irabinna Rigney's (2011, p. 210) request to interact actively with the complex settler-state interface with actions and ideals for conscious-raising. He argues this should include increasing the level of community engagement, nurturing and sustaining cultural identity, increasing regional authority, autonomy and Indigenous representation, instilling community cohesion, creating coherent structures for dialogue, and maintaining ethical and transparent processes – all of which underpin this course.

Further, in support of recent writing by Muller, Hemming, and Rigney (2019, p. 399), who have built up a number of case studies focusing on the role of Indigenous nations as change makers, this course, set up in 1994, has played one minor part in what they call the "redefining and reimagining of environmental management based on Indigenous sovereignties, knowledges, and ways of seeing". In one small way, the course has attempted to move positively with this 'fracturing' to counter the domination of colonial knowledge. It closely navigates through the politics of knowledge and ensures we interrogate the assumptions behind this knowledge (Nakata & Maddison, 2019, p. 416). This is an example of one strategy to decolonise the curricula by putting front and centre the alternative perspectives that are designed to acknowledge and increase the focus on new ways of seeing and managing land in Australia. The course also reinforces this by arguing academic staff can walk alongside students to "strengthen their positions and aspirations" (Land, 2001, p. 7). As Barbour and Schlesinger (2012) have commented when asking 'Who's the boss?', when it comes to conservation research on Indigenous lands, "We need to discuss what the cross-cultural priorities for land management are, value different world views and respect the equal legitimacy of different knowledges grounded in these ontologies" (p. 39).

Maggie Walter (2018) recently wrote a paper entitled 'The voice of Indigenous data: Beyond the markers of disadvantage'. In it, she argued there is very "little data that truly reflects or expresses the lifeworlds of Aboriginal and Torres Strait Islander people" or the embodied experience of social, political, economic and cultural realities (p. 258). She also comments that, as it stands, "the capacity for a two-way data exchange remains untapped" (p. 260). Hopefully, the writing of other stories about course development and further research into Aboriginal and Torres Strait Islander student employment experiences will further enrich this data.

In January 2020 many parts of the Australian landmass were on fire. World media projected the spotlight on Australia and its bushfires as another reminder that a heating planet can bring with it intense bushfires. A few days after the danger had abated, I heard an Aboriginal woman on national radio talking about the Aboriginal practice of customary burning as a form of age-old land management. Unsurprisingly, the interviewee was a past graduate of the course and as I listened to her talking, I realised her contribution to this current conversation was just as powerful as the class contributions she made all those years ago. After thinking more about her conversation on the radio, I knew that Aunty Dawn, who worked tirelessly for the course a number of years ago, would be extremely proud.

Notes

1. RAPS are the traditional and legal source of advice and knowledge on matters that relate to Aboriginal cultural heritage management and safeguarding in the state of Victoria.
2. See https://en.unesco.org/
3. In 2020, the Institute of Koorie Education (IKE) was renamed the National Indigenous Knowledges, Education, Research and Innovation (NIKERI) Institute.
4. Keeping Places are distinctly Victorian spaces that were built to house and safeguard Aboriginal cultural matter, as well as repatriating human remains from overseas.
5. The term Koorie derives from the word for 'people' in the Indigenous languages of the coastal groups of Central and Northern New South Wales. The term slowly drifted southwards as people found themselves in their colonised world.
6. Community Based Delivery (CBD) is the description used by the IKE to describe its delivery mode. It is a combination of intensive on-campus delivery plus studying at home in community. Students do not have to actually move to the university, rather study in a mixed mode.
7. The Tindale Collection is a repository of records and over 50,000 genealogies that were gathered in the 1920s and 1930s. They are housed at the South Australian Museum.
8. The course names have included the Graduate Certificate in Environment and Heritage Interpretation, the Graduate Diploma of Applied Science (Environmental and Heritage Interpretation), the Graduate Diploma of Natural Resource Management and the Graduate Diploma of Natural and Cultural Resource Management.
9. These projects include claiming, testimonies, storytelling, celebrating survival, indigenising, intervening, revitalising, connecting, reading, writing, representing, gendering, envisioning, reframing, restoring, returning, democratising, networking, naming, protecting, creating, negotiating, discovering and sharing.

References

Altman, J., Buchanan, G., & Larson, L. (2007). *The environmental significance of the Indigenous estate: Natural resource management as economic development in remote Australia.* Centre for Aboriginal Economic Policy Research Discussion Paper 286. Australian National University.

Altman, J., & Kerins, S. (Eds.). (2012). *People on country: Vital landscapes, Indigenous futures*. The Federation Press.

Barbour, W., & Schlesinger, C. (2012). Who's the boss? Post-colonialism, ecological research and conservation management on Australian Indigenous lands. *Ecological Management and Restoration, 13*(1), 36–40.

Cameron, P., & Miller, L. (2011). Reclaiming history for Aboriginal governance: Tasmanian stories. In S. Maddison & M. Brigg (Eds.), *Unsettling the settler state: Creativity and resistance in Indigenous settler-state governance* (pp. 32–50). The Federation Press.

Carter, J. (1993). The place of story in the study of teaching and teacher education. *Educational Researcher, 1*, 5–18.

Clandinin, D., & Connelly, F. (1987). Teacher's personal practical knowledge: What counts as personal in studies of the personal. *Journal of Curriculum Studies, 19*(6), 487–500.

Deakin University. (1994). *Minutes of fifth steering committee meeting* (Unpublished manuscript). Author.

Deakin University. (1995, Winter). *Alumni news*. Author.

Deakin University. (2016). *Thirtieth anniversary: Institute of Koorie education*. Author.

Elbaz, F. (1991). Research on teacher's knowledge: The evolution of a discourse. *Journal of Curriculum Studies, 23*(1), 1–19.

Fogarty, B. (2012). Country as classroom. In J. Altman & S. Kerins (Eds.), *People on country: Vital landscapes, Indigenous futures* (pp. 162–174). The Federation Press.

Hjort, M., & Morrie, M. (2012). Institutional culture: A manifesto with rules. In M. Morris & M. Hjort (Eds.), *Creativity and academic activism: Instituting cultural studies* (pp. 19–23). Duke University Press.

Land, R. (2001). Agency, contexts and change in academic development. *International Journal of Academic Development, 6*(1), 4–20.

Maddison, S., & Brigg, M. (Eds.). (2011). *Unsettling the settler state: Creativity and resistance in Indigenous settler-state governance*. The Federation Press.

Mertens, D. (2010). Transformative mixed methods research. *Qualitative Inquiry, 16*(6), 469–474.

Morris, M., & Hjort, M. (Eds.). (2012). *Creativity and academic activism: Instituting cultural studies*. Duke University Press.

Muller, S., Hemming, S., & Rigney, D. (2019). Indigenous sovereignties: Relational ontologies and environmental management. *Geographical Research, 57*(4), 399–410.

Nakata, S., & Maddison, S. (2019). New collaborations in old institutional spaces: Setting a new research agenda to transform Indigenous-settler relations. *Australian Journal of Political Science, 54*(3), 407–422.

Nunn, S., & Sutton, K. (2016). *An experiential review of joint management of Victorian National Parks: Learning from Traditional Owners and National Park managers*. Parks Victoria and Institute of Koorie Education, Deakin University.

Pascoe, B. (2014). *Dark Emu: Black seeds: Agriculture or accident*. Magabala Books.

Rigney, L.-I. (2011) Epilogue: Can the settler state settle with whom it colonises? Reasons for hope and priorities for action. In S. Maddison & M. Brigg (Eds.), *Unsettling the settler state: Creativity and resistance in Indigenous settler-state governance* (pp. 206–211). The Federation Press.

Robson, J., Miller, A., Idrobo, C., Burlando, C., Deutsch, N., Kocho-Schellenberg, J., Pengelly, R., & Turner, K. (2009). Building communities of learning: Indigenous ways of knowing in contemporary natural resources and environmental management. *Journal of Royal Society of New Zealand, 39*(4), 173–177.

Smith, L. T. (1999). *Decolonizing methodologies: Research and Indigenous peoples*. Zed Books.

Trowler, P. (1998). *Academics responding to change: New higher education frameworks and academic cultures*. Society for Research into Higher Education & Open University Press.

Walter, M. (2018). The voice of Indigenous data: Beyond the markers of disadvantage. *Griffith Review, 60*, 256–263.

Zurba, M., Ross, H., Izurieta, A., Rist, P., Bock, E., & Berkes, F. (2012). Building co-management as a process: Problem solving through partnerships on Aboriginal Country, Australia. *Environmental Management, 49*, 1300–1142.

CHAPTER 3

Indigenous Knowledges and Global Knowledge Systems: Co-Actioning Thresholds in Australian Science Curricula and Initial Teacher Education

Gabrielle Fletcher and Kate Chealuck

Abstract

The compartmentalisation and fixity of western science as part of a deeply entrenched positivist cache of knowledge and how and what to know, has been historically reproduced in curriculum in terms of what is science and how to apply this science, to the exclusion of all 'other' ways of knowing and doing (Denzin & Lincoln, 2008). Indigenous Knowledges, in contrast, have been represented as "unscientific" (Martin, 2012, p. 21), or even "inferior and primitive" (Kincheloe & Steinberg, 2008, p. 136), and part of a storying process that is incommensurate with the dominant western culture of validation and credibility. In an epoch where the variance of knowledges, and the credentialing of Indigenous Knowledge is making increasing sense in a global context of crisis – one where problems are reaching for 'different' solutions (Finlayson, Preuss, Jackson, & Holcombe, 2012; Mazzocchi, 2018; Nakata, 2002), this chapter considers the complexity of pedagogical transformations from a colonised academy to a co-actioning of Indigenous Knowledge and western science within primary schools for pre-service and in-service teachers. The 'troublesomeness' of 'accepting' and actioning Indigenous Knowledges as a valid component of the science curriculum represent threshold concepts that teachers must engage with to truly embody and work within and around the cultural interface to transform science teaching and learning.

Keywords

Australian Indigenous Knowledges – pedagogy – relationality – threshold concepts – science curriculum – pre-service teaching

1   Introduction

There are multiple ways of seeing, understanding and being in the world. The entrenchment of western knowledges, paradigms and the concomitant centrality of non-pluralistic logics have been ideologically, conceptually and intellectually privileged to make sense of the world and order reality. This self-referent world-view recircuits a 'natural' authority to diminish or exclude other forms of knowledge, its disseminations, expression, credibility or indeed existence. To 'make room' for diverse knowledges creates enormous tensions and challenges. On the one hand, a more entrenched universalist approach to knowledge and science insists that "knowledge and truth are not relative to a particular culture or social context" (Green, 2008, p. 145); and on the other, a relativist approach can recognise different knowledge organisation "precisely because scientific knowledge practices discard so much of what they know to be useful" (Green, 2008, p. 147). This sets up ongoing oppositions between science and Indigenous Knowledges, that loosely resonate with Khun's conception of "incommensurability" and a kind of "no-overlap principle" (Kuhn, 2000, p. 125). This is mediated around preclusion and taxonomies of 'common' language in shifting (revolutionary) science paradigms. An argumentative absolutism about 'useful' knowledge legitimated through power, dominant culture and its reproduction has historically subsumed other 'forms'. Knowledge systems, rather than knowledge or the content of 'truth', must take into account epistemological and knowledge production contexts and subjectivities of 'knowers' and practitioners to provide a re-consideration of an understanding of knowledge that can "advance understanding" (Green, 2008, p. 153) and be appropriately and respectfully represented.

This chapter takes at its core the epistemic, subjective and produced/practiced context of diverse knowledge systems and the understanding that Indigenous Knowledge is distinct and valid on this basis. What is considered is this apparent 'incommensurability' of knowledge systems, and the questions arising around 'finding space' in a contemporary western science curriculum. In particular, this work has emerged from an Indigenous space within an Australian University delivering science curriculum to Aboriginal and Torres Strait Islander pre-service teachers. It has been co-written by two colleagues: one non-Indigenous science educator, and the other an Indigenous specialist in Indigenous Studies and Social Sciences. The aim of this chapter is to reflect upon and consider situated Australian Indigenous Knowledges as a formative possibility of culturally-responsive pedagogy within the Australian Science Curriculum, and for both Aboriginal and Torres Strait Islander and non-Indigenous teachers to navigate authentically across these domains. Further, it seeks to re-cast these tensions as considerations beyond 'simply' embedding meaningful Indigenous content as framework efficacy. It considers Indigenous Knowledges as a threshold concept that takes into account the subjectivities, epistemologies and context of such systems, and provides relevance and inclusion for Aboriginal and

Torres Strait Islander pre-service teachers themselves. This creates a means of embracing the multiple possibilities for the transmission of knowledge and an understanding that knowledge is a bearer of agency. This argument therefore becomes one of exploring a co-actioning of thresholds, underpinned by the centring of Indigenous Knowledges, perspectives and experience in creating a cultural interface where science and Indigenous Knowledges can inform science curriculum.

This chapter also finds voice in speaking back to some of the disparaging and depleting responses to the recent recommendation by the Australian Curriculum, Assessment and Reporting Authority (ACARA) to incorporate Indigenous perspectives and Knowledges into the Australian Science Curriculum. Reports from the *Daily Telegraph*, for example, suggests 'outrage' that:

> Science teachers are being told to incorporate Aboriginal culture into their lessons – a move slammed by critics as nothing more than a silly distraction to appease the PC crowd when our kids are already falling behind the rest of the world. (Daily Telegraph, 2018, p. 1)

This tabloid representation was accompanied by an image of a 'traditional' Aboriginal Elder 'teaching' mathematics to two young Aboriginal children inside a cave. This representation underscores the apparent 'incommensurability' of science and Indigenous Knowledges. It also significantly reproduces the ideological sediments and discursive disavowal of diverse Knowledge systems as irrelevant and 'primitive', if they are permitted to exist at all, through such destructive, retrograde hegemonic circuitry. This lends further consideration to the role of western knowledge and the Academy as a site of knowledge 'production' that forms part of the reiterative exclusionary instrumentation at the disposal of dominant culture and its determination of what is 'useful' or 'relevant'. It also underscores the need for de-colonising the academy and curriculum, in order to co-create a workable cultural interface that is translatable in the science classroom.

This chapter provides some understanding of Indigenous Knowledges; traces some of the tensions of encounter between science and Indigenous Knowledges and explores the need to de-colonise the academy. It then reflects upon transformations in science education. It foregrounds teacher education in Australia to then finally contextualise and propose a co-actioning threshold model for Indigenous Knowledges in the Australian science curriculum, inclusive of Indigenous pre-service teachers. The final argument is for a transformative 'becoming', with agency of and in knowledge that informs identity and enacts an inclusive 'both ways' approach. This chapter argues for a co-actioned threshold paradigm between Aboriginal and Torres Strait Islander Knowledges and practices and the knowledge systems from within which science curricula are informed and created.

2   Indigenous Knowledges – An Understanding

For Indigenous peoples, Indigenous Knowledge is mediated around and within relationality, situatedness and collectivism. Holistic, experiential and evolving, it is the relationship between people and the environment that is "the organising foundation of knowledge, the categorisation of life experiences, and the shaping of attitudes and patterns of thinking" (Durie, 2005, p. 303). Identity is ineluctable to the world and cosmology. There are clear links between physical and social environments, and resources are collective and intergenerational, with land featuring as a core to health and wellbeing (p. 304). The basis for knowledge, its creation, circulation and maintenance is: "the dynamic relationships that arise from the interaction of people with the environment, generations with each other, and social and physical relationships. Relationships form a substrate for indigenous knowledge" (Tau, 1999, p. 12).

Relationship to land is central to Indigenous peoples. It is not a 'making of home' upon an area of ground or part of the earth that is 'owned'. It is inherent to all things, inextricably linked, co-existent and both sentient and sapient "like our bodies and our parents" (Trask, cited in Blair, 2015, p. xxiii). Indigenous Knowledge and worldviews are characterised by their relational aspects; they cannot be separated from the people, the land, spirituality, and the universe (Chilisa, 2011). "Indigenous knowledge is inherently tied to the land ... to particular landscapes, landforms and biomes where ceremonies are properly held ... Stories properly recited, medicines properly gathered, and transfers of knowledge properly authenticated" (Battiste, 2008, p. 8).

The concept of 'the individual' set apart from creation and the world, or existing "for the purpose of human domination and exploitation is absent from Indigenous world-views" (Duran & Duran, 1995, cited in Durie, 2004). As Rose (1996) points out, a significant aspect of Indigenous Knowledge is that it "does not universalise" (p. 32). Knowledge systems are entwined in "multiple and messy" ontological and epistemological positions (Acton, Salter, Lenoy, & Stevenson, 2017, p. 1311). The emphasis on Indigenous Knowledge is based upon the specificity of situatedness and is mediated from and in place. Within an Australian Indigenous context, this complex and sophisticated interconnectedness and web of relationships is named as Country, with land (as tangible) and being (as temporal). Country is "a living entity with a yesterday, today and tomorrow ... a nourishing terrain" (Rose, 1996, p. 7); "Country is a space where knowledge is learnt, lived, practiced, renewed, regenerated through ceremony" (Blair, 2015, p. xxiii). The ineluctable Being of Country is not imagined or represented, rather it is "lived in and lived with ... Country knows, hears, smells, takes notice, takes care, is sorry or happy" (Rose, 1996, p. 7). Contextualised, then, and as an attempt to distil apprehension, Country is knowledge: it is whole, circular (not linear) and without it there is no self (Watson, 2017, p. 32). What is of further significance is that,

> Indigenous peoples make place by relating both personal and communal experiences and histories to certain locations and landscapes – maintaining these spatial relationships is one of the most important components of identity ... land is a storied site of human interaction ... [and] ... a reality to be clarified and understood from the perspectives of the people who have given it meaning ... Experiences of space become expressions of self. (Goeman, 2008, pp. 22–24)

While European colonisation disrupted Indigenous lives and ways of living, Indigenous Knowledge systems remain intact and continue developing as living, social schemas (Moreton-Robinson & Walter, 2009, p. 3). According to Kincheloe and Steinberg (2008), Indigenous Knowledge is a multidimensional body of understandings: "knowledges, epistemologies, ontologies and cosmologies that construct ways of being and seeing in relationship to their physical surroundings" and have been "viewed by Euroculture as inferior or primitive" (p. 136), especially since the scientific revolution in 17th and 18th century Europe. What does need to be flagged is the need to be careful in the use of the term Indigenous as it "appears to conflate numerous separate groups of people whose histories and cultures may be profoundly divergent" (Kincheloe & Steinberg, 2008, p. 136).

3 Tensions of Encounter: Indigenous Knowledges and Global Knowledge Systems

There are multiple tensions when considering Indigenous Knowledges and global knowledge systems. The utilisation of the term Indigenous Knowledge first began to appear in scholarly literature in the 1980s, growing out of disciplines of anthropology and ethnoscience as a means of interrogating environmental concerns and the link to culturally-driven behaviour (Lanzano, 2013). The concept "was a tool to discuss eurocentrism in the natural sciences and to acknowledge the positive role of non-Western technical knowledge" (Lanzano, 2013, p. 2). To circumvent problematics around Indigenous and thus Indigeneity as contested labels, other terms featured were 'local' or 'traditional' or, less commonly, 'autochthone', a synonym for 'Indigenous'. Interestingly Heidegger's use of "autochthonology" or "rootedness-in-soil" in the 1940s (Heidegger, Macquarrie, Robinson, & Carmen, 2008, p. 60), is an example of one of many Heideggerian phenomenological propositions to consider Being and its essence. It also considers the impact of technology upon 'civilisation', with a specific notional use of Indigenous connected to 'rootedness'. It refers to a 'within' groundedness, where understanding is generative from this origin as a way of articulating 'homeland', belonging and human-ness as "the indigenous-character/groundedness of conceptuality'" (p. 61). This may loosely intersect in considering complex First Nations' conceptions beyond 'coming from' a geography or ecological topography. Ironically, if this were decontextualised philosophically, this would go some way to capturing this relationship and the process of deracination or up-rootedness and loss of origin experienced by Indigenous peoples. Finally, however, Heidegger's terminological use was a part of broader ontological project that drew from "Greek science" (p. 61), which was used to promote German Nationalism and anti-Semitism during the Second World War.

More contemporaneously, Nakata (2002) discusses the contentious labelling of Indigenous Knowledge: "from what constitutes 'Indigenous' to whose interests are being served by the documentation for such knowledge, there lies a string of contradictions, sectoral interests, local and global politics, ignorance and hope for the future" (p. 19). And as Kovach (2009, p. 30) points out,

> Introducing Indigenous knowledges into any form of academic discourse (research or otherwise) must ethically include the influence of the colonial relationship, thereby introducing a decolonising perspective to a critical paradigm ... Knowledge is neither acultural or apolitical.

Western research and knowledge have conveniently not recognised this relationship, and have situated Indigenous peoples as the 'other' rather than "equal holders of knowledge or collaborators in the creation of knowledge" (Smith, 1999, p. 198). In short, and most powerfully, "Indigenous epistemologies challenge the very core of knowledge production and purpose" (Kovach, 2009, p. 29). This does raise another layer of consideration from the perspective of Indigenous researchers themselves, in having to understand and dismantle a western knowledge apparatus in terms of how it is produced, and how it might be 'read' from the position of 'other'.

This notion of reading position highlights the need for Indigenous researchers and scholars to understand the way (western) knowledge construction and legitimation works, how it represents and misrepresents so we can "develop strategies that will assist us to read these knowledges (texts), as others read them, but in full cognisance of their relation to our history, our current position and us" (Nakata, 2007, p. 32). Of concern is the burden placed upon Indigenous researchers and scholars to develop textual strategies of reading as the 'other', rather than the possibility of western researchers also developing cultural and critical competencies in developing ways to engage with Indigenous ontologies and knowledges as an equal and equalising strategy. As Royal (2007) points out, the challenge is to "recover and revitalise existing Indigenous knowledge held within our communities and elsewhere ... [and] reworking of our fragmentary existing knowledge in new creative ways" (p. 1).

> It is the immersion of Indigenous peoples and knowledges beyond the limits of western scientific and textual culture, into the excesses of western consciousness that is the same place that Indigenous people will begin to reconnect with a former temporality – a temporality that is still available to us. (Moreton, 2006, p. 54)

These tensions, collisions and fragmentations have radically exposed the privileging of the monocultural project, de-historicising and (at minimum) neutralising multiplicity. Thus, through this filter of singularity, Indigenous Being and cosmology, reliant upon the collective, have been further diminished according to western knowledge systems of ordering the material world. Additionally, there have been bodied and embodied violations enacted upon Indigenous peoples historically through research: "Aboriginal peoples have been weighed, given blood, urine, faeces and hair samples, given their stories, explained their existence, been interviewed, questioned, observed, followed, interpreted, analysed and written about for years" (Fredericks, 2008, p. 25). This is extended to measured, categorised, classified, indexed, sampled, determined, surveyed and unearthed – the surviving remains of equal empiric import as survivors remaining. This objectification has been called into question with Indigenous researchers reclaiming their own subjectivity and knowledge production as former objects of research in historic ethnographic practice.

These practices become part of a formation of 'epistemic violence' (Foucault, 1982; Spivak, 1988). This is a process of actively "subjugating knowledge" through "obstructing and undermining non-Western concepts, approaches or understandings of knowledge in the construction of the 'Other' as a subtextual palimpsestic narrative of Imperialism" (Spivak, 1988, p. 101). Non-western epistemologies have been "disqualified as inadequate ... insufficiently elaborated ... naive ... beneath the required level of cognition or scientificity" (Foucault, 1982, p. 82) and the western episteme is re-inscribed over the colonised subject. In simpler terms, the mobilisation of objectivity becomes an instrument to further distance, objectify and diminish to maintain its own subjectivity. The dichotomous object/subject is applied as an apparatus to reify dominance. This reinscribes the "monological authority of the Western narrative" (Rigney, 2001, p. 7), giving primacy to sites of its own knowledge and knowledge production though exclusionary practices. In many instances, the subjugation of knowledge as a (Western) global, unitary hegemony has been so absolute that self-knowledge has been denied by those who have been subjugated, oppressed or who have experienced violence enacted upon them (Hartman, 1992, p. 483).

Western knowledge "has become a dominant global knowledge system and has often been accused of intolerance towards other persuasions" (Durie, 2005, p. 305). Australia's Eurocentric education system places western knowledge as front and centre, and "continues to exclude and marginalise Indigenous presence, perspectives and ways of knowing" (Hauser, Howlett, & Matthews, 2009, p. 47) in both school and university settings. Before we can move forward into culturally responsive pedagogy, it is important to de-colonise the academic milieu in which teachers engage, both in their initial teacher education and as they enter classrooms.

4 Decolonising the Academy

Early governments entrenched western knowledge as the dominant way of knowing in public education systems "through its assumed authority over all 'Other' ways of knowing" (Hauser et al., 2009, p. 48). A consequence of this hegemony is that all other knowledge systems are devalued and even 'silenced'. Global western knowledge systems are normative and 'ideal', and all others are marginalised. Foucault's ideas on knowledge as a strategy of power, argue Hauser et al. (2009), "provides a theoretical perspective of how Western [knowledge] has maintained its privileged position [in education institutions], and thus, how Indigenous ways of knowing in this context have been marginalised and excluded" (p. 48). Discourse in these areas is central to enabling the operation of hegemony, not only by the dominator, but also by the dominated: "the ways of knowing and power inherent in discourses reinforce one another to determine the circumstances under which knowledge can be deemed as truth or delegitimised and excluded (Hauser et al., 2009, p. 48).

Aboriginal and Torres Strait Islander students' academic performance in schools (or even participation/non-participation) is often experienced from a deficit framework "without interrogation of the schooling context, curriculum and pedagogies involved ... The power relations underpinning these educational provisions have to be interrogated" (Hart, Whatman, McLaughlin, & Sharma-Brymer, 2012, p. 707) in order to see the bigger picture. Until then, any 'closing the gap' initiative or social justice reforms will continue to be unfulfilled. Interrogation of the system and de-colonisation of the academy will help in rethinking and transforming the colonising encounter and may lead to positive social transformation, indeed, "an academy that honors difference and promotes healing ... and is not constrained by positivist assumptions" (Denzin & Lincoln, 2008, p. 15).

It is vitally important that, if it is indeed a priority to include Indigenous Knowledges in school curriculum, that universities and places of initial teacher education first be transformed. The academy must acknowledge and address its own ignorance if there is to be genuine acceptance and inclusion of Indigenous ways of Knowing, Being and Doing (Howlett, Ferreira, Seini, & Matthews, 2013). Otherwise, there is the potential for 'tokenism' as Indigenous Knowledges are added into curriculum, and this will filter down through teacher education candidates and into the teaching workforce (if it has not already). University staff must reflect on the foundations on which their discipline knowledge is based. This is particularly pertinent to disciplines such as science, where only one knowledge has been historically accepted:

> the hegemonic role of science in the curriculum, the lack of ontological pluralism within the academy, and finally, about [academics'] own privileged position within the academy. (Howlett et al., 2013, p. 70)

Incorporating Indigenous Knowledge into education programs "allows for the epistemological interrogation of knowledge production" (Baynes, 2015, p. 81) and, as well as helping to decolonise the curriculum in all learning areas, the benefit to education, teachers and students is multifaceted and numerous (Baynes, 2015). As Denzin and Lincoln (2008, p. 15) state:

> It turns the academy and teaching classrooms into sacred spaces, sites where Indigenous and non-Indigenous scholars interact, share experiences, take risks, explore alternative modes of interpretation and participate in shared agenda, coming together in a spirit of hope, love and shared community.

And that:

> an appreciation of Indigenous epistemology ... provides Western peoples with another view of knowledge production in diverse cultural sites. Such a perspective holds transformative possibilities, as people from dominant cultures come to understand the overtly cultural processes by which information is legitimised and delimited. (Kincheloe & Steinberg, 2008, p. 4)

5 Transformation in Science Education and Co-Actioning the Knowledges

The global knowledge system of western science is certainly the most encouraged form of knowing taught and learned in Australian classrooms. Global knowledge systems are accepted without question, and Indigenous ecological understandings are dismissed as exotic, irrelevant and distracting. Academics and teachers privilege a form of knowledge that presumes the cultural neutrality of science and technology education disciplines. Rather than disparaging or ignoring Indigenous values and choices, educators should seize a potent opportunity for a cross-cultural critique. Increasingly, this opportunity has been included in academic discourse, with a recent recognition and acknowledgement that there are other equally valuable ways to understand the world (Martin, 2012). According to Carter (2011)

> ... postcolonial perspectives can offer science education at once political analysis, cultural critique and philosophical insight to disrupt the continuing Eurocentrism of normative assumptions of cultural diversity. These assumptions are bound to stable and unitary ideas of nation, culture, identity, comparison and difference that, though now outdated, remain embedded within much of science education's take on cultural diversity. Postcolonial perspectives can help science education develop more appropriate and complex conceptualisations that include cultural translation and representation, difference, hybridity, localism, boundaries and borders, fragmentation, and pluralism in ways that reshape the categories of culture, identity and difference better suited to contemporary global culture. They can also expose some of the new forms of imperialism being entrenched within globalised approaches to science education reform. (p. 318)

Discussions and research on incorporating alternative ways of Knowing, such as Indigenous Knowledges, into the science classroom are also starting to become more common (Martin, 2012; Michie, Hogue, & Rious, 2018). However, some educators in both schools and higher education continue to dismiss the importance of Indigenous Knowledges in content and pedagogical practice:

> The incongruities between Western institutional structures and practices and Indigenous cultural forms is not easy to reconcile. The complexities that come into play when two fundamentally different worldviews converge present a formidable challenge. (Maher, 2012, p. 485)

It may be challenging but it is important to consider the relationship between Indigenous Knowledges and global knowledge systems as complementary rather than contradictory. Acknowledging that reference to the cultural context of learners may afford a more meaningful science education, particularly in our multicultural society, we can recognise that Indigenous Knowledges and perspectives can play a valid role in teaching and learning the science curriculum. As Michie and colleagues (2018, p. 1208) note "to define science only through the dominant Western lens has serious and detrimental ramifications as it leaves out critically important alternative knowledge".

For Indigenous and western scientific ways of Knowing to co-exist in the Australian science curriculum, a type of ontological pluralism is needed, where "western science is realised outside its universal framework and in its social context of locality, time and place" (Hauser et al., 2009, p. 49). Research widely recognises the need to develop co-action between knowledge systems in science education, although this discourse has tended to promote 'integration' of Indigenous Knowledges and perspectives into western science programs (Hauser et al., 2009; Howlett et al., 2013; Michie et al., 2018). More recent discourse is moving away from the idea of 'integrating', promoting instead a parallel approach for developing synergies across knowledge systems that highlights the complementary aspects of each. That is, a parallel approach recognises that each system is legitimate in its own right and utilising both in parallel maintains the possibility of interacting with, and mutually enriching the curriculum whenever possible and needed (Mazzocchi, 2018). Parallel approaches better represent the co-action and ontological pluralism than an integration approach entails. Integrated approaches have been noted by Mazzocchi (2018) as façade pluralism, whereby the 'other' knowledge system is incorporated into the dominant system and the dominant system has not been critically de-colonised. By co-actioning global knowledge systems and Indigenous Knowledges in science teaching and learning programs, recognition and validation are given to diverse ways of Knowing that have historically been silenced. This promotes reconciliation and enhanced outcomes for Aboriginal and Torres Strait Islander children.

6 Australian Experiences in Teaching and Learning Science

The Australian Curriculum (Australian Curriculum and Assessment Authority (ACARA), 2019) and its state/territory-based variations across the country promote the global knowledge system of western science. This is a reflection of the aforementioned Eurocentric and hegemonistic discourse around science understanding and knowledge creation, which may be distinct from students' cultural values and backgrounds. Since its inception as the national curriculum in 2008, the Australian Curriculum has included cross-curricular priorities, one of which is Aboriginal and Torres Strait Islander Histories and Cultures. This is an area to be 'integrated' across discipline learning areas, and specifically working towards the following goals, that:

– Aboriginal and Torres Strait Islander students are able to see themselves, their identities and their cultures reflected in the curriculum of each of the learning areas, can fully participate in the curriculum and can build their self-esteem;
– the Aboriginal and Torres Strait Islander Histories and Cultures cross-curriculum priority is designed for all students to engage in reconciliation, respect and;
– recognition of the world's oldest continuous living cultures (ACARA, 2019).

Until recently, this cross-curricula priority was rarely included in the science learning area. In response to feedback from community and educators, ACARA now has 95 new examples (elaborations) of how teachers can incorporate Aboriginal and Torres Strait Islander histories and cultures into science teaching and learning programs. These elaborations demonstrate the connections between Aboriginal and Torres Strait Islander histories and cultures and core science concepts in the Australian Curriculum. Importantly, the elaborations were developed with the assistance of ACARA's Aboriginal and Torres Strait Islander Advisory Group and Task Force, and Science and Aboriginal and Torres Strait Islander curriculum specialists. They acknowledge that Aboriginal and Torres Strait Islander peoples have "worked scientifically for millennia and continue to contribute to contemporary science" (ACARA, 2019).

Also relevant is the recent implementation of the Australian Professional Standards for Teachers by the Australian Institute for Teaching and School

Leadership (AITSL, 2017). These seven Standards hold teachers more accountable for what it is they should know and do and are engaged with in initial teacher education courses, teacher registration, classroom teaching, and job/promotion opportunities. They include Standards 1.4 and 2.4, which focus on: Demonstrating knowledge and understanding of the impact of culture, cultural identity and linguistic background on the education of students from Aboriginal and Torres Strait Islander backgrounds; and understanding and respecting Aboriginal and Torres Strait Islander people to promote reconciliation between Indigenous and non-Indigenous Australians (AITSL, 2017).

Even with the above inclusions in the national curriculum, and the expectations inherent in the Australian Professional Standards for Teachers, primary teachers in Australian schools are often reluctant to engage with Indigenous Knowledges and perspectives within their teaching and learning programs. In general, pre-service teachers and practicing teachers feel uncertain and ill-prepared to teach Indigenous Knowledge or even Aboriginal and Torres Strait Islander students themselves in culturally appropriate ways (Baynes, 2015; Moodie, 2017; Nakata, 2010). As Harrison and Greenfield (2011, p. 74) state: "teachers lament they do not possess the knowledge to teach about Aboriginal Australia".

Baynes (2015) reports that teachers are hesitant to include Indigenous Knowledges as they feel they do not have the expertise to do it authentically. Yunkaporta and McGinty (2009) found that teachers avoided Indigenous perspectives because they felt uncomfortable and were "fearful of overstepping cultural boundaries, whether real or imagined" (p. 63). This is concerning for a number of reasons. Most obviously this may have an impact on the learning, development, and perhaps even feelings of identity and belonging experienced by Aboriginal and Torres Strait Islander children in the classroom. It also maintains validation of the hegemony, even though it is an expectation within the teaching profession that teachers are proficient and active in this area. In the science learning area, there is even more reluctance by teachers to engage with Indigenous Knowledges and pedagogies (that is, if science is even taught at all in primary schools, but that is a topic for another time). Michie (2002) claims that teachers have little knowledge about Indigenous Science. Baynes and Austin (2012) also report that science teachers' initial reactions to the cross-curricular priorities in the Australian Curriculum were negative ("Is this really science?" (p. 61)), and that teacher apathy and lack of knowledge were challenges to implementation.

Co-actioning and parallel ontological methodologies in implementing Indigenous Knowledges into school science may be helpful in reconsidering teaching and learning science. Some examples include using Both ways (Michie, Hogue,

& Rious, 2018) or 2Ways Education (Michie, Anzelark, & Uibo, 1998), and/or pedagogical practices that draw on Indigenous pedagogies, such as affective storytelling (Brits, de Beer, & Mabotja, 2019), or the 8 Ways Aboriginal Pedagogy (Yunkaporta, 2009). These can also play a role in making the curriculum more inclusive. Chinn (2007) found that when teachers shared stories, critiqued the curriculum and discussed issues of power and knowledge, it allowed them to consider the purpose of science education from a de-colonising perspective to include 'serving the common good' (p. 1262). This allowed those teachers to recognise the potential for Indigenous Knowledges in their teaching practice. Considering and implementing the co-action of two knowledge systems is still a challenging area for many academics and teachers and may be better represented as thinking and working across the cultural interface (Nakata, 2002) or liminal space (Hogue & Forrest, 2018).

7   Working across a Cultural Interface

The current education system is based on dualities of western and 'other', of culture and 'mainstream' and, until recently, few researchers have considered the complexities at the intersection between them. Nakata (2002) names this intersection the cultural interface, a space where knowledge systems meet, interact, develop, change and transform. It is not about replacing one system with another or about undermining one or the other (Nakata, 2002), and it can be considered from both Indigenous and non-Indigenous perspectives.

For Aboriginal and Torres Strait Islander teachers, the notion of cultural interface represents what they may need to navigate the two knowledge systems to learn and teach science in a way that represents their two worlds. As Nakata (2002, p. 28) states:

> The notion of the Cultural Interface as a place of constant tension and negotiation of different interests and systems of Knowledge means that both must be reflected on and interrogated. It is not simply about opposing knowledges and discourses that compete and conflict with traditional ones. It is about seeing what conditions the convergence of all these and of examining and interrogating all knowledge and practices associated with issues so that [Indigenous people] take a responsible but self-interested course in relation to our future practice.

For non-Indigenous pre-service and practicing teachers it represents what they may need to navigate to engage with and 'accept' 'other' knowledges. It represents more a liminal space as they move from perhaps only considering or understanding one worldview, into considerations and understandings of multiple (Indigenous) worldviews. The challenge is to stimulate conversations and focal points, perhaps beyond framework or fixity, to engage and embed "situated, plural and reflexive knowledges that work together in inherently relational ways to nourish the cultural sustainability of Indigenous knowledges" (Acton et al., 2017, p. 1311).

There is a canon of literature that highlights the role of teacher education in any successful attempt at education reform (for example, Austin & Hickey, 2011; Rudduck, 1991; Rutherford, 1971). Perhaps movement within the cultural interface and liminal space represents such transformation of ideas and perspectives that it can be construed as education reform. Universities and initial teacher educators have a responsibility and influence in helping pre-service and graduating teachers navigate this space, in order to not only de-colonise the academy, but to enable and build capacity to work with Indigenous Knowledges in future classrooms. It will be important then for Faculty members to firstly engage in the cultural interface and liminal spaces themselves, challenging their own preconceptions, prejudices and hegemony of their discipline area, and acknowledge the transformations that may be necessary to co-action the knowledge systems and pedagogies within their initial teacher education spaces.

8 Co-Actioning Indigenous Knowledges and Global Knowledge Systems as a Threshold Concept

According to Meyer and Land (2005), a threshold concept can be considered "akin to a portal, opening up a new and previously inaccessible way of thinking about something" (p. 3). It represents a transformed way of understanding or interpreting subject matter or worldview; without this transformation a learner cannot progress. It is different from a core concept, which is a key concept or idea that progresses understanding in a learning area, instead, threshold concepts enable new and different ways of thinking. They tend to contain similar characteristics that cross disciplinary areas and contexts. According to Meyer and Land (2005), threshold concepts are transformative "in that, once understood, its potential effect on student learning and behaviour is to occasion a significant shift in the perception of a subject" (p. 7). This transformed perspective may mean a shift in affect, values, attitudes and beliefs. This change is unlikely to be forgotten, and so is likely to be irreversible; it tends to demonstrate the interrelatedness of areas (integrative); and the concepts are often 'troublesome' or problematic for learners.

This troublesome knowledge represents a liminal space that learners need to move through in order to have a transformative effect: "Difficulty in understanding threshold concepts may leave the learner in a state of liminality" (Meyer & Land, 2005, p. 16), with liminality being a variable state of being, and a useful metaphor to aid understanding of conceptual transformations. This liminal state equates well with Nakata's (2002) cultural interface discussed previously. The liminal state and the perceived 'crossing the threshold' might be unsettling for some learners, involve a sense of loss, or even an identity transformation. It is these characteristics that form an effective representation of, and an argument for, the movement of practice from a purely western science teaching and learning program to a co-actioned Indigenous/western science teaching and learning program as a threshold concept for both pre-service and in-service teachers.

For Aboriginal and Torres Strait Islander pre-service and in-service teachers, this threshold concept may involve movement within the cultural interface (and liminal space) of western science and Indigenous Knowledge – 'unlearning' to preface/prioritise western knowledges in their teaching; and 'relearning' the strength and validity of Indigenous Knowledges and the intricate links and interrelatedness of and between the knowledge systems (that often western science has stemmed from Indigenous Knowledges in the first place).

One example where this is seen is in the tensions and anxieties experienced by Aboriginal and Torres Strait Islander pre-service teachers during their (western) degrees and on teaching practicum. Aboriginal and Torres Strait Islander pre-service teachers are presumed to have a superior ability and understanding of Indigenous Knowledges simply by virtue of their own Indigeneity (Hart et al., 2012), and unrealistic expectations to know all things Aboriginal (Santoro, 2007). They must negotiate the pedagogical demands and expectations of university first, then the school/classroom of their practicum, both of which have historically privileged western knowledge and tended to silence Indigenous Knowledges. This can be represented as a threshold concept, as for these learners it is full of 'troublesomeness' – the tension in the cultural interface of the two competing systems of knowledge. It may be "manifested by rejection, resistance, ambivalence and accommodation" (Hart et al., 2012, p. 710) as learners move within and between the knowledge systems. To move within this cultural interface and to engage with the transformative possibilities, learners must be able to navigate with agency (Nakata, 2010). Aboriginal and Torres Strait Islander pre-service teachers must have respectful and equal relationships with education staff, a right to negotiate curriculum, and validation of their Knowledges and lived experiences.

For non-Indigenous pre-service and in-service teachers, the threshold concept might involve movement into the liminal space of experiencing, understanding and even 'accepting' Indigenous Knowledges as a valid perspective in science teaching and learning. This is troublesome knowledge for non-Indigenous people, and although it is important and exciting, it can be 'alien' and "surprisingly difficult to get students to engage with" (Meyer & Land, 2005, p. 19). This disengagement, apathy, reluctance, and even outright refusal to engage with the troublesome knowledge of co-actioning Indigenous Knowledges into a western knowledge system, has been demonstrated repeatedly in the literature (Baynes, 2015; Yunkaporta & McGinty, 2009). In addition, it is recognised within threshold concept discussions, noting that while some students will "productively negotiate the liminal space, others will find difficulty in doing so" (Meyer & Land, 2005, p. 27). As a threshold concept, the importance of emphasising the multiplicity of thinking and doing science needs engaging with. Learners should take seriously the fact that Indigenous Knowledges are a valid and appropriate vehicle for science. They may find the different knowledges alluring, but also counterintuitive to what they have experienced in previous education. This may challenge understandings of a singular science viewpoint and suggest the need for pluralism and co-action in their teaching and learning.

This troublesome knowledge includes recognising the 'boundedness' of one knowledge system that rejects 'others'. That is, moving to complex new perspectives that acknowledge the implications of hegemony as culturally constraining and determining of behaviours and choices. It may also include interrogating perceptions of 'other', 'otherness' and 'otherising' and even interrogating perceptions of 'culture' itself. Indigenous Knowledges in science cannot be simply reduced to distinct understandings or skills to be learned, rather as a shared way of perceiving the way in which concepts are related and relational, from an epistemological and ontological foundation. This movement through the threshold concept and through the liminal space will transform learners' perceptions of themselves as well as perceptions of the subject. Undoubtedly this will cause some learner discomfort (Meyer & Land, 2005), as they move beyond 'their' world to expose the previously hidden interrelatedness and complex interconnectivities, the tensions and contradictions inherent in engaging with different knowledge systems and de-colonising the learning. It is about 'becoming', transforming teaching identities to include that of an 'informed ally' in order to enact a teaching and learning program in science that encompasses both ways of Knowing and Doing.

8   Conclusion

Critically questioning and interrogating the ideas embodied in the previous sections of this chapter will influence the way pre-service teachers approach teaching and learning when they enter the teaching workforce. This includes questioning: the complexities of defining Indigenous Knowledges; de-colonising the Eurocentric curriculum in universities and schools; the absence and silence of Indigenous Knowledges within universities and schools; and the critical pedagogies and perspectives developed through working in the cultural interface and liminal space of the global and Indigenous Knowledge systems. Taking account of not only the epistemological contexts, subjectivities and knowledge production/practices of Aboriginal and Torres Strait Islander pre-service teachers, but also the knowledge systems from within which science curricula are created, offers multiple sediments for reflection in co-actioning and informing what appear to be divergent frameworks. Diverse knowledges, and Indigenous Knowledge systems have relevance and meaning in western science. A threshold paradigm that encompasses co-actioning as a reciprocal rigour of value, legitimacy and interfacing seems an agent of transformation, and one that transforms agency in the 'becoming' of authentic understanding and paucity to a reflected, diverse reality.

References

Acton, R., Salter, P., Lenoy, M., & Stevenson, R. (2017). Conversations on cultural sustainability: Stimuli for embedding Indigenous knowledges and ways of being into curriculum. *Higher Education Research and Development, 36*(7), 1311–1325.

Austin, J., & Hickey, A. (2011). Incorporating Indigenous knowledge into the curriculum: Responses of science teacher educators. *The International Journal of Science in Society, 2*(4), 139–152.

Australian Curriculum and Assessment Authority (ACARA). (2019). *Australian Curriculum*. Retrieved October 29, 2019, from https://www.australiancurriculum.edu.au/f-10-curriculum

Australian Institute for Teaching and School Leadership (AITSL). (2017). *Australian professional standards for teachers*. Retrieved October 29, 2019, from https://www.aitsl.edu.au/teach/standards

Bala, A., & Joseph, G. (2007). Indigenous knowledge and western science: The possibility of dialogue. *Race and Class, 49*(1), 39–61.

Battiste, M. (2008). *Indigenous knowledge foundations for first nations*. Retrieved April 1, 2020, from https://gov.viu.ca/sites/default/files/indegenousknowledgepaperbymariebattistecopy.pdf

Baynes, R. (2015). Teachers' attitudes to including Indigenous knowledge in the Australian science curriculum. *The Australian Journal of Indigenous Education, 45*(1), 80–90.

Baynes, R., & Austin, J. (2012). *Indigenous knowledge in the Australian national curriculum for science: From conjecture to classroom practice.* Paper presented at the International Indigenous Development Research Conference, Auckland, NZ.

Blair, N. (2015). *Privileging Australian Indigenous knowledge sweet Potatoes, Spiders, Waterlilies and Brick Walls.* Common Ground Publishing.

Brits, S., de Beer, J., & Mabotja, S. (2019). *Through the eyes of a puppet: A pedagogy of play for the incorporation of Indigenous knowledge in the life and natural sciences curriculum.* Retrieved November 1, 2019, from http://uir.unisa.ac.za/bitstream/handle/10500/22898/Sanette%20Brits,Josef%20de%20Beer,%20Sam%20Mabotja.pdf?sequence=1

Carter, L. (2011). The challenge of science education and Indigenous knowledge. *Counterpoints, 379*, 312–329.

Chilisa, B. (2011). *Indigenous research methodologies.* Sage Publications.

Chinn, P. (2007). Decolonizing methodologies and Indigenous knowledge: The role of culture, place and personal experience in professional development. *Journal of Research in Science Teaching, 44*(9), 1247–1268.

Cronje, A., de Beer, J., & Ankiewicz, P. (2015). The development and use of an instrument to investigate science teachers views on Indigenous knowledge. *African Journal of Research in Mathematics, Science and Technology Education, 19*(3), 319–332.

Daily Telegraph. (2018, November 1). *Science kooriculum outrage over Indigenous school scheme.* Retrieved November 28, 2019, from https://www.dailytelegraph.com.au/news/science-kooriculum-outrage-over-indigenous-school-scheme/news-story/2991d2acec1ec3b7e8b651409da827e5

de Beer, J., & Whitlock, E. (2009). Indigenous knowledge in the life sciences classroom: Put on your de Bono hats! *The American Biology Teacher, 71*(4), 209–216.

Denzin, N. K., & Lincoln, Y. S. (2008). Introduction: Critical methodologies and Indigenous inquiry. In N. Denzin, Y. S. Lincoln, & L. Smith (Eds.), *Handbook of critical and Indigenous methodologies* (pp. 1–20). Sage.

Devie Naidoo, P., & Vithal, R. (2014). Teacher approaches to introducing Indigenous knowledge in school science classrooms. *African Journal of Research in Mathematics, Science and Technology Education, 18*(3), 253–263.

Duran, E., & Duran, B. (1995). *Native American postcolonial psychology.* State University of New York.

Durie, M. (2004). Understanding health and illness: Research at the interface between science and Indigenous knowledge. *International Journal of Epidemiology, 33*(1), 1138–1143.

Durie, M. (2005). Indigenous knowledge within a global knowledge system. *Higher Education Policy, 18*, 301–312.

Ens, E., Finlayson, M., Preuss, K., Jackson, S., & Holcombe, S. (2012). Australian approaches for managing 'country' using Indigenous and non-Indigenous knowledge. *Ecological Management and Restoration, 13*(1), 100–107.

Foucault, M. (1982). Two lectures. In *Power/knowledge* (pp. 82–85). Pantheon Press.

Fredericks, B. L. (2007). Utilising the concept of pathway as a framework for Indigenous research. *Australian Journal of Indigenous Education, 36*, 15–22.

Goeman, M. (2008). From place to territories and back again: Centering storied land in the discussion of Indigenous nation-building. *International Journal of Critical Indigenous Studies, 1*(1), 23–34.

Green, L. (2008). 'Indigenous knowledge' and 'science': Reframing the debate on knowledge diversity. *Archaeologies: Journal of the World Archaeological Congress, 4*(1), 144–163.

Harrison, N., & Greenfield, M. (2011). Relationship to place: Positioning Aboriginal knowledge and perspectives in classroom pedagogies. *Critical Studies in Education, 52*(1), 65–76.

Hart, V., Whatman, S., McLaughlin, J., & Sharma-Brymer, V. (2012). Pre-service teachers' pedagogical relationships and experiences of embedding Indigenous Australian knowledge in the teaching practicum. *Compare: A Journal of Comparative and International Education, 42*(5), 703–723.

Hartman, A. (1992). In search of subjugated knowledge. *Social Work, 37*(6), 483–484.

Harvey, A., & Russell-Mundine, G. (2019). Decolonising the curriculum: Using graduate qualities to embed Indigenous knowledge at the academic cultural interface. *Teaching in Higher Education, 24*(6), 789–808.

Hauser, V., Howlett, C., & Matthews, C. (2009). The place of Indigenous knowledge in tertiary science education: A case study of Canadian practices in indigenising the curriculum. *The Australian Journal of Indigenous Education, 38*, 46–58.

Heidegger, M., Macquarrie, J., Robinson, E., & Carmen, T. (2008). *Being and time.* HarperCollins.

Hogue, M., & Forrest, J. (2018). Bridging cultures over-under: Digital navigation to create liminal spaces of possibility. *Canadian Journal of Family and Youth, 10*(2), 67–84.

Howlett, C., Ferreira, J., Seini, M., & Matthews, C. (2013). Indigenising the Griffith school of education curriculum: Where to from here? *The Australian Journal of Indigenous Education, 42*(1), 68–74.

Kidman, J., Abrams, E., & McRae, H. (2011). Imaginary subjects: School science, Indigenous students and knowledge-power relations. *British Journal of Sociology and Education, 32*(2), 203–220.

Kincheloe, J., & Steinberg, S. (2008). Indigenous knowledges in education: Complexities, dangers, and profound benefits. In N. Denzin, Y. S. Lincoln, & L. Smith (Eds.), *Handbook of critical and Indigenous methodologies* (pp. 135–155). Sage.

Kovach, M. (2009). *Indigenous methodologies: Characteristics, conversations, and contexts.* University of Toronto Press, Scholarly Publishing Division.

Kuhn, T. (2000). Reflections on my critics. In J. Conant & J. Haugeland (Eds.), *The road since structure* (pp. 123–175). University of Chicago Press.

Lanzano, C. (2013). What kind of knowledge is 'Indigenous knowledge'? Critical insights from a case study in Burkina Faso. *Transcience, 4*(2), 3–18.

Maher, M. (2012). Teacher education with Indigenous ways of knowing, being and doing as a key pillar. *AlterNative: An International Journal of Indigenous Peoples, 8*(3), 343–356.

Martin, D. (2012). Two-eyed seeing: A framework for understanding Indigenous and non-Indigenous approaches to Indigenous health research. *Canadian Journal of Nursing Research, 44*(2), 20–42.

Mazzocchi, F. (2018). Under what conditions may Western science and Indigenous knowledge be jointly used and what does this really entail? Insights from a Western perspective stance. *Social Epistemology, 32*(5), 325–337.

Meyer, J., & Land, R. (2005). Threshold concepts and troublesome knowledge: Epistemological considerations and a conceptual framework for teaching and learning. *Higher Education, 49*, 373–388.

Michie, M. (2002). Why Indigenous science should be included in the school science curriculum. *Australian Science Teachers Journal, 48*(2), 36–41.

Michie, M., Anlezark, J., & Uibo, D. (1998, July). Beyond bush tucker: Implementing Indigenous perspectives through the science curriculum. In *Proceedings of the 47th Conference of the Australian Science Teachers Association* (pp. 101–110). Northern Territory Department of Education, Australia.

Michie, M., Hogue, M., & Rious, J. (2018). The application of both-ways and two-eyed seeing pedagogy: Reflections on engaging and teaching science to post-secondary Indigenous students. *Research in Science Education, 48*, 1205–1220.

Moodie, N. (2017). Learning about knowledge: Threshold concepts for Indigenous studies in education. *The Australian Educational Researcher, 46*, 735–749.

Moreton, R. (2006). *The right to dream* (Doctoral thesis). University of Western Sydney. Retrieved December 19, 2019, from https://researchdirect.westernsydney.edu.au/islandora/object/uws%3A2495/datastream/P DF/view

Moreton-Robinson, A., & Walter, M. (2009). Indigenous methodologies in social research. In A. Bryman (Ed.), *Social research methods*. Oxford University Press.

Nakata, M. (2002). Indigenous knowledge and the cultural interface: Underlying issues at the intersection of knowledge and information systems. *IFLA Journal, 28*(5), 281–291.

Nakata, M. (2007). *Disciplining the savages: Savaging the disciplines*. Aboriginal Studies Press.

Nakata, M. (2010). The cultural interface of Islander and scientific knowledge. *The Australian Journal of Indigenous Education, 39*, 53–57.

Page, S. (2014). Exploring new conceptualizations of old problems: Researching and reorienting teaching in Indigenous studies to transform student learning. *The Australian Journal of Indigenous Education, 43*(1), 21–30.

Rigney, L. (2001). *A first perspective of Indigenous Australian participation in science: Framing Indigenous research towards Indigenous Australian intellectual sovereignty*. Retrieved April 1, 2020, from https://ncis.anu.edu.au/_lib/doc/LI_Rigney_First_perspective.pdf

Robertson, D. (2005). Re-imagining and rescripting the future of education: Global knowledge economy discourses and the challenge to education systems. *Comparative Education, 41*(2), 151–170.

Rose, D. (1996). *Nourishing terrains: Australian Aboriginal views of landscape and wilderness*. Australian Heritage Commission.

Royal, C. (2007). *Creativity and matauranga maori: Towards tools for innovation*. Hau Taumatu Trust Publishing.

Rudduck, J. (1991). The language of consciousness and the landscape of action: Tensions in teacher education. *British Educational Research Journal, 17*(4), 319–331.

Rutherford, F. (1971). Preparing teachers for curriculum reform. *Science Education, 55*(4), 555–568.

Santoro, N. (2007). 'Outsiders' and 'others': 'Different' teachers teaching in culturally diverse classrooms. *Teachers and Teaching: Theory and Practice, 13*(1), 81–97.

Smith, L. T. (1999). *Decolonising methodology: Research and Indigenous peoples*. Zed Books.

Spivak, G. (1988). Can the subaltern speak? In C. Nelson & L. Grossberg (Eds.), *Marxism and the interpretation of culture* (pp. 99–111). Macmillan.

Tanaka, M., Williams, L., Benoit, Y., Duggan, R., Moir, L., & Scarrow, J. (2007). Transforming pedagogies: Pre-service reflections on learning and teaching in an Indigenous world. *Teacher Development, 11*(1), 99–109.

Tau, T. (1999). Matauranga Maori as an epistemology. *Te Pouhere Korero: Maori History Maori People, 1*, 10–23.

Watson, I. (2017). Standing our ground and telling the one true story. In D. Dudgeon, J. Jeannie Herbert, J. Milroy, & D. Oxenham (Eds.), *Us women, our ways, our world* (pp. 128–143). Magabala Books.

Yunkaporta, T. (2009). *Aboriginal pedagogies at the cultural interface*. Retrieved November 1, 2019, from https://researchonline.jcu.edu.au/10974/

Yunkaporta, T., & McGinty, S. (2009). Reclaiming Aboriginal knowledge at the cultural interface. *Australian Educational Researcher, 36*(2), 55–72.

CHAPTER 4

Passing Time

Kelly Menzel

Abstract

American author Nella Larson (1929) wrote the acclaimed novel *Passing*. The novel's protagonist, Irene Redfield, is a light-skinned black woman, hiding her true identity while 'passing' as a white woman. The novel explores the social and economic advantages and disadvantages associated with racial passing. Passing is a process by which a person can move from one cultural or racial group to another undetected. For Australia's Indigenous people, this was different as passing was the policy. The government undertook a form of biological genocide to 'breed out' dark skin, to dilute by cross breeding and force people to separate from Indigenous language, culture and family. The policy meant death by integration and assimilation, and while there were segregation policies as well, these were stop-gaps for the 'final solution' of passing and the total annihilation of the Indigenous population. The shame of ancestors being forced to pass, as well as the threat of fake Aboriginality labels, or 'Johnny come lately' status, has prevented any study of passing as a phenomenon from an Indigenous perspective. It shapes our lives, but none of us want to see it. In this chapter, I explore my grandfather's story of racial identity denial and how this legacy of cultural genocide, through alternative means, has been passed down in my family.

Keywords

passing – racism – internalised racism – Indigenous

1 Introduction

American author Nella Larson (1929) wrote the acclaimed novel *Passing*. The novel's protagonist, Irene Redfield, is a light-skinned black woman, hiding her true identity while 'passing' as a white woman. The novel explores the social and economic advantages and disadvantages associated with racial passing. Passing is a process by which a person can move from one cultural or racial group to another undetected. For Australia's Indigenous people, this was different as passing was the policy. The government undertook a form of biological genocide to 'breed out' dark skin, to dilute by cross breeding and force people to separate from Indigenous language, culture and family. The policy meant death by integration and assimilation, and while there were segregation policies as well, these were stop-gaps for the 'final solution' of passing and the total annihilation of the Indigenous population. The shame of ancestors being forced to pass, as well as the threat of fake Aboriginality labels, or 'Johnny come lately' status, has prevented any study of passing as a phenomenon from an Indigenous perspective. It shapes our lives, but none of us want to see it. In this chapter, I explore my grandfather's story of racial identity denial and how this legacy of cultural genocide, through alternative means, has been passed down in my family.

Wald (cited in Godfrey & Ashanti Young, 2018) argues "[p]assing is a social construction. In order for a person to pass for an identity unlike the one socially ascribed, the viewer of the person must hold essentialist ideas about what constitutes and looks like a given identity" (p. 193). Passing is an adaptation to the circumstances of oppression.

Passing is an American concept (and a concept within queer literature; Butler, 1990; Pfeffer, 2014) that is different within the Australian political context. This is because passing came out of abolition times, when former slaves who were 'high yellow' passed for white to 'hack the system', improve their lives and survive. Passing was resisted by the system that wanted segregation, so the 'one drop' (of black blood) rule was enforced. The one-drop rule was a social and legal principle of racial classification. The rule asserted that any person, even with only one ancestor from sub-Saharan Africa, was considered black (Tallbear, 2003).

For Australian Indigenous people, passing was different because it was the policy (McCorquodale, 1987). The idea was the government undertook a form of biological genocide to 'breed out' dark skin, to dilute by cross breeding and force people to separate from Indigenous language, culture and family (Anderson, 2006; Levine & Bashford, 2010). The policy meant death by integration and assimilation, and while there were segregation policies as well, these were stop-gaps for the 'final solution' (James, 2018) of passing and the total annihilation of the Indigenous population (Australian Human Rights Commission [AHRC], 1997).

So, today we have the opposite of the one drop rule. This is called 'pan Indigeneity' (Kowal & Paradies, 2017; Watt & Kowal, 2019). Pan Indigeneity is a concept that was introduced in the 1960s, with the argument that "all people of Indigenous descent who self-identified as such were equally Indigenous, vigorously opposing views that people with less Indigenous ancestry were not authentic" (Kowal & Paradies, 2017, p. 105). However, this has created division within some Indigenous communities, with people being shamed and berated for being on the wrong end of the blood quantum scale (Denholm, 2015; Tomlinson, 2008). The shame of ancestors being forced to pass, as well as the threat of fake Aboriginality labels, or 'Johnny come lately' (a newcomer to their Indigeneity) status (Carlson, 2013), has prevented any study of passing as a phenomenon (Rowley, 1971). It shapes our lives, but none of us want to see it.

In this chapter, I explore my grandfather's story of racial identity denial and how this legacy of cultural genocide, through alternative means, has been passed down in my family.

2   To Pass or Not to Pass

There are very few pieces written about passing from an Indigenous Australian perspective. One is a small publication from Darlene Johnson's (1993) Honours thesis: *Ab/originality: Playing and Passing versus Assimilation*. Johnson discusses racial identity strategies and passing as performance. Her argument is that "the production of Aboriginal identities has been contingent on a negotiation, a dependence and an enduring subjugation that has also been a struggle for resistance and survival; a struggle that IS not so easily articulated" (1993, p. 19). She, like me, is fair skinned and has experienced racism from outside and from within the Indigenous community. She has been asked such questions as "how much of you is Aboriginal?" (p. 21). This question is rooted in the assumption that there is such a thing as a 'real Aborigine' (Carlson, 2016); that blood quantum is relevant to what is considered 'authentic' Indigeneity (Bennett, 2015; Dodson, 2017); and that someone who is not a 'full blood' must justify their identity. I too have been asked such questions. As Johnson's work illustrates, this reduces my Aboriginality in "terms of fractions" (p. 21) and then begs the question 'who is an 'authentic' Aborigine'? Because my ancestry includes the colonised and colonising, does this also mean, according to some, I am a 'Johnny come lately'? The trauma of the legacy of colonisation means that some stereotypes still hold strong and I do not fit the stereotype perpetuated.

Interestingly, Johnson (1993) also argues passing can be a positive performance. She suggests:

> ... an understanding of passing as an alternative form, as an identity strategy and representation that makes it possible to construct new ways for thinking about the limitations of Aboriginality and identity politics. Passing then can be read as a positive cultural construction of acting out

> identity at different moments. It emerges here, as a specific articulation of identity as strategic and performative. (p. 21)

Johnson goes on to posit passing as a way of concealing one's identity at certain moments in time. She contends, "[i]t is not simply about denying your Ab/originality or abandoning a part of yourself, but rather it's about protecting it. Passing refuses any idea of a sovereign master and the idea of self-renunciation" (p. 22). I feel uncomfortable agreeing with Johnson's tenet that passing is a positive act of "refusing the permanent boundaries of a fixed identity" (p. 23); that it is a masquerade performed to negotiate walking in two worlds. Whilst eloquent and I see the point she is making, from my lived experience, Johnson's thesis that passing is "masquerade as a strategy" is almost too grandiloquent for me. I acknowledge and respect this is her position and I judge her in no way, but I have always felt being fair skinned and inadvertently passing for a white person has placed me in a position of privilege. I have had access to certain things that my friends and members of my family have not, simply based on the colour of my skin. Historically, I sometimes passed because I felt too unsafe to declare my Indigeneity. I heard the terrible racist things other people said about the Aboriginal community and I did not want that vitriol aimed at me. The ramifications were too high. The consequences were too violent. I felt forced into the dilemma of choosing between complicity and confrontation. I often opted out. I am ashamed of that now. I wish I had the strength to confront the racism I witnessed and vicariously experienced. I am now interested in the way individuals manage social stigma by constructing and enacting passing as a strategy to survive.

3   The P/pas(sed)

It is important to consider the concept of Aboriginal identity within the context of the systemic and institutionalised genocide and the regime of control and 'protection' that took place after the colonisation of Australia (Johnson, 1993; Grant & Wronski, 2008). The implementation of colonial policies that targeted Aboriginal and Torres Strait Islanders resulted in significant physical, emotional and spiritual ill-health and the death of many people (Durie, 2003). Although colonial governments in the nineteenth century professed abhorrence at the brutality of colonial settlers, they were unwilling or unable to stop their activities (Grant & Wronski, 2008). Upon hearing of the mistreatment of the Indigenous population in Australia in 1838, the British Parliament appointed a Select Committee to inquire into the condition of Aboriginal people. They subsequently passed a bill to protect Aboriginal people from being massacred by colonial settlers (Sherwood, 2010). This resulted in the creation of Aboriginal Protection Boards, legislation and policy developed to 'protect' the Indigenous population (Sherwood, 2010).

The Victorian Central Board for the Protection of Aborigines, established by the *Aboriginal Protection Act 1869*, made Victoria the first state to enact comprehensive regulations on the lives of the Aboriginal population. Western Australia passed an equivalent statute in 1886 and in 1909 the New South Wales government passed the *Aborigines Protection Act NSW*. These Acts provided for the establishment of the Aborigines Protection Boards (McCorquodale, 1987). Each states' Board was "charged with the duty of controlling and promoting the welfare" of Aboriginal people (Macilwain, 2011).

However, the legislation and policies were not enacted as they were intended; the 'protection policies' became a notorious outcome of colonialism, mandating near total control over Aboriginal peoples (Lapham, 2016). During the late 1800s and early 1900s, the lives of Aboriginal people were regulated to such an extent that governments controlled where Aboriginal people lived; where they worked; what kind of work they did; who they could associate with; who they could marry; the language they could speak; where they could eat; what they could eat; or whether or not they could use public transport or move from one area to another (McCorquodale, 1987).

Policies of removal also saw Aboriginal people moved off traditional land and placed in missions, largely to allow for the ongoing expansion across Aboriginal Country to enclose it as the settler's own (Standfield, 2011). Missions consisted of poor housing, were largely over-crowded and disease flourished. Food rations were supplied to some people, generally consisting of only flour, sugar and tea (Sherwood, 2010). Elsie Roughsey (1984) described her own experience: "[l]ife was regimented and far removed from the natural, rhythmic and family oriented bush life" (p. 24).

All of the above needs to be taken into consideration when thinking about identity, how to stay safe and how to keep one's children, family and community safe, and why an Indigenous person would consider passing for white. It is a cultural strategy for survival. Passing for white becomes a strategy for attaining the necessary distance "between oneself and one's image" (Doane, 1987, p. 82) and could have meant the difference between life and death.

4   My Grandfather Passed

My grandfather was the poster child for passing. He was born around 1915. He was just dark enough to have his identity questioned but just fair enough to pass as white. His peers would call him 'Kanaka Keith'. He would angrily reply "I am not a fucking Kanaka!". Which was true. He was not a fucking Kanaka.[1] He was also referred to as 'Aborigine Keith'. There was nowhere to hide from this 'accusation'. He really was Aborigine Keith. His Aboriginality caused him great shame. He experienced violence and abuse and as such, he wanted nothing to do with his Indigeneity. He would occasionally say we were "licked by the tar brush" or "black Irish" but never more than this. His shame caused him to drink himself into obscurity, but not before he took the violence out on his wife and children.

He never spoke about his family history or his cultural identity. Maybe he even talked himself into believing he was not really black? His denial of his cultural identity laid itself bare on his body and psyche. By midlife, he was a violent but functional alcoholic, depressed and massively overweight. I have no doubt he would have been diagnosed a diabetic with hypertension and cardiac concerns, if he ever bothered to see a doctor. He was depressed and repressed and he acted out his anger on those around him. He died in his late 50s in the early 1970s. The family rarely spoke about him after he died. My grandmother despised him. She scattered his ashes out the front of the pub where he spent most of his time (not at sea, as he had romanticised about). She burned every photograph of him and destroyed every item of his that existed. I have learned more about him from my father, his son-in-law, than any other family member. Apparently, I have his infectious laugh and green eyes. He was incredibly bright, a prolific reader and a bastard to the core, except at Christmas when life was happy for one beautiful but brief moment.

Townsend, Markus, and Bergsieker (2009) state "[m]ixed-race individuals often encounter situations in which their identities are a source of tension, particularly when expressions of multiracial and biracial identity are not supported or allowed" (p. 185). My grandfather's experiences and actions went far beyond this statement. His identity denial was deeply rooted in self-hatred. Originally, I assume his (my) family encouraged denial of our Indigeneity as a form of self-preservation and protection. As already discussed, structural violence, assimilation and the forced removal of children were governmental policy at that time in Australia (Ellinghaus, 2003). In this context of violence, it makes perfect sense that my family wanted to protect itself from such things. There were also no terms such as 'Indigeneity' or 'Aboriginality' (Langton, 2003) at this time. As Indigenous people, we were denied the right to name ourselves and reclaim the nations that were usurped by colonisation (Maddison, 2013). Indigenous people were to be 'bred out' or 'blended' into the colonial population, thus rendering us invisible (Maddison, 2013). As part of his self-preservation process and as an effect of the colonial narrative, my grandfather developed a deeply entrenched internalised racism and self-loathing and this was passed on to his children in varying degrees.

Racism is a system of oppression based on race and is perpetrated by those in a position of power, generally white people against people of colour (Freire, 1970). It involves an unequal distribution of systemic power and perpetuates white privilege. Racism is "pervasive, operating at the interpersonal and institutional levels simultaneously, its effects are cumulative, spanning generations, individuals, time, and place – encompassing much more than discrete acts" (Speight, 2007, p. 126). Because of this, the psychological injury that can be caused by racism is not limited to that caused by one individual, at one time or one place. Internalised racism stems from racism but is also a systemic form of racism. Internalised racism is about cultural imperialism, dominance and power (Bennett, 2014; Carter, 2007; Speight, 2007). Not only is there a system in place that upholds the power of white people, there is a system in place that undermines the power of people of colour and teaches us to fear our own power and difference (Paradies, 2006).

Seeing internalised racism as systemic oppression allows us to distinguish it from other human conditions like self-hatred or low self-esteem, to which all people are vulnerable. Internalised racism is not just an issue of individuals (Graham, West, Martinez, & Roemer 2016). It refers to "the acceptance, by marginalized racial populations, of the negative societal beliefs and stereotypes about themselves" (Williams & Williams-Morris, 2000, p. 255), and it can significantly affect how an individual views themselves and their identity. The internalising of this negative erroneous self-belief is internalised racism. Internalised racism occurs in a racist system when a racial group oppressed by racism supports the supremacy and dominance of the dominating group by maintaining or participating in the set of attitudes, behaviours, social structures and ideologies that underpin the dominating group's power (Paradies, 2005). Through internalised racism, oppression becomes self-sustaining or domesticating (Freire, 1970). This happened to my grandfather and he did everything he could do to distance himself from the reality of his Indigenous identity. He internalised a negative sense of himself as a marginalised negative population.

My grandfather also experienced what I am naming as externalised racism along with violence. Externalised racism comes in the forms of external messages that interact with internalised self-loathing and racism. These messages are borne of prejudice, bias and negative stereotypes. Prilleltensky and Gonick (1996) argue, "images of personal inferiority are formed following experiences of shame and humiliation that erode self-confidence" (p. 132). One of the greatest injuries caused by both externalised internalised racism is shame (Watts-Jones, 2002). My grandfather felt great shame. Shame, for Indigenous people is very unlike the western concept of shame. Shame has different meaning. It describes stigma and embarrassment associated with gaining attention through certain behaviour or action. Shame can be overwhelming and disempowering (Mental Health First Aid [MHFA] Australia, 2014), and can be argued to be a form of "psychological slavery" (Akbar, 1984). I contend shame recolonises the colonised.

The consequences of invasion and colonisation have been experienced and re-experienced through the generations in my family. This is referred to as 'intergenerational or transgenerational trauma' (Dudgeon, Wright, Paradies, Garvey, & Walker 2014). This trauma is "the transfer of the impacts of historical trauma and grief across successive generations of Aboriginal people" (Ralph, Hamaguchi, & Cox, 2006, p. 118). Milroy (2005, cited in Ralph et al., 2006, p. 119) argues that "when considering ... impacts from a psychological perspective, the historical denial of Aboriginal humanity, existence and identity emerge as critical themes".

This is particularly relevant to my grandfather, my mother and me. My grandfather's shame and denial of his Indigeneity reached such a point that he was racist towards others. He externalised the violence he had experienced. He perpetrated violence against others. This is called 'lateral violence'. Bennett (2014) maintains "[l]ateral violence is thought to occur in Aboriginal communities due to their continued oppression, marginalization and colonization" (p. 182). There is also a connection between this form of trauma and illness and disease. My grandfather's father was a violent alcoholic and my grandfather was a violent alcoholic. He was also chronically depressed. The violence my mother endured growing up meant she has been conditioned to tolerate bullying behaviour from my father and I have been conditioned to tolerate bullying and violent behaviour in my relationships. We have both experienced depression and anxiety. I have also experienced alcohol and drug misuse issues. Just because I am aware of transgenerational trauma, does not make it easier to change behaviour.

Additionally, 'epigenetics' proposes that we pass along more than DNA in our genes. There is a suggestion that genes can also carry the memories of trauma experienced by our ancestors and this can then influence how we respond to stress and trauma (Yehuda & Lehrner, 2018). Yehuda and Lehrner (2018, p. 243) state:

> [o]n the simplest level, the concept of intergenerational trauma acknowledges that exposure to extremely adverse events impacts individuals to such a great extent that their offspring find themselves grappling with their parents' post-traumatic state.

Whether trauma is transmitted in our genes, along with what we see, experience and learn growing up, is not the point here. The point is that trauma is passed down through generations and this significantly effects the physical, social and emotional wellbeing of individuals and the community. This is referred to as "cumulative emotional and psychological wounding" (Mu'id, 2004, p. 9).

The Aboriginal and Torres Strait Islander Healing Foundation Development Team (2009, cited in Atkinson, 2013) state:

> many of the problems prevalent in Aboriginal and Torres Strait Islander communities today – alcohol abuse, mental illness and family violence ... have their roots in the failure of Australian governments and society to acknowledge and address the legacy of unresolved trauma still inherent in Aboriginal and Torres Strait Islander communities. (p. 6)

The above statement echoes the experiences of my grandfather and my family. My family's denial of our Indigeneity resulted in the perpetration of violence within the family, and our disconnection from ancestry, our community and our culture.

5 I Will Not Pass

Brown (1995) states that passing is "an adaptation to circumstances of oppression" (p. 36) "wherein individual members of various minority/subordinate groups will achieve an identity as a member of the dominant/superordinate group" (p. 33). This is a way of attempting to conceal or play down someone's origins for the purposes of surviving. Here the concept of race and trust is important.

Individuals learn to trust, or not, through early life experiences and this establishes what individuals expect of each other (Rotenberg, 1995; Weissman & LaRue, 1998). However, there are individual and community based factors that account for variations in the ability to trust, such as gender, age, education, and socio-economic status. Socio-economic status is correlated with levels of trust/distrust in community. Generally speaking, marginalised (black) groups, such as the Indigenous community, are socio-economically disadvantaged and this means levels of trust in my community are lower than less disadvantaged (white) groups (Smith, 2010). Additionally, distrust in Indigenous community can be attributed to the socio-political history of Australia. This being the "ethnoracial socialization or the mechanisms, whether subtle or overt, deliberate or unintentional, through which verbal and nonverbal messages are conveyed to the younger generation about race and ethnicity" (Smith, 2010, p. 461). These would be the messages conveyed about the relationship between the Indigenous community and wider Australia: that Australia is an unsafe place for Indigenous people. Thus, the skills with which one survives are paramount.

Wald (cited in Godfrey & Ashanti Young, 2018) poses the question "[w]hy would someone want to publicly embrace and acknowledge Native American ancestry when that ancestry is not otherwise readily knowable?" (p. xiii). Although this is written from an African-American perspective, it struck a chord with me. Why would I elect to disclose my Indigeneity if I am not outwardly 'Aboriginal looking'? Wald's question clearly identifies the disconnect between the African-American political context and the Australian Indigenous context. My Indigeneity is part of my being, knowing and doing, not just my outward appearance. My culture is fundamental to who I am and how I live. I cannot be anything other than Indigenous, so to pass would be a lie, disingenuous and disrespectful to my community.

As an Indigenous person of mixed heritage, I am fair skinned and, in a social space, I am often assumed to be white by non-Indigenous people, who speak freely around me as if I am an 'insider'. When I was younger, I used to debate in my head whether to disclose my Indigeneity or not, because it is not until I disclose that my place as an 'outsider' is made known. This is usually followed by 'gee, you don't look Aboriginal' or 'you know you aren't black, right'. In general, identity claims are more likely to invite scrutiny when physical appearance, dress, language, accent, history or the status of the individual is incongruous with what the viewer expects (Kowal & Paradies, 2017, p. 102). This is because as a fair skinned Aboriginal, I disrupt the white skinned social space and my Indigeneity often makes non-Indigenous people uncomfortable. My Indigeneity challenges their perception of what an 'authentic Aborigine' looks like. In addition, Kessaris (2006) identifies a phenomenon where non-Indigenous people believe they have the right to discuss the Indigenous community as if they are experts. This frequently occurs in the presence of Indigenous people. She has coined this "unconstrained Mununga (white) talk" (p. 355). This kind of talk is destructive because of its frequency and the fact that it dismisses the Indigenous person entirely.

As an Aboriginal woman I demonstrate my Indigeneity by refusing to be white. This is a form of "race discordance", argue Kowal and Paradies (2017), "affects almost one in five Indigenous people" (p. 107). Race refusal (my refusal to be white) can be demonstrated in a multitude of ways, such as casually identifying/correcting someone in conversation that I am Indigenous, through my actions, or when someone else identifies me as Aboriginal in a collective setting. According to Kowal and Paradies (2017), three things are also refused when whiteness is refused: "assimilation, white sociality and everyday racialisation" (p. 108). By refusing whiteness I refuse the goals of assimilation, the perpetuation that all spaces are white spaces and deny non-Indigenous people the privilege of "reading race from the body of the observed, and faced with the accusation that they have misread the signs" (Kowal & Paradies, 2017, p. 110). My refusal of whiteness is my way of challenging systemic racist practices and policy that were established when Australia was invaded and colonised. It is also about exhibiting hope. I hope to be part of a regenerative conversation that challenges stereotypes and sows the seeds of transformation.

6   Conclusion

In this chapter, I have explored the concept of passing and the story of my grandfather. Because of systemic racism, colonial settler violence and a profound self-hatred, my grandfather attempted to pass for white his entire life. Whilst, fundamentally, this was a self-preservation strategy, passing has left an indelible scar on my family. My family lost our connection to Country, community and culture and I have spent much of my adult life attempting to reclaim this.

Note

1   I mean no disrespect to people of Hawaiian or Pacific Islander descent whose ancestors were brought to Australia to work in slave conditions.

References

Akbar, N. (1984). *Chains and images of psychological slavery*. New Mind Productions.
Anderson, W. (2006). *The cultivation of whiteness. Science, health, and racial destiny in Australia*. Basic Books.
Atkinson, J. (2013). *Trauma-informed services and trauma-specific care for Indigenous Australian children*. Resource sheet No. 21, produced for the Closing the Gap Clearinghouse. Australian Institute of Health and Welfare.
Australian Human Rights Commission (AHRC). (1997). *Bringing them home report. National inquiry into the separation of Aboriginal and Torres Strait Islander children from their families*. Commonwealth of Australia.
Bennett, B. (2014). How do light-skinned Aboriginal Australians experience racism? Implications for social work. *AlterNative, 10*(1), 181–192.

Bennett, B. (2015). *Developing identity as a light-skinned Aboriginal person with little or no community and/or kinship ties* (Doctoral thesis). Australian Catholic University.

Brown, L. S. (1995). Lesbian identities: Concepts and issues. In A. R. D'Augelli & C. J. Patterson (Eds.), *Lesbian, gay and bisexual identities over the lifespan* (pp. 3–23). Oxford University Press.

Butler, J. (1990). *Gender trouble: Feminism and the subversion of identity*. Routledge.

Carlson, B. (2013). The 'new frontier': Emergent Indigenous identities and social media. In M. Harris, M. Nakata, & B. Carlson (Eds.), *The politics of identity: Emerging indigeneity* (pp. 147–168). University of Technology Sydney E-Press.

Carlson, B. (2016). *The politics of identity: Who counts as Aboriginal today?* Aboriginal Studies Press.

Carter, R. T. (2007). Racism and psychological and emotional injury: Recognizing and assessing race-based traumatic stress. *The Counseling Psychologist, 35*, 13–105.

Denholm, M. (2015, February 16). Brawl over 'wannabe' and 'tick-a-box' Aborigines. *The Australian*.

Doane, M. A. (1987). *The desire to desire*. Indiana University Press.

Dodson, S. (2017, June 8). Too White, too Black, or not Black enough? This is not a question for others to decide. *The Guardian*.

Dudgeon, P., Wright, M., Paradies, Y., Garvey, D., & Walker, I. (2014). Aboriginal social, cultural and historical contexts. In P. Dudgeon, H. Milroy, & R. Walker (Eds.), *Working together: Aboriginal and Torres Strait Islander mental health and wellbeing principles and practice* (pp. 3–24). Commonwealth of Australia.

Durie, M. (2003). The health of Indigenous people [Editorial]. *British Medical Journal, 326*, 510–511.

Ellinghaus, K. (2003). Absorbing the 'Aboriginal problem': Controlling interracial marriage in Australia in the late 19th and early 20th centuries. *Aboriginal History, 27*, 183–207.

Freire, P. (1970). *Pedagogy of the oppressed*. The Continuum International Publishing Group.

Graham, J. R., West, L. M., Martinez, J., & Roemer, L. (2016). The mediating role of internalized racism in the relationship between racist experiences and anxiety symptoms in a Black American sample. *Cultural Diversity and Ethnic Minority Psychology, 22*(3), 369–376.

Grant, M., & Wronski, I. (2008). Aboriginal health and history. In S. Couzos & R. Murray (Eds.), *Aboriginal primary health care. An evidenced-based approach* (pp. 1–28). Oxford University Press.

Gross, A. J. (2008). *What blood won't tell: A history of race on trial in America*. Harvard University Press.

James, D. (2018, August 14). Put your dog whistles away, the 'final solution' is here. *Indigenousx*.

Johnson, D. (1993). Ab/originality: Playing and passing versus assimilation [Online]. *The Olive Pink Society Bulletin, 5*(2), 19–23.

Kessaris, T. (2006). About being Mununga (Whitefella): Making covert group racism visible. *Journal of Community and Applied Social Psychology, 16*, 347–362.

Kowal, E., & Paradies, Y. (2017). Indigeneity and the refusal of whiteness. *Postcolonial Studies, 20*(1), 101–117.

Langton, M. (2003). Aboriginal art and film: The politics of representation. In M. Grossman (Ed.), *Blacklines: Contemporary critical writings by Indigenous Australians* (pp. 109–124). Melbourne University Press.

Lapham, A. (2016). Stanley Middleton's response to assimilation policy in his fight for Aboriginal people's equality, 1948–62. *Aboriginal History, 40*, 27–64.

Levine, P., & Bashford, A. (2010). Introduction: Eugenics and the modern world. In A. Bashford & P. Levine (Eds.), *The Oxford handbook of the history of eugenics*. Oxford Handbooks Online.

Macilwain, M. (1987). Aborigines protection board. *SA History Hub*. History Trust of South Australia.

Maddison, S. (2013). Indigenous identity, 'authenticity' and the structural violence of settler colonialism. *Identities, 20*(3), 288–303.

McCorquodale, J. (1987). *Aborigines and the law: A digest*. Aboriginal Studies Press.

Mental Health First Aid (MHFA) Australia. (2014). *Communicating with an Aboriginal or Torres Strait Islander adolescent: Guidelines for being culturally appropriate when providing mental health first aid*. Author.

Mu'id, O. (2004). '... Then I lost my spirit': An analytic essay on transgenerational trauma theory as applied to oppressed people of color nations (Master's thesis). State University of New York.

Paradies, Y. (2005). Anti-racism and Indigenous Australians. *Analyses of Social Issues and Public Policy, 5*, 1–28.

Paradies, Y. (2006). *Race, racism, tress and Indigenous health* (Doctoral thesis). Centre for Health and Society, The University of Melbourne.

Pfeffer, C. A. (2014). 'I don't like passing as a straight woman': Queer negotiations of identity and social group membership. *American Journal of Sociology, 120*(1), 1–44.

Prilleltensky, I., & Gonick, L. (1996). Polities change, oppression remains: On the psychology and politics of oppression. *Political Psychology, 17*(1), 127–148.

Ralph, N., Hamaguchi, K., & Cox, M. (2006). Transgenerational trauma, suicide and healing from sexual abuse in the Kimberley Regions, Australia. *Pimatisiwin, 4*(2), 117–136.

Rotenberg, K. J. (1995). The socialisation of trust: Parents' and children's interpersonal trust. *International Journal of Behavioural Development, 18*(4), 713–726.

Roughsey, E. (1984). *An Aboriginal mother tells of the old and the new*. McPhee Gribble.

Rowley, C. D. (1971). *Outcast in white Australia. Aborigines in Australian society* (Aboriginal Policy and Practice, Vol. II). ANU Press.

Sherwood, J. (2010). *Do no harm: Decolonising Aboriginal health research* (PhD thesis). University of New South Wales.

Sherwood, J., & Geia, L. K. (2014). Historical and current perspectives on the health of Aboriginal and Torres Strait Islander people. In O. Best & B. Fredericks (Eds.), *Yatdjuligin. Aboriginal and Torres Strait Islander Nursing and Midwifery Care* (pp. 7–30). Cambridge University Press.

Smith, S. S. (2010). Race and trust. *Annual Review of Sociology, 36*, 453–475.

Speight, S. L. (2007). Internalized racism: One more piece of the puzzle. *The Counseling Psychologist, 35*(1), 126–134.

Standfield, R. (2011). 'The vacillating manners and sentiments of these people': Mobility, civilisation and dispossession in the work of William Thomas with the Port Phillip Aboriginal protectorate. *Law Text Culture, 15*, 162–184.

Tallbear, K. (2003). DNA, blood, and racializing the tribe. *Wicazo Sa Review, 18*(1), 81–107. doi:10.1353/wic.2003.0008

Tomlinson, D. (2008). *Too White to be regarded as Aborigines: An historical analysis of policies for the protection of Aborigines and the assimilation of Aborigines of mixed descent, and the role of Chief Protectors of Aborigines in the formulation and implementation of those policies, in Western Australia from 1898 to 1940* (Doctoral thesis). University of Notre Dame Australia.

Townsend, S. S. M., Markus, H. R., & Bergsieker, H. B. (2009). My choice, your categories: The denial of multiracial identities. *Journal of Social Issues, 65*(1), 185–204.

Wald, G. (2018). Foreword: Passing and 'post-race'. In M. Godfrey & V. Ashanti Young (Eds.), *Neo-passing. Performing identity after Jim Crow* (pp. 1–6). University of Illinois Press.

Watt, E., & Kowal, E. (2019). To be or not to be Indigenous? Understanding the rise of Australia's Indigenous population since 1971. *Ethnic and Racial Studies, 42*(16), 63–82.

Watts-Jones, D. (2002). Healing internalized racism: The role of a within-group sanctuary among people of African descent. *Family Process, 41*(4), 591–601.

Weissman, M., & LaRue, C. M. (1998). Earning trust from youths with none to spare. *Child Welfare, 77*(5), 579–594.

Williams, D. R., & Williams-Morris, R. (2000). Racism and mental health: The African American experience. *Ethnicity and Health, 5*(3–4), 243–268.

Yehuda, R., & Lehrner, A. (2018). Intergenerational transmission of trauma effects: Putative role of epigenetic mechanisms. *World Psychiatry, 17*, 243–257.

CHAPTER 5

Where the Rivers Meet

Jodie Satour, Naomi Nirupa David, Rosemarie Garner and Gracie Scala Adamson

Abstract

This chapter seeks to consider the teaching experiences, practices and relationships that occur in one Aboriginal and Torres Strait Islander tertiary learning space. It draws from a small study that focused on the teaching practices of five staff members from the National Indigenous Knowledges, Education, Research and Innovation (NIKERI) Institute at Deakin University in Melbourne, Australia. Teaching can be complex and offer both challenge and opportunity as staff and students mediate the multilayered environment. The study found that three key areas emerged as significant for those teaching in this space: the role of community; the contextual teaching and learning practices; and issues of power that underpin the performance of the teachers and students. In order to capture the dynamic nature of teaching in the Institute and the relationships between Australian Indigenous knowledges and Western perspectives we wanted to use a metaphor that illustrated the ways in which learning is reciprocal and teaching is not just directed by lecturers. In this educational place, there is a journey undertaken over time that takes the individuals, their perspectives, the content of the Western degree and Australian Indigenous knowledge to embody a pedagogy that embraces 'other' ways of knowing and being. This journey can be represented in the metaphor of confluence. The metaphor of confluence draws from notable confluence rivers around the world that are described in terms of their contribution, to culture and history as powerful symbols of wisdom, knowledge and transformation, each river drawing from the other in order to reach its destination (Coates, 2015). They are unified in the journey, which is characterised by partnership and relationship.

Relationships especially in the context of community was found to be an important influence on teacher identity. This encompassed many 'types' of community, such as the students' home communities, the community created in the classroom, the community of teachers within the NIKERI, and the wider university community within which the NIKERI resides. The practice of teaching and learning at the NIKERI was another important influence on teacher identity, with issues of power and agency, as well as community, interwoven within this aspect of the teacher's role. Issues of power were found to influence teacher identity, both in the classroom between teacher and

© JODIE SATOUR, NAOMI NIRUPA DAVID, ROSEMARIE GARNER AND GRACIE SCALA ADAMSON, 2021 | DOI: 10.1163/9789004461642_005

student, and also within the larger university community. The privileging of knowledge was linked to issues of power.

Adjusting to these issues and the decisions made to address them were found to influence how the teacher perceived themselves and their role as a teacher at the NIKERI.

Keywords

higher education – Aboriginal and Torres Strait Islander knowledge and perspectives narrative – community – power – teaching and learning – professional teacher identity

1   Introduction

This chapter examines the narratives of five lecturers, a mixed group of both Indigenous Australian and non-Indigenous academics employed in the National Indigenous Knowledges, Education, Research and Innovation (NIKERI) Institute at Deakin University, Melbourne, Australia. The project that led to this chapter emerged in response to the increasingly neo-liberal agenda that enforces universities to adopt matrices that focus on numbers and easily quantifiable data. The project seeks to give voice to the 'other' story, which is less tangible and harder to share, because it lies in the history, people and educational landscapes of learning spaces that are outside the dominant discourse of white tertiary settings. The project discussed in this chapter was focused deeply on the teaching and learning landscape; forged by the staff, students and the curriculum in the confluence of western degree journeys with Aboriginal and Torres Strait Islander knowledges and perspectives. The study's foci was the perspectives of the five lecturers based on their experiences working at NIKERI.

The participating lecturers in the study were interested in investigating the pedagogical and philosophical elements that shaped teaching pedagogy and practice at NIKERI (n = 5 academic staff; 2 Indigenous, 3 non-Indigenous). This led to a project that was developed over 18 months as a reflective community of practice (Wenger, 2000) through regular meetings (n ≈ 9). The meetings considered key reflective questions that support inquiry into teaching practice. The reflective questions and the meetings were developed in three phases. Reflective practice in educational communities of practice are particularly useful in order to make meaning and develop greater insights into the abstract and concrete elements that influence teaching practices and perspectives (Wenger-Trayner, 2015).

2 Research Design

Narrative analysis (NA) was engaged throughout the project and the first phase considered the stories of the teachers in terms of teaching and learning experiences in NIKERI. For example, questions such as, 'what were the teaching moments that profoundly shaped philosophies and pedagogies?' The second phase considered the key themes that emerged in the data collected in phase one. The meetings analysed the themes that emerged through the lens of respective disciplines, teaching practices and current educational discourses. The third phase considered a critical reading of the data and the analysis. The central question was 'What themes have emerged most frequently, how we have analysed this data and why is it so important in the landscape of NIKERI?' All lecturers involved in the study shared in the evolving thematic analysis and iterative shifting, discussing and refining of themes.

Over time, as the participating members shared their stories, an investigation of the key themes led to particular areas emerging as the pillars of practice in this Indigenous learning place. The method of analysing key themes used during the project privileged narrative and oral story in order to respect and embrace the unique role that oral history plays in the cultural stories, historical accounts and ecological knowledges of the land (Gwatkin-Higson, 2018). Narrative analysis as a method is attentive to the stories of the participants and seeks to integrate the story for meaning, emphasis and insight (Riessman, 2008). In order to develop a foundational understanding of the context to this chapter, we first introduce the Community Based Delivery (CBD) model, followed by discussions of the key themes identified through the project.

3 The Community Based Delivery (CBD) Model: The Community as the Pulse of Teaching Practice

The word 'community' is integral to courses delivered courses at NIKERI. The roles of the typical student enrolled are multifaceted in that they often present with multiple family, community and work responsibilities (White, 2005). The CBD model includes a combination of both on- and off-campus teaching, designed to enable Aboriginal and Torres Strait Islander students to study without being removed from their communities for substantial periods of time; a reported challenge of study for Indigenous students (Foley, 2010). This provides students with the flexibility to access higher education in a space with shared cultural values and belief systems whilst maintaining their family, community and cultural commitments (Deakin University, 2016a). The need for culturally safe support systems to alleviate the challenges of study has often been emphasised (Fleet, Kitson, Cassady, & Hughes, 2007).

The CBD mode of delivery lessens the pressure on students, who are more likely to stay engaged in study if financial and logistical burdens are mitigated whilst studying (Fleet et al., 2007). However, it is not solely these practical elements that are apparent; the underlying theory framing the CBD model is also significant. May's (1999) long-established view of this community framework as "beginning with people and their immediate reality" and allowing the members within to" become meaningfully involved in shaping their own futures" (p. 10) is indicative of the aspirations of the CBD model delivery in this instance. This also reverberates with Paulo Freire's efforts to empower groups through feelings of assurance (Hooley, 2009). Indeed, in their research on the role of universities in releasing the potential of Indigenous students, Andersen, Bunda, and Walter (2008, p. 4) found a "degree of comfort" when realising the course provider in their study utilised CBD type models of delivery. Furthermore, Simpson (cited in MacDonald, 2006, p. 52) denotes "affective support" alongside academic support as an underlying key feature of CBD type models. Deliberate emphasis on these aspects of CBD delivery is offered here as these features are exist at NIKERI and are fundamental to enabling student success.

4 Method: Narrative Analysis

Narrative analysis (NA), like many methods, has a range of possible operations to examine the narrative construct effectively (Van Manen, 1988). NA explores the inclusions/exclusions and emphases/silences in order to pick up the threads of meaning and significance that are embedded in the narrative reconstruction of experience, life and history. The storied nature of self is instrumental in demystifying the complexity of time and the temporal nature of experience (Inglis, 2000). Through narrative it is possible to move backward, forward, into the experience and beyond it in order to be informed by the author's rich meaning, invaluable insights and contextual memories (Riessman, 2008). In NA, the methods form a body of techniques that play a crucial role in a project as the tools are used as interpreters of knowledge. The devise in the hand of the researcher is applied with great forethought to make meaning. This chapter draws in particular on the work and insights of Catherine Riessman (2008) in relation to typologies of practice in NA and their significance.

5. Looking at Language and Narrative

Catherine Riesman's recognition of narrative formats and their significance in human interaction and reflection, builds on the longstanding linguistic trends set by scholars such as William Labov (Gordon, 2013). Labov's (1972) emphasis on language and linguistic theory may not stem from a sociological perspective, however it is deeply immersed in people's language and, therefore, people's stories and considers the significance of language in the rich discourse of identity. Labovian research methods privilege personal narrative and in doing so privilege heterogeneous voices in research (Johnstone, 2016). Therefore, there is a sociological ramification in the acknowledgement of the narrative as the vehicle for understanding storied human lives. The results of this are evident in the findings of Language in the inner city: Studies in Black English vernacular (1972). Labov's seminal work provides an undercurrent for these themes where close attention is paid to the ways in which language is used. Linguistic features of speech particularly in relation to speech structure are analysed (Riessman, 2008), where data is examined and attention is given to the phonology of particular sounds, the choice of key words and the emphasis on key terms (Riessman, 2008).

Narrative practices embrace the broad and fine linguistic strokes that are applied to sharing a storied life. Narratives become acts of agentic negotiation by the storyteller used to inform the listener. They include necessary adaptations, important exclusions and blaring silences. The researcher is accountable to the story and the negotiations that the storyteller is making. Through the analysis that is undertaken the story needs to be appreciated in terms of complexity and, at times, contradiction (Mishler, 2005). The investigator is then tasked with sharing dialogue with the story to contextualise it, interpret it and often present it.

6. Culture, Context and Narrative

Riesman's (2008) analysis builds on the work of socio-linguists with a collection of tools that look at various ways of analytically approaching texts. But NA also draws from the rich complexities of Bakhtin's theories (Bakhtin, 1981), particularly narrative and its relationship to other narratives, context, genre and discourse. Bakhtin's advocacy of the narrative polyphony: many perspectives, stories, dislodged binaries and disrupted categories, all value the individual, the 'other story' (Owen, 2007). According to Riessman (2015), the narrative analyst engages in dialogue with the stories (data) and, through their analysis, they dialogue with the storyteller. She would also argue that the researcher takes on the role of producer and is reflexive in the methods applied during the analysis. The researcher shares the ways of knowing and doing that underpin how the narrative research was conducted. The choice of questions, the specific methods, and the planning of the research are all part of the production. The production process recognises how the story is studied, the context of the audience and the importance of individual voices.

Narrative privileges the individual story but also enables the individual (the storyteller) to articulate happenings that are complex and do not always unfold in a linear sequence. As an example, Riessman (1990, p. 155) reflects on the experience of hearing a participant's response to questions about his divorce. His initial reply was simple: that the reasons for his separation could only be explained in a really long story. Riessman noted that narrative played a pivotal role in the participant being able to engage with the events that had taken place in his own life. Analysing and investigating the narratives provided Riessman (1990) with opportunities to uncover the themes, underlying areas of emphasis and reoccurring phrases which led to a greater understanding of divorce as a significant sociological event. Story becomes a relational pivot point linking the experiences of many and creating the context of an event. The relationships between narratives as a response to cultural discourse, are embedded in the ubiquitous nature of intertextuality. The intertextuality of narrative and the cultural capillaries that run through human stories embrace the important roles that place and audience play on narrative formation and delivery (Hyvarinen, 2010). Stories reflect the identity kaleidoscope of the teller, welcoming fragments and disconnections. The significance of this is the inclusion of diverse views, their contribution to cultural discourse and their influence on identity as negotiated in narratives. Narratives reflect historical and cultural nuances, as well as individual interpretation. Therefore, the analysis of narrative is irrevocably linked to the analysis of cultural discourse and lends itself to sociological questions asked in the social sciences (Riessman & Quinney, 2005). Riesman's (2015) attention to stories recognises that there are many different types of communication and not all speech or writing is a story. Narratives are distinguishable by their inclusion of place, time and the teller's emphasis on what happened and why those events may be significant. The common thread in NA is its storied beginning. However, there are various types of NA methods, supporting a range of disciplines.

The significance of this is the ways in which the methods compliment diverse methodologies that are made richer from the inclusion NA methods. Braun and Clarke (2006), for example, refer to the growing use of narrative in research conducted in health-related research.

Riessman (2008, pp. 2–4) captures the importance of NA methods in three questions:
1. How is the idea of narrative employed in a research project?
2. To what degree does an investigation attend to narrative features?
3. How do narrative analysts take into consideration the 'worlds' that surround a narrative text?

The third question which is particularly focused on oral narratives is relevant to this project. Being attentive to oral narrative enables participants to reflect deeply on their experiences and actions as well as interact with the narratives of other participants in the organic forms of conversation. This was also essential in order to privilege Aboriginal Knowledges that are fostered, shared and developed through narrative (Dean, 2010). The application of the question and a thematic analysis (one form of NA) of the data followed. Riesman's definitions of thematic analysis (2004) argue that this typology pays close attention to what is being said or written rather than how it is being said.

There are many lenses that can be applied to NA two in particular define thematic analysis (Braun & Clarke, 2006). Thematic analysis is developed either with a particular theme that the researcher is searching for in the data set or through thorough examination of the data in order to explore what themes naturally emerge (Maguire & Delahunt, 2017). In the case of this project, examining the data through discussion, reflection and re-storying uncovered the themes that are discussed in this chapter.

7 Theme 1: Community

7.1 *Introduction*

Community, in the landscape of the Institute, consists of a series of significant intersections rife with histories, both personal and national, that contextualise the teaching here. In broad terms, a community consists of members whose roles and responsibilities are based on and/or influenced by a common idea. The teaching staff can be likened to individual streams, derived from different sources contributing to their character. As they journey along the way, they encounter many factors that shape the type, quality, purposes of that river. The histories and her-stories trickle and flow with languages, people, families, losses and gains. It is in this merging of waters where the discussions for this project took place and where the significance of community to pedagogical practice was revealed. As the hidden transcript in the classroom (Holland & Lave, 2001), the tributaries of histories merging with daily classroom practices, shape and re-shape our teacher identity. At the confluence, the individual streams and waterways merge to create a new space that ebbs and flows. The streams feed into and draw from each teacher allowing for growth, shaping and re-shaping. When these rivers meet, it can both enrich and be tumultuous, thus prompting continuous reassessment of what it means to teach at NIKERI.

7.2   Community Landscapes

The significance of community for Aboriginal and Torres Strait Islander people surfaced early in our initial discussions in this project and deepened as the consequent reflection, conversations and written narrative occurred. It is important to clarify that there are three significant community 'landscapes' (Wenger-Trayner & Wenger-Trayner, 2015) navigated by the teachers in this space. These are: the students' home community; the Institute community created within the classroom by the Institute teachers and students; and the larger university community within whose strictures the Institute resides. Each of these landscapes encompasses obligations, connections, perspectives and pressure on the students and the lecturers and provides the context of how we negotiate these landscapes in our role of teacher. These community environments thus both inform and influence our practice, within which our teacher identity is contextualised.

7.3   Space of Confluence

The confluence created by the merging streams is awash with different knowledge systems that are considered and respected. Having a physical place within the wider university community where Aboriginal and Torres Strait Islander students can come together to learn, share, and preserve their own philosophies as well as attain a western university degree, attests to the belief that Aboriginal pedagogy is equally important as learning western knowledge. Both are seen as important so that both can be used to benefit our communities. This forges the Institute community both as a place for transformation but also a place of challenge with "potential misunderstanding and confusion" (Wenger-Trayner & Wenger-Trayner, 2015, p. 17). Underlying this is the notion of a counter-narrative, whereby one knowledge system parallels another. This is evident when students are able to weave cultural knowledge that differs from western-based perspective into their academic journey and find the intersections that enable their identity to be recognised and thrive. The confluence asks the lecturer to be a facilitator and a contributor and thus shapes the type of interactions and considerations that are to be respected and acknowledged.

Etienne Wenger (2015) describes the collective process of learning and shared dialogue as establishing a 'community of practice' that actively creates opportunities for discussion, joint activity and reflection. The community of practice model provides the platform for both staff and students to safely share perceptions and practices and, in doing so, intersect boundaries of practice (Edwards, 2011) and encourage the appreciation of other 'professional and personal landscapes' (Britt & Sumsion, 2003, p. 116). Via 'border crossing' the lecturers are presented with multicentric perspectives that prompt reflection and re-consideration that lead towards a shared understanding (Britt & Sumsion, 2003; Hartley, Rogers, Smith, Peters, & Carr, 2010; Carr, 2012; Peters & Dunlop, 2014) and informs our notion of what a teacher must do. The space of confluence however can equally be a challenging space that shapes our teacher identity with constant negotiation and contestation, competing for validity for Aboriginal and Torres Strait Islander knowledge in a western curricula perspective (Nakata, Nakata, Keech, & Bolt, 2012). Time pressures such as university assignment deadlines and community pressures such as a student's family, work and community obligations can collide. Decisions need to be made about how best to negotiate the conflicting roles of advocate for the student and agent for the university program. The teachers' perspective of the content is deepened by the increased awareness of current community views and sensitivities that the Aboriginal and Torres Strait Islander Elders and students bring.

7.4   Cultural Interface

The community at the Institute is navigated by lecturers and students and, although challenging, creates a space for opportunity and affirmation of students' Aboriginal and Torres Strait Islander culture. Here, a new narrative is at play that is contrary to colonising priorities. Nakata (2007a) describes this type of changing and evolving meeting place as a "cultural interface" that is a "multi-layered and multi-dimensional space of dynamic relations" (p. 323). The interface is more than a theoretical concept, it is tangible, with intentional practices, designed to acknowledge students' community and learner identities and simultaneously foreground these with course specific academic content and university priorities. These practices shape the teacher's identity and pedagogical practices.

By applying Aboriginal and Torres Strait Islander ways of relating and being, an individualised approach is utilised. Teaching strategies are modified to make time for developing authentic relationships and two-way exchanges that are not typical of current university practices. Together with the students, a community is created at NIKERI that is respectful and valorises scaffolded learning. It thus acknowledges the importance of relational connection. In so doing, NIKERI disrupts the neo-liberalist agenda by swimming against the tide, valuing people and promoting a culturally safe atmosphere (Yelland & Kilderry, 2006).

Further, by recognising the students' home communities and their influence on the students' priorities and needs, the content and delivery become nuanced and more relevant. Teachers are also cognisant that students, who are often leaders in their communities, must deal with the added pressure of assigning priorities between their studies and their community expectations. The added pressure on the students impacts the teacher's practice such as prompting re-consideration and negotiation of university priorities. By supporting the students as leaders, power is maintained in the community and adds another layer of complexity to the teacher's role further influencing their teacher identity. The teacher must balance not only pedagogical practice and the greater university community via its academic administrative requirements, but also the larger commonwealth government initiatives that provide funding. In effect, the histories of students and their communities become intertwined with the history of NIKERI.

8 Theme 2: Teaching and Learning

Universities attempt to address inclusivity in various ways. However, the practice of everyday teaching and learning is largely underpinned by western pedagogies and dominant western perspectives. These give privilege to how knowledge is formed and transmitted between the teacher as the knower and the student as the learner. Teaching this way ignores the opportunities in valuing and applying other knowledge systems and perspectives.

Educational success can be linked to culturally responsive learning environments, yet alternate perspectives in higher education have rendered Aboriginal and Torres Strait Islander students disembodied from their knowledge and culture (Osborne & Guenther, 2013). In demonstrating their commitment to addressing these challenges, Deakin University published the Aboriginal and Torres Strait Islander Higher Education Agenda and action plan. This states that Aboriginal and Torres Strait Islander knowledge, skills and practices are to be embedded throughout the curricula and for the university to provide a safe and productive learning environment for all Aboriginal and Torres Strait Islander students (Deakin University, 2016b). These actions are pivotal to optimising student and teacher learning across the University.

NIKERI exists as an exclusive space at Deakin University where Aboriginal and Torres Strait Islander students have come for over twenty years to learn, share and maintain their cultural connections; fostering a sense of belonging and wellbeing whilst engaged in study. NIKERI's CBD model creates a student experience that includes negotiating their cultural, personal and work experiences as well as attending face-to-face classes and online activities (Keppell, Souter, & Riddle, 2012). The yarning discussions amongst the five teacher participants; a mixed group of both Indigenous Australian and non-Indigenous academics in this project highlighted that their identity and the student identity was informed by, and connected to, their work experience, and personal and cultural narratives shared in and outside the classroom. This process provided a space to validate the multiple experiences that enrich and influence their learning, connected to local community and various experiences (Yunkaporta, 2009; Martin, 2008). Aboriginal and Torres Strait Islander pedagogies are crucial for re-claiming their knowledges and de-colonising the traditional teaching process (Biermann & Townsend-Cross, 2008).

Intrinsically linked to the CBD model is cultivating an environment that builds on forming authentic relationships between students and teachers. Building these genuine relationships is integral to teaching in this space, and this contributes to teacher identity formation. In her well-known book, Please Knock Before You Enter, Aboriginal scholar Karen Martin (cited in Skattebol & Hayes, 2016), detailed her work on Aboriginal methodologies for engaging in relational epistemologies in ways of knowing, being and doing. Osbourne and Guenther (2013, p. 5) argue that applying Indigenous ways of knowing into teaching and learning activities provides alternative knowledge structures and learning styles that are given equal status to wester knowledge constructs. The five teacher participants of this project found that by being respectful and taking responsibility in this exchange at the cultural interface is a necessity.

They also considered the method of storying to make connections between students' discourses and unit content essential. In this context, relatedness in educational settings can be achieved by centering knowing on the stories shared, community knowledge, traditional and contemporary knowledge, history and their cultural dispositions. The teacher participants found the transference of information in sharing these stories is intrinsically tied with a person's identity and belonging of their past, present and future.

Using story as a method provides a vessel for many standpoints in hearing the struggles and ways in which students share their knowledge, life experiences in community and the land in which they are located. Being culturally responsive can be achieved by creating a safe place to share these stories; by being accountable in relation to one's own knowledge and how this can be transmitted to learning (Skattebol & Hayes, 2016). The doing is how these attained skills can be taken back to community, and how reciprocated learning occurs amongst students and between students and teachers. This includes considerations for the complexities in the delivery of student and teacher identities. The five teacher participants found the yarning discussions and the process of negotiating relational and cultural practices had its challenges.

Education cannot be improved simply with a 'tick and flick' approach by including, for example, cultural content and without deep meaning and perspective that also includes connections and collaboration with local Aboriginal and Torres Strait Islander people (Nakata, 2007b; Yunkaporta, 2009; Osborne & Guenther, 2013). To achieve authenticity, teachers require the skills, knowledge and values to build their capacity in Aboriginal and Torres Strait Islander pedagogy and epistemology 'in learning through culture not just about culture' (Yunkaporta & Kirby 2011, p. 206). The yarning discussions between the teacher participants revealed that teaching styles vary, as does the way a student learns. The teacher may draw on their strengths, often reverting to western perspectives. Yunkaporta (2009, p. 5) stresses, however, that doing this, and not confronting Aboriginal perspectives, marginalises them once again and damages any relationships formed. In creating a confluent space for Aboriginal and Torres Strait Islander pedagogy, the teacher participants spoke of observation skills, of non-verbal body language, deep listening of stories being told, learning by doing and learning in real life narratives and how this relates to identity. In terms of the listening and taking notice, Nakata (2007a, p. 95) likens this to "driving with the windows down" in terms of the sensory connections that can be made between non-Aboriginal and Torres Strait Islander and Aboriginal and Torres Strait Islander people. Approaching the learning and teaching in this way creates opportunities for students and teachers to re-imagine possibilities beyond binary colonial paradigms (Nakata et al., 2012).

9   Theme 3: Identity, Power and Agency

The open discussion and reflective written exercise held during the project shaped this chapter with an examination of the teacher participant's educational 'praxis' and a questioning of taken-for-granted actions and thinking about who one is as a teaching professional in the unique space at the Institute (Yunkaporta & Kirby, 2011). Here, Indigenous and non-Indigenous staff work alongside each other facilitating a range of course disciplines solely to students who identify as Aboriginal or Torres Strait Islander. Several authors highlight how one's own experience shape their professional identities, entrenching certain qualities, values and practices that form their own teaching constitution, or the habitus they bring to the field of education (Bourdieu & Wacquant, 1992; Oakes, Townley, & Cooper, 1998; Bräuchler & Postill, 2010). Indeed, Malterud (2001) emphasises that people are both motivated by and compelled towards certain avenues of research because of their entrenched professional identities. This, in turn, maintains the momentum for the research journey, affording that desire for 'deeper insight' into an issue through a genuine drive for understanding (Bell, 2005; Maxwell, 2005). An initial search for answers or perceived formula for success leads to a deeper critical reflexivity and, while some answers are revealed, more questions are created to increase the depth of understanding (Moles, 2012). It is hoped that through the surfacing, questioning and justifying of our own underlying assumptions and taken-for-granted habits and positions (Forbes, 2008) will lead to a greater understanding and further expose ignorance or blind spots (Wagner, 2010) so as to learn from them.

In writing this chapter, the teacher participants were also drawn to the analogy of viewing an upright stick in a pond, offered by Sandra Harding (2004). This highlights the need to consider different 'locations' of practice; to not be fixed on looking at an issue from one dimension or angle. In Harding's analogy, if one remains in one spot, they cannot possibly describe the view of the stick from the other side. One needs to "walk around the pond to observe the stick from different angles" (p. 257). Thus, this chapter endeavours to reflect Harding's belief by highlighting both our customised and flexible teaching and learning strategies, as well as consideration of the individual habitus of our Indigenous and non-Indigenous colleagues.

In so doing, a sense of "polyvocality" is offered (Finlay, 2003, p. 215). Polyvocality provides a way of legitimising and valuing each teacher participants perspectives and experiences. This notion of giving voice is a common theme in this discussion and, indeed, should be a prerequisite for working in this space for both staff working alongside each other and when working with students. Unforeseen 'silences' can occur if nurturing of voice is not maintained and cultural considerations are not evident (Milner, 2007; Rizvi, 2015). Milner (2007) posits that their efforts in giving voice to what they do and to those who may have been misinterpreted, misrepresented, marginalised or silenced, are indeed worthwhile and must be maintained. The teacher participants see their role is also that of ally (Bishop, 2002; Perso & Hayward, 2015) to Indigenous and non-Indigenous colleagues and students, with a commitment to avoiding a shallow 'hit and run' approach (Bishop, 2002, p. 127). The Institute nurtures a genuine "bicultural" approach where difference is appreciated and cultures are validated (Perso & Hayward, 2015, p. 22).

Finally, it is pertinent to mention that it does indeed require immense effort and dedication to work within a specialised education institute such as the one described here. Whilst the Institute actively campaigns for equity and parity in educational opportunities for Aboriginal and Torres Strait Islander students, which is a truly remarkable and a worthy cause, the political and bureaucratic facets of working within a broader university context can be incredibly challenging. This reflects Sennett's (2006) description of a rather sombre commodity-driven, competitive, sometimes non-collegial environment. However, as Sennett also states, "unhappiness with an institution can coexist with a strong commitment to it" (p. 36). The core business is important not the place itself. Also, as teaching is a chosen vocation rather than simply an occupation, there is some natural philanthropic disposition or "primary habitus" (Zippin & Brenan, 2003) to making a difference.

10   Conclusion

This chapter has given voice to a particular educational landscape and learning space that is outside the dominant discourse of non-Indigenous tertiary settings. It has focused on the teaching and learning landscape, forged by the staff, students and curriculum, and the confluence of western degree journeys and Aboriginal and Torres Strait Islander knowledges and perspectives. Using NA afforded the opportunity for the authors and teachers in this space to discuss, reflect and re-story experiences. These were subsequently clustered into the key themes: community landscapes; teaching and learning; and identity, power and agency. These are significant features of this teaching space and the combined effect of their interaction is part of the teaching landscape.

The contours of our lives were particularly important in the context of the research, as we found ourselves drawing from our experiences and our own teaching journeys in the data collection meetings. During the meetings we talked, listened, storied and re-storied our experiences having closely studied the themes that were emerging. As the themes surfaced in our writing and collective discussions, it became apparent that in the landscape of this Indigenous learning place, people were at the nucleus of every aspect of the institution. The people form the community that is integral to the relationships that underpin the teaching and learning taking place. People are the keepers of knowledge that is embedded in culture, family, kinship and identity, shaping the great appreciation that lecturers have for students. The acknowledgement of shared knowledge disrupts the binary between teacher and learner, ensuring that neither position is fixed. There is a confluence between an Indigenous learning environment that pursues western tertiary qualifications in a university. This forms an essential resistor identity whose role and function are to tell the 'other' story and celebrate the strength of the interactions, conflicts, concerns and disjuncture that take place in the confluence of perspectives. Bachelard (2014) would describe such a house of human resistance as bound by its roots and not its surroundings, stating that:

> Everything swayed under the shock of this blow, but the flexible house stood up to the beast. No doubt it was holding firmly to the soil of the island by means of the unbreakable roots from which its thin walls of mud-coated reeds and planks drew their supernatural strength. (p. 28)

In the context of a neo-liberal agenda, with its pursuit of productive knowledge in particularly neat columns and rows, the flesh and bones of this project was a timely reminder for us that education can and must seep beyond the column and rarely fits neatly in the rows.

Acknowledgement

We would like to acknowledge the contributions of Jamie Anderson (Gangulu/Kanolu) and Anne Ryan in assisting in the collection of data used throughout this chapter.

References

Andersen, C., Bunda, T., & Walter, M. (2008). Indigenous higher education: The role of universities in releasing the potential. *The Australian Journal of Indigenous Education, 37*(1), 1–8. doi:10.1017/S1326011100016033

Bachelard, G. (2014). *The poetics of space*. Penguin Classics.

Bakhtin, M. M. (1981/1930). *The dialogic imagination*. University of Texas Press.

Bell, J. (2005). *Doing your research project: A guide for first time researchers in education, health and social science* (4th ed.). Open University Press.

Biermann, S., & Townsend-Cross, M. (2008). Indigenous pedagogy as a force for change. *The Australian Journal of Indigenous Education, 37*(1), 146–154. doi:10.1375/S1326011100000048X

Bishop, A. (2002). *Becoming an ally breaking the cycle of oppression*. Allen & Unwin.

Bourdieu, P., & Wacquant, L. (1992). *Invitation to reflexive sociology*. Polity Press.

Bräuchler, B., & Postill, J. (2010). What is practice theory? In B. Bräuchler & J. Postill (Eds.), *Theorising media and practice* (pp. 8–12). Berghahn Books.

Braun, V., & Clarke, V. (2006). Using thematic analysis in psychology. *Qualitative Research in Psychology, 3*(2), 77–101.

Britt, C., & Sumsion, J. (2003). Within the Borderlands: Beginning early childhood teachers in primary schools. *Contemporary Issues in Early Childhood, 4*(2), 115–136.

Carr, M. (2012). Making a borderland of contested spaces into a meeting place – The relationship from a New Zealand perspective. In P. Moss (Ed.), *Early childhood and compulsory education*. Taylor and Francis.

Deakin University. (2016). *Deakin University Aboriginal and Torres Strait Islander higher education agenda 2016–2020*. Author.

Dean, C. (2010). A yarning place in narrative histories. *History of Education Review, 39*, 6–13.

Edwards, A. (2011). Building common knowledge at the boundaries between professional practices: Relational agency and relational expertise in systems of distributed expertise. *International Journal of Educational Research, 50*, 33–39.

Finlay, L. (2003). The reflexive journey: Mapping multiple routes. In L. Finlay & B. Gough (Eds.), *Reflexivity: A practical guide for researchers in health and social science* (pp. 3–20). Wiley-Blackwell.

Fleet, A., Kitson, R., Cassady, B., & Hughes, R. (2007). University-qualified Indigenous early childhood teachers: Voices of resilience. *Australian Journal of Early Childhood, 32*(3), 17–25.

Foley, D. (2010). Can we educate and train Aboriginal leaders within our tertiary education systems? *The Australian Journal of Indigenous Education, 39*, 138–150.

Forbes, J. (2008). Reflexivity in professional doctoral research. *Reflective Practice, 9*(4), 449–460.

Gordon, M. J. (2013). *Labov: A guide for the perplexed*. Bloomsbury Academic.

Gwatkin-Higson, P. (2018). What is the role of oral history and testimony in building our understanding of the past? *NEW: Emerging Scholars in Australian Indigenous Studies, 4*(1), 39–44.

Harding, S. (2004). *The feminist standpoint theory reader: Intellectual and political controversies*. Routledge.

Hartley, C., Rogers, P., Smith, J., Peters, S., & Carr, M. (2010). Building relationships between early childhood and school: Mutually interesting projects. In A. Meade (Ed.), *Dispersing waves innovation in early childhood education* (pp. 19–26). NZCER Press.

Holland, D., & Lave, J. (2001). *History in person: Enduring struggles, contentious practice, intimate identities* (1st ed.). SAR Press.

Hooley, N. (2009). *Narrative life: Democratic curriculum and Indigenous learning*. Springer.

Hyvarinen, M. (2010). Revisiting the narrative turns. *Life Writing, 7*(1), 69–82.

Inglis, F. (2000). *Clifford Geertz: Culture, custom and ethics*. Polity.

Johnstone, B. (2016). 'Oral versions of personal experience': Labovian narrative analysis and its uptake. *Journal of Sociolinguistics, 20*(4), 542–560.

Keppell, M., Souter, K., & Riddle, M. (2012). *Physical and virtual learning spaces in higher education: Concepts for the modern learning environment*. IGA Global.

Labov, W. (1972). *Language in the inner city: Studies in the Black English vernacular*. University of Pennsylvania Press.

MacDonald, J. (2006). *Blended learning and online tutoring: A good practice guide*. Gower Publishing Company.

Maguire, M., & Delahunt, B. (2017). Doing a thematic analysis: A practical, step-by-step guide for learning and teaching scholars. *AISHE-J: The All Ireland Journal of Teaching & Learning in Higher Education, 9*(3), 3351–3354.

Malterud, K. (2001). Qualitative research: Standards, challenges and guidelines. *The Lancet, 358*, 483–488.

Martin, K. (2008). *Please knock before you enter: Aboriginal regulation of outsiders and the implications for researchers*. Post Pressed.

Maxwell, J. A. (2005). *Qualitative research design: An interactive approach*. Sage.

May, S. (Ed.). (1999). *Indigenous community-based education*. Multilingual Matters.

Milner, R. (2007). Race, culture and researcher positionality: Working through dangers seen and unseen. *Educational Researcher, 36*, 388–400.

Mishler, E. (2005). Patient stories, narratives of resistance and the ethics of humane care: A la recherche du temps perdu. *Health, 9*(4), 431–451.

Moles, J. (2012). *Path to reflective practice: A guide for professional practitioners in education*. Deakin University.

Nakata, M. (2007a). *Disciplining the savages: Savaging the disciplines*. Aboriginal Studies Press.

Nakata, M. (2007b). The cultural interface. *The Australian Journal of Indigenous Education, 36*(S1), 7–14.

Nakata, M., Nakata, V., Keech, S., & Bolt, R. (2012). Decolonial goals and pedagogies for Indigenous studies. *Decolonisation: Indigeneity, Education and Society, 1*(1), 120–140.

Oakes, L., Townley, B., & Cooper, D. (1998). Business planning as pedagogy: Language and control in a changing institutional field. *Administrative Science Quarterly, 43*(2), 257–292.

Osborne, S., & Guenther, J. (2013). Red dirt thinking on power, pedagogy and paradigms: Reframing the dialogue in remote education. *The Australian Journal of Indigenous Education, 42*(2), 111–122.

Owens, J. (2007). Liberating voices through narrative methods: The case for an interpretive research approach. *Disability and Society, 22*(3), 299–313.

Patterson, W. (2013). Narratives of events: Labovian narrative analysis and its limitations. In M. Andrews, C., Squire, & M. Tamboukou (Eds.), *Doing narrative research* (pp. 27–46). Sage Publications, Ltd. doi:10.4135/9781526402271

Perso, T., & Hayward, C. (2015). *Teaching Indigenous students cultural awareness and classroom strategies for improving learning outcomes.* Allen & Unwin.

Peters, S., & Dunlop, A. W. (2014). Editorial. *Early Years, 34*(4), 323–328.

Riessman, C. K. (1990). *Divorce talk: Women and men make sense of personal relationships.* Rutgers University Press.

Riessman, C. K. (2008). *Narrative methods for the human sciences.* Sage Publications.

Riessman, C. (2015). Twists and turns: Narrating my career, Catherine Kohler Riessman. *Qualitative Social Work, 14*(1), 10–17.

Riessman, C. K., & Quinney, L. (2005). Narrative in social work: A critical review. *Qualitative Social Work, 4*(4), 391–412.

Rizvi, F. (2015). Mobilities paradigm and policy research in education. In K. N. Gulson, M. Clarke, & E. B. Peterson (Eds.), *Education policy and contemporary theory: Implications for research* (pp. 171–182). Routledge.

Sennett, R. (2006). *The culture of the new capitalism.* Yale University Press.

Skattebol, J., & Hayes, D. (2016). Cracking with affect: Relationality in young people's movements in and out of mainstream schooling. *Critical Studies in Education, 57*(1), 6–20. doi:10.1080/17508487.2015.1096803

van Manen, M. (1998). Modalities of body experience in illness and health. *Qualitative Health Research, 8*(1), 7–24.

Wagner, J. (2010). Ignorance in educational research, how not knowing shapes new knowledge. In P. Thomson & M. Walker (Eds.), *The Routledge doctoral student's companion: Getting to grips with research in education and the social sciences* (pp. 31–42). Routledge.

Wenger, E. (2000). *Communities of practice learning, meaning and identity.* Cambridge University Press.

Wenger-Trayner, E., & Wenger-Trayner, E. (2015). Learning in a landscape of practice: A framework. In E. Wenger-Trayner, M. F. O'Creevy, S. Hutchinson, & C. Kubiak (Eds.), *Learning in landscapes of practice boundaries, identity, and knowledgeability in practice-based learning* (pp. 13–29). Routledge.

White, C. (2005). Contribution of distance education to the development of individual learners. *Distance Education, 26*(2), 165–181.

Yelland, N., & Kilderry, A. (2005). Against the tide: New ways in early childhood education. In N. Yelland (Ed.), *Critical issues in early childhood education* (pp. 1–14). Open University Press.

Yunkaporta, T., & Kirby, M. (2011). Yarning up Indigenous pedagogies: A dialogue about eight Aboriginal ways of learning. In R. Bell, G. Milgate, & N. Purdie (Eds.), *Two way teaching and learning: Toward culturally reflective and relevant education* (pp. 205–213). ACER Press.

Yunkaporta, T. (2009). *Aboriginal pedagogies at the cultural interface* (Professional Doctorate [Research] thesis). James Cook University.

Zippin, L., & Brennan, M. (2003). The suppression of ethical dispositions through managerial governmentality: A habitus crisis in Australian higher education. *International Journal of Leadership in Education, 6*(4), 351–370.

CHAPTER 6

Thought Ritual: An Indigenous Data Analysis Method for Research

Tyson Yunkaporta and Donna Moodie

Abstract

There is an absence of studies on discrete Indigenous data analysis methods in the literature on Indigenous research methodologies. However, data analysis is occasionally incorporated as an aspect of Indigenised research frameworks (Elder & Kersten, 2015; Suaalii-Sauni & Fulu-Aiolupotea, 2014) or, more often, follows emic academic techniques mediated by etic values and paradigms (Hill, Pace, & Robbins, 2010; Gillies, Burleigh, Snowshoe, & Werner, 2014; Castleden, Garvin, & Huu-ay-aht First Nation, 2008; Wright et al., 2012). This chapter proposes a standalone Indigenous data analysis tool that is a hybridisation of ancient oral culture practice and contemporary thought experiment. It is grounded in Aboriginal protocols of communal knowledge production that are aligned with principles of complexity theory. This analysis tool represents a significant departure from western academic approaches, while promoting high levels of intellectual rigour. It also offers the intriguing possibility of examining non-Indigenous data sets using an Indigenous Knowledge process, potentially resolving the issue described by Walters (2005) of quantitative data being, to date, largely ignored in Indigenous research.

Keywords

Indigenous data analysis – Indigenous research methodologies – qualitative data analysis – Australian Aboriginal research

1   The Status of Data Analysis in Indigenous Research

While Indigenous research frameworks, methodologies and paradigms have emerged strongly in the academy in recent decades, most of these innovations have involved plundering 'the master's toolbox' and slightly modifying standard approaches in an effort to de-colonise research practice and centre

Indigenous voices (Walters, 2005). Indigenous methods are mostly concerned with data collection rather than analysis, despite insistence by theorists that Indigenous perspectives and customary practice should inform the design of every step in the research process (Drawson, Toombs, & Mushquash, 2017). Kovach (2010) asserts that Indigenous research paradigms should shape not only the choice of methods, but how the data are analysed and interpreted.

When Indigenous methodologies focus primarily on data collection in their design, the result can be a perpetuation of colonisation through the data analysis phase (Willox et al., 2013). This issue has been addressed by some practitioners through extra diligence in the prioritisation of Indigenous values and voices within the data analysis process (Hill et al., 2010), self-location within the data as a potential resolution (or defiance) of subjectivity challenges (Gillies et al., 2014), including participants in data analysis in community-based participatory projects (Castleden et al., 2008), and incorporating sentient non-human elements such as animals, water and wind through storied approaches to data analysis (Wright et al., 2012).

Most Indigenised approaches to data analysis lack a detailed sequence of steps grounded in customary ritual processes of knowledge production. However, there are some notable exceptions, such as the Kaupapa Maori practice of data analysis moving through stages of *noho puku* (self-reflection), *whanaungatanga* (connection), and *kaitiakitanga* (guardianship) (Elder, 2013). Another effective Polynesian approach to analysis involves mapping the data onto a culturally relevant narrative (Suaalii-Sauni & Fulu-Aiolupotea, 2014).

Some particularly radical approaches include attempts to remove the researcher from data analysis and interpretation entirely (Willox et al., 2013) and turning over ethnographic data collected by western researchers for a reflexive, narrative-based analysis by local Indigenous participants (Botha, 2012). Another radical departure from the mixed-methods toolbox is relationally responsive analysis (Yunkaporta, 2019) which is a free-ranging method of analysis based on the process of 'walking Country' in Australian Aboriginal contexts. While this approach has been effective, it is also vague and subjective, offering little by way of a generalisable sequence of explicit steps for other researchers to follow, or a theoretical grounding recognisable within the academy.

In order to resolve this issue, Yunkaporta designed the Indigenous data analysis approach outlined in this chapter. This aligns a relationally responsive approach with hybridised Indigenous versions of complexity theory and thought experiment in order to make the approach recognisable to the academy. The method emerged from a three-year process of relationally responsive analysis of the Yunkaporta's home language and auto-ethnographic data from cultural activity on-Country (Yunkaporta, 2019). At this point, however, the method was merely theoretical. It was made 'real' through a collaborative and practical application with another Indigenous researcher, Moodie, bringing the approach into proper relation through her doctoral research project (Moodie, 2021) and associated networks of affiliation on-Country and in community.

2 A Proposed Indigenous Data Analysis Method

A thought ritual is a method of data analysis that is a hybridisation of Indigenous oral culture practice and thought experiment. While western thought experiments involve creating purely abstract simulations of events and fields, thought ritual comprises four stages grounded in Aboriginal protocols of communal knowledge production (Sheehan, 2003). This involves practical activity and generation of images, objects, relationships and story (Jones, Moodie, & Hobson, 2014). As Indigenous Knowledge systems are regarded in this method as complex adaptive systems (Rose, 2005), these activities are also aligned with principles of complexity theory, particularly the way agents behave in complex adaptive systems (Pintea, Tripon, Avram, & Crisan, 2018). Those principles are distilled here into the descriptors of connection, diversity, interaction and adaptation, sitting within a framework of pattern-thinking. They reflect Indigenous ways of valuing, being, knowing and doing (Martin, 2008).

The stages in this process may overlap in the cultural activities employed in analysis, or may take a different order, or be altered from what is described here, but the overall process is as follows:

1. Connection: Identify the relational pairs of agents (participants), data points, variables etc. and the networks of pairs these form, and the pairs of networks (i.e. different systems or data sets or thematic categories interacting), using visual modalities to express these relations.
2. Diversity: Use narrative in collaboration with other participants to identify similarities, differences and areas of overlap between different variables, agents and data points.
3. Interaction: Use oral culture metaphors and forms of expression to replicate the exchanges of energy, information or matter between the different agents, variables and data points in the field.
4. Adaptation: Use supra-rational moments of ancestral connection to identify transformative feedback loops and chains of cause and effect in which data points change, attract change or interact with other data points to produce change events. Time is non-linear in this process, so the changes you perceive might be in past, present or future.

The first principle is connection, which involves locating yourself as the researcher within the field by defining all of the relationships in the field and your belongingness in that network of relations. This means extending your ontology to include Indigenous pronouns of I, we-two, we-only, we-all (rather than the limited range of single and plural forms in academic English). This means that every agent (a participant or sentient entity in the field), variable, datum and theme in the data set is defined by relationships within pairs, networks of pairs and pairs of networks. Every item is connected to multiple pairs that form exclusive networks and then connections with other networks within an inclusive whole. These data groupings reflect the independent and interdependent relations that form complex systems.

Inclusion of the researcher as a related element within the data recognises observer effects and uncertainty by embracing subjectivity and belongingness within the field. Rather than contaminating the data (or ignoring contamination through false claims of objectivity), the presence of the Indigenous researcher only enriches the data set by increasing complexity through relatedness and adherence to oral culture knowledge protocols. Observer effects are neutralised as the researcher ceases to be a solitary analyst and becomes part of a self-organising system reflexively observing itself. It is recommended that this stage be executed using visual modalities (images, maps, diagrams, or genealogy-like frameworks), to access supra-rational ways of thinking that enable the perception of complexity. Computer modelling or digital simulations may be used here also.

The second principle is diversity, which involves identifying the individual elements (agents, variables, data points, themes, data sets) within the relationships explored in the first principle, then telling the stories of each element to identify similarities, differences and overlaps between them. It is important to examine these through narrative and yarning (Indigenous modality of dialogue) to ensure adherence to Indigenous protocols of communal knowledge production. Indigenous Knowledge is only valid if it is produced in groups or pairs; individual analysis is considered to be invalid and lacking intellectual rigour.

So, this stage of the process must be completed by the researcher in a group or pair, preferably with research participants who were involved with the data collection but also with mentors, peers, knowledge keepers or Elders. It is storied in order to adhere to Indigenous narrative modalities of knowledge production. The process of seeking similarities, differences and dynamic overlaps is patterned on the practice of 'reading Country'. This involves seeking the changes and forces of change in between different elements and systems to find areas of increase and significance.

The third principle is interaction, which involves the continuous transfer of energy, matter and information between elements in the system (or data set). Without this flow, the spirit of a system becomes stagnant and results in collapse. This stage of the data analysis involves using oral culture metaphors and expression (e.g. dancing, weaving, imaging, storying, carving, walking Country) to perceive the 'forces in between' that are influencing all of the elements in the field. It involves translating the elements of your data sets into oral culture metaphors and moving them into an abstract/spiritual space to create a simulation of the field. You can then manipulate or examine those elements through cultural practice before translating your findings back into the tangible reality. For example, you might represent a data set from interviews with a dance about eagle flight, then an empirical data set of test scores with a dance about that eagle making a kill and feeding. Similarly, cultural metaphors might be employed in a painting, weaving, carving, journey or story. The purpose of this stage is to acknowledge the influences of spirit on the field and find deeper understandings and patterns in your analysis. The intense concentration involved in this process may give rise to the heightened mental state required for the final stage of the analysis.

The fourth principle of adaptation builds on the third by seeking revelatory or ancestrally connected insights about feedback loops, chain reactions and transformations in the field. In Indigenous Knowledge systems these dynamic instances of convergence produce adaptation and increase; these are the rich areas of data that produce the most interesting and transformative findings. The purpose of this stage in the analysis is to achieve an altered state of consciousness through cultural activity, creating a moment of inspiration or realisation. Key findings may emerge in the analysis through extra-cognitive, supra-rational reasoning accessed through a dream, a trance, deep reflection, revealed knowledge (e.g. cellular memory), meaningful coincidence or 'signs' observed on-Country. These are regarded in Indigenous ontologies as ancestral communications, including the observation of unusual phenomena such as sudden wind gusts in treetops, lightning strikes, rainbows, fires and the behaviour of animals. Such occurrences are known as 'a Something' in Aboriginal English.

A Something can also be experienced as a startling moment of synchronicity and convergence in the researcher's lived reality, whether on-Country or in cyberspace or a workspace. It may emerge as an unexpected or unexplainable synchronicity within the data itself. A Something will often indicate the presence of a strange attractor in a complex system – an agent or element in the field that precipitates transformations and adaptation. There will be feedback loops and chain reactions of cause and effect surrounding that strange attractor – data points that do not exist in isolation but that change in interactions with other data points or combine with others to create new ones. This means your data is not static or fixed, but a living system of knowledge patterned on creation. Time is not linear in this way of knowing, so the changes you perceive in the system may occur in past, present or future. Future changes, when carried back into the linear paradigms of print-based academic reality (i.e. writing up findings), may be reported as extrapolations, predictions or projections.

The overarching framework of pattern-thinking is not a stage in this process but runs as a common thread through all four principles. It involves seeking the trends and relational forces within data sets that might be missed with more linear and analytical modes of thought. During the simulation you are creating through the thought ritual process, you will overlay networks of relationships between data points with storied sites of overlap between those networks and the flows of energy, matter and information across the whole field. While working with the data using Indigenous modalities, the patterns you perceive through cultural practice and ancestral connection will yield deeper understandings, richer findings and emergent applications for those findings.

3 Trialling the Indigenous Data Analysis Method

This data analysis approach was applied to a doctoral research project examining cross-cultural engagement issues at the interface between Indigenous and non-Indigenous systems (Moodie, 2021). The researcher organised data sets around three case studies that were reframed as 'life projects' within her Indigenous methodology. The data sets included all of the relations within Country and community in the dynamic contexts of the life projects, storied in print, yarns and paintings. Each instance of data analysis was carried out with a partner to establish collaborative rather than individual understandings of the patterned knowledge revealed in the data.

In the initial process of identifying the relationships between every element in the data sets (including sacred sites, stories, artists, art dealers, plant and animal species, Elders, marketplaces, economic transactions, programs, managers, quotes, outcomes, events and more), a significant correlation was found almost immediately that would not have been apparent in a standard thematic analysis.

As the bunya pine was included in the analysis as a sentient participant in the field, interspecies communication and cooperation were considered in the patterning of the data. The three-yearly cycle of peak bunya-nut production that facilitates periodic multi-national gatherings on that country for feasting, trade and ceremony was examined as an ancient practice of inter-cultural engagement. The elements of engagement in this process were outlined in yarns with a partner and then similar patterns were sought in the data. Another three-year cycle was perceived in the funding rounds of a failed co-management project. All the data associated with this project was brought alongside the bunya feast data and the two engagement processes were analysed in terms of similarities, differences and dynamic overlap.

The researcher inscribed the names of each data point, agent and variable on objects and arranged then rearranged them in different groupings. She began to colour-code them according to the networks they belonged to and began to move these around in simulations of the field for different case studies. Up until this point she expressed a sense of being 'lost' in the complex relations of the data, which triggered a feeling of being lost in forest Country. She had a vivid recollection during this process of her father telling her as a child how to find north when lost by observing the growth of moss on trees. She allowed this to guide the directionality of her practice in this stage of the analysis.

A north to south map of the Great Dividing Range was created and the data were arranged around storied locations on that map. Sites of productive and disruptive engagement on Aboriginal land along that massive songline were perceived at various points of intersection between significant sites and the narrative data about the lives of program participants. A pattern emerged whereby instances of disruptive engagement occurred around activities based on extraction, while productive engagement activities were grounded in the Indigenous concept of 'increase'. Analysis of the data grouped around these themes yielded common traits of both extractive and increase models of engagement that formed a major part of the findings and recommendations from this research.

There were many moments in which a Something was perceived during the thought ritual process. Some of these were previous occurrences that had been forgotten or ignored in the course of the research. In one such example, the researcher moved to a new office in a different state to find a painting there by an Elder who was one of her research participants, now deceased. This Elder had shared a lot of knowledge about the Country and sacred site reported on in the research and continued to do so non-locally through this painting, so the messages perceived in this Something were allowed to guide the researcher's attention in the data analysis.

4 Conclusions

Mario Blaser and Marisol de la Cadena (2018) articulate a concept they call 'Pluriverse', a world of many worlds in the cosmologies of Indigenous South America. The Indigenous cultures of the continent currently known as Australia also comprise a world of many worlds. We have multiple cosmologies inscribed in the landscape and diverse ritual practices centred around thousands of sacred increase sites. Despite this startling diversity, there is a shared pattern of inquiry and analysis across this pluriverse of knowledge systems that the thought ritual method has sought to utilise in a way that is generalisable for all of the custodial groups keeping these diverse knowledges. This patterning of knowledge practice has always involved productive engagement with Country as sentient kin, an increase paradigm giving rise to complexity and sustainability in living systems.

In the project we used to trial this Indigenous data analysis method (Moodie, 2021), complex relations between extractive and increase paradigms emerged that had been overlooked in the initial standard thematic analysis. Extractive paradigms informing settler policies in relation to Indigenous people were revealed in places they had previously been invisible, once the entities of increase sites were viewed as sentient participants and engaged with appropriately.

Non-Indigenous analysis promises much but delivers little from an Indigenous standpoint grounded in an increase paradigm. Manning Clark (1997) wrote of the great forest and the analyses of this ecosystem in the early 1800s that predicted centuries of lumber harvest, while in reality it was depleted within 25 years. Accurate understandings of abundance and sustainability are not possible using analysis tools grounded in extractive paradigms seeking short-term profit from water, earth, Intellectual Property, DNA and other Indigenous resources that are destroyed by this unproductive form of engagement.

The emerging data analysis approach was experienced by the participants in this project as a way of honouring a world of many worlds, worlds including sentient beings usually regarded as inanimate, reinstating their knowledges and healing Country through interaction with increase sites. This work came about through a relationship based on a professional encounter. The encounter became a Something that was found to have a pre-existing presence throughout the entire project, resulting in a realisation that Indigenous analysis is embedded at every stage of a research project, not just following data collection. Further, the analysis could not be constrained by constructs of linear time and was often understood to have predated the research project itself, or even its own 'design' by the researchers.

Family, community, Aboriginal students, academics, and a small cohort of visiting international academics at Deakin University all entered the yarns and rituals of this analysis, co-creating a consensus of shared understandings in a process of joint discovery, speaking, being and thinking. These encounters were physicalised through the art of making and the practice of walking Country. From the practice of art making in land-based cultural contexts, we two found that Country is always at the core of this data analysis method: geological (basalt, sandstone, water, ochre); geographical (cultural boundaries); ecological (flora and fauna); legal (kinship, law, governance); economic (trade routes, resources, industry); and profoundly cultural in ways that make it impossible to separate any of these elements within the process of data analysis.

References

Botha, L. (2012). Mixing methods as a process towards Indigenous methodologies. *International Journal of Social Research Methodology, 14*(4), 313–325.

Blaser, M., & de la Cadena, M. (Eds.). (2018). *A world of many worlds*. Duke University Press.

Castleden, H., Garvin, T., & Huu-ay-aht First Nation. (2008). Modifying photovoice for community-based participatory Indigenous research. *Social Science and Medicine, 66*(6), 1393–1405.

Clark, M., (1997). *History of Australia*. Melbourne University Press.

Drawson, A. S., Toombs, E., & Mushquash, C. J. (2017). Indigenous research methods: A systematic review. *The International Indigenous Policy Journal, 8*(2).

Elder, H., & Kersten, P. (2015). Whakawhiti kōrero, a method for the development of a cultural assessment tool, Te Waka Kuaka, in Māori traumatic brain injury. *Behavioural Neurology, 1*, 1–8.

Gillies, C., Burleigh, D., Snowshoe, A., & Werner, D. (2014). Walking in circles: Self-location in Indigenous youth violence prevention research. *First Nations Perspectives, 6*(1), 5–25.

Hill, J. S., Pace, T. M., & Robbins, R. R. (2010). Decolonizing personality assessment and honoring Indigenous voices: A critical examination of the MMPI-2. *Cultural Diversity and Ethnic Minority Psychology, 16*(1), 16–25.

Jones, J., Moodie, D., & Hobson, N. (2014). Dinawan dreaming: Seeing the darkness or the stars. In J. K. Jones (Ed.), *Weaving words: Personal and professional transformation through writing as research* (pp. 81–102). Cambridge Scholars Publishing.

Kovach, M. (2010). Conversational method in Indigenous research. *First Peoples Child & Family Review, 5*(1), 40–48.

Martin, K. (2008). *Please knock before you enter: Aboriginal regulation of outsiders and the implications for researchers*. Post Pressed.

Moodie, D. (2021). *Inclusive engagement and development: An Indigenous perspective on business, sustainable and community development* (Doctoral thesis). School of Agriculture and Foods Systems, University of Queensland.

Pintea, C., Tripon, A., Avram, A., & Crisan, G. (2018). Multi-agents features on Android platforms. *Complex Adaptive Systems Modeling, 6*(10).

Rose, D. (2005). An Indigenous philosophical ecology: Situating the human. *The Australian Journal of Anthropology, 16*(3), 294–305.

Sheehan, N. (2003). *Indigenous knowledge and higher education: Instigating relational education in a neocolonial context* (Doctoral thesis). School of Education University of Queensland.

Suaalii-Sauni, T., & Fulu-Aiolupotea, S. M. (2014). Decolonising Pacific research, building Pacific research communities and developing Pacific research tools: The case of the talanoa and the faafaletui in Samoa. *Asia Pacific Viewpoint, 55*(3), 331–344.

Walters, M. (2005). Using the 'power of the data' within Indigenous research practice. *Australian Aboriginal Studies, 2*, 27–24.

Willox, A. C., Harper, S. L., Edge, V. L., 'My Word': Storytelling and Digital Media Lab, & Rigolet Inuit Community Government. (2013). Storytelling in a digital age: Digital storytelling as an emerging narrative method for preserving and promoting Indigenous oral wisdom. *Qualitative Research, 13*(2), 127–147.

Wright, S., Lloyd, K., Suchet-Pearson, S., Burarrwanga, L., Tofa, M., & Country, B. (2012). Telling stories in, through and with country: Engaging with Indigenous and more-than-human methodologies at Bawaka, NE Australia. *Journal of Cultural Geography, 29*(1), 39–60.

Yunkaporta, T. (2019). Wik pedagogies: Adapting oral culture processes for print-based learning contexts. *The Australian Journal of Indigenous Education*.

CHAPTER 7

The Value of an Integrated Relational and Culturally Responsive Pedagogy in Teaching Aboriginal and Torres Strait Islander Teacher Education Students

Lisa Bell and Kate Chealuck

Abstract

Sidorkin (2002, p. 88) defines education as "a process of building relationships". There is a considerable body of research demonstrating that positive teacher-student relationships are associated with a variety of desired academic outcomes in children (Aspelin, 2012; Hattie, 2012; Reeves & Le Mare, 2017; Shor, 1992). We propose that this relational pedagogy is important for all learners, both school children and university students, with important implications for the retention of students within higher education degrees.

This chapter discusses the value of an integrated relational and culturally responsive pedagogical approach used in teacher education degrees in a Victorian university setting. This approach fosters reciprocal relationships between university academics and Aboriginal and Torres Strait Islander teacher education students with cyclical engagement in teaching and learning (Rishel & Zuercher, 2016). Within this engagement, academics learn as much as they teach. This approach involves building positive relationships and interactions between academics and Aboriginal and Torres Strait Islander teacher education students that break down the power relations inherent in both student-teacher and student-institution relations (Pearce & Down, 2011). It also utilises culturally relevant and respectful pedagogy, where academics utilise students' culture as a vehicle for learning. This is a pathway for students to maintain their cultural identity while succeeding academically (Ladson-Billings, 1995).

Keywords

teacher education – relational pedagogy – culturally responsive pedagogy – Aboriginal pre-service teachers – indigenous students

1 Positive Teacher-Student Relationships and Relational Pedagogy

"At the heart of education is the relationship between learners and their teachers" (Martin & Pirbhai-Illich, 2016, p. 355). It is well-known within education literature that positive teacher-student relationships are associated with a variety of desired academic outcomes in children (Aspelin, 2012; Hattie, 2012; Reeves & Le Mare, 2017; Shor, 1992). This includes children's positive development, which "depends to a considerable degree, on whether the contexts in which they develop, including schools, are reliable sources of supportive relationships" (Reeves & Le Mare, 2017, p. 86). As Sidorkin (2002, p. 88) contends, education is a "process of building relations", and Ikpeze (2018, p. 112) states, "the caring work of teaching is premised upon having a reciprocal relationship between students and teachers". Hattie (2009) describes the influence of teachers on student achievement as critical in two ways: "the quality of the teacher, and the nature of the teacher-student relationship" (p. 126). In a literature review related to such relationships, Aspelin (2012) cites many European studies and notes that the majority of studies in the field "have shown that the teacher is the single most important factor in student learning" (p. 45).

Relational competency, as highlighted by the Danish Clearinghouse for Educational Research (2008, cited in Aspelin, 2012), is emphasised as having the largest impact on the wellbeing of students, as well as on measurable knowledge: "teachers who are able to enter into friendly, respectful and positive relations with the pupils generate far better pupil achievements" (p. 45). Students are attracted to education facilities because of the quality of relationships and communal experiences that can occur in them. That is, the innate desire to 'belong' can be facilitated through educational experiences and the relationships forged within them.

Relational pedagogy treats relationships as the foundation of good pedagogy and emphasises the interpersonal skills of teachers and learners (Sabol & Pianta, 2012) in developing positive and caring relations. According to Reeves and Le Mare (2017, p. 86), relational pedagogy manifests in "teachers who are aware and explicitly focus on the quality of their interactions with students to develop classroom communities that promote academic, social and emotional growth". Brownlee (2004) elaborates, stating that relational pedagogy values students as knowers who bring their experiences to the class. Teachers adopting this approach, therefore, know, relate to, and utilise students' experiences and social constructivist approaches to enhance student outcomes.

Whilst much of the research focusing on relational pedagogy is centred on children at school, we agree with other studies (Biesta, 2004; Pearce & Down, 2011) that suggest relational pedagogy is important for *all* learners. This includes not only school children, but also university students, with relational pedagogy having important implications for the retention of students within higher education degrees.

2 Relational Pedagogy in Higher Education

Within higher education settings, relational pedagogy has been shown to have a significant impact on the retention of students experiencing disadvantage. Pearce and Down (2011) found two inter-related dimensions of relational pedagogy as experienced by students in their study:

> Firstly, the support and resources that enable students to build powerful relations with academics (both tutors and lecturers) and secondly, the constraints and interferences that students face in establishing these relationships. (p. 486)

The support and resources that assisted student learning included inviting interactions between academics and students at a variety of times; 'counting on' academics to be there if students had problems; and just academics 'having time' for students (Pearce & Down, 2011, p. 486).

Inviting interactions between academics and students opens communication styles and friendly relationships that can also be used for pedagogical purposes (Margonis, 2004) to engage students in learning within discipline areas. Particularly, 'participatory' forms of communication, whereby the positive teacher-learner relationship facilitates participation in communication and hence the construction of shared understandings and meaning-making (Biesta, 2004). Shor (1992) states that academics who engage with students through participatory and affective communication have a profound impact on student learning. Pearce and Down (2011) also found that participatory communication enhanced connectedness and belonging in university settings. Positive interactions with academics reduced the isolation of studying, and affirmed students' 'rights' to be at university. In other words, this style of communication often reduced the relational power imbalances inherent in student-academic and student-institution relations. These studies suggest this relational pedagogy was also crucial to the wellbeing of students and their feelings of belonging, as summed up eloquently by Berryman (2013, p. 3):

> The sense of belonging to, or marginalisation from, education affects every aspect of participation and, therefore, learning within it. This in turn

affects students' behaviours and their self-perception. Failing to support the development of students' understandings and ability to act in a social context risks marginalising and alienating young people and rendering them incompetent.

We would suggest this is then particularly important to students who are from cultural backgrounds underrepresented in higher education.

3   Aboriginal and Torres Strait Islander Students in Higher Education Settings

It is well-documented that Aboriginal and Torres Strait Islander people continue to be the most disadvantaged group in Australian education (see for example Gillan, Mellor, & Krakouer, 2017). Aboriginal and Torres Strait Islander students also remain underrepresented in universities, with "Indigenous people comprising only 1.7% of the domestic student population, compared with 3.1% of the Australian working age population" (Australian Government Department of Prime Minister and Cabinet, 2018).

The authors of this chapter work with Aboriginal and Torres Strait Islander students within a four-year Bachelor of Education degree at an Australian university, where students graduate as primary school teachers. The importance of increasing the number of Aboriginal and Torres Strait Islander qualified teachers has been well-recognised by Government and within policy documents (Buckskin, 2016; Australian Government Department of Prime Minister and Cabinet, 2018). Nevertheless, the statistics and literature show that despite ongoing policy attempts and substantial budget allocations, few targets to 'close the gap' and increase the number of Aboriginal and Torres Strait Islander teachers have been achieved (Australian Government Department of Prime Minister and Cabinet, 2018). There are many reasons for this which are beyond the scope of this chapter, however in describing this, we wanted to highlight the ongoing challenges that Aboriginal and Torres Strait Islander people face when engaging with higher education.

Within university settings, Aboriginal and Torres Strait Islander students may be first generation university attendees, and many have had limited or negative previous educational experiences. These negative experiences may have included racism, deficit model learning, or low expectations by teachers, as well as recognising the 'hidden curriculum' that has historically silenced Aboriginal culture within Australian educational settings (Guywanga, 1991). The literature acknowledges that participating in this system may be potentially very daunting for prospective students (Day & Davidson, 2005; Ragoonaden & Mueller, 2017), particularly if they know few people who have previously pursued tertiary education and who can provide support or act as role models (Lampert & Burnett, 2012; White, 2009).

Furthermore, universities are represented by the dominant western knowledge paradigms and may have little acknowledgement of Indigenous Knowledge systems, pedagogy and forms of governance and leadership (Lampert & Burnett, 2012). This is consistent around the world, where Indigenous Knowledges and meaning construction are rarely validated or legitimised by the western Academy or formal schooling systems (Battiste & Youngblood Henderson, 2000; Ortiz, 2009).

In contrast to this, the idea of culturally relevant pedagogy has been around for decades (Ladson-Billings, 1995) although the uptake in Australian Universities has been on an individual unit or subject basis and is not well-represented in the literature.

4 Culturally Responsive Pedagogy

Ladson-Billings (1995) defines culturally responsive pedagogy as committed to collective empowerment of cultures. It is premised on the academic success of students, cultural competence and critical consciousness, and uses "the cultural knowledge, prior experiences, frames of reference and performance styles of ethnically diverse students to make learning encounters more relevant and effective for them" (Gay, 2013, p. 50). According to Gay (2013), culturally responsive pedagogy uses cultural resources to facilitate better teaching and learning and highlights positive learning possibilities for marginalised students, rather than being based on a deficit model. Gay goes on to state, "it is a means of improving achievement by teaching diverse students through their own cultural filters" (2013, p. 50) and should teach "to and through" (p. 51) students' personal and cultural strengths, capabilities and accomplishments. It is a framework that recognises the "rich and varied cultural wealth, knowledges and skills of diverse learners" (Ragoonaden & Mueller, 2017, p. 23) and seeks to develop and nurture students' academic, social, emotional, cultural, psychological and physiological well-being (Ragoonaden & Mueller, 2017). As acknowledged by Berryman (2013, p. 9), "engagement is more effective when individuals feel they are able to initiate learning interactions and when they are able to use their own cultural experiences as the basis for constructing new understandings".

Culturally responsive pedagogy has its roots in Vygotskian theories of learning (1978), which stressed the importance of social interactions and community in the process of learning and meaning-making. Vygotsky advocated for the use of cultural tools and the prior knowledge and experience of learners to help construct knowledge in a social manner. A culturally responsive pedagogy utilises this information by first building relationships with students and drawing on their culture, backgrounds, and experiences to facilitate learning opportunities, as well as understanding and acknowledging the social, political and cultural context in which the learner resides (Quillinan, MacPhail, Dempsey, & McEvoy, 2019). Quillinan and colleagues (2019) stress that learning is an active process that is participatory rather than transmissive and that teachers must connect and interact with learners in an effective manner if learning is to occur. This includes connecting with the whole learner, their prior experiences, knowledge and understandings, and also the experiences and understandings they share with others in their families and communities. Culturally responsive teaching therefore "requires a thoughtful consideration of what curriculum to use (place-based, culturally relevant) and how to structure the teaching and learning relationship (cyclic-relational instruction) in culturally respectful ways" (Rishel & Zuercher, 2016, p. 48). The aim is to create contexts for learning "where the students' home-cultural experiences, as determined by them, can be used in the construction of new knowledge, rather than those experiences being marginalised, ignored or belittled" (Berryman, 2013, p. 9).

5 Positioning a Framework for Integrated Relational and Culturally Responsive Pedagogy

These theories particularly resonate with us. We the authors, Lisa and Kate, are non-Indigenous teacher-educators working exclusively with Aboriginal and Torres Strait Islander pre-service teachers throughout their higher education degrees. The pre-service teachers travel to the NIKERI Institute at Deakin University in Victoria, Australia, for block intensive teaching seven times a year. The rest of the year, students live in their home communities (all around Australia) and maintain ongoing access to the university online learning environment and communication platforms to access all teaching and learning materials.

This chapter evolved from the authors' collaborative self-study using dialogue as a method of examining our practice for the purpose of improving our teaching (East, Fitzgerald, & Heston, 2009). As suggested by East and colleagues (2009), our professional conversations provide a stimulus for understanding our discipline areas and teaching practices and modelling the collaborative meaning-making we hope to achieve with our students. From these regular conversations it became clear we were utilising the best of both worlds by integrating relational and culturally responsive pedagogies into our teaching practices. These practices started off organically, since both of us were primary school teachers ourselves and we recognise the importance of first establishing positive and caring relationships with students in our care – of course it would be the same with our university students! Using this relationality as a centralising point, our professional conversations led us to recognise the other pedagogical approaches we were using within the areas we taught (and beyond, into our everyday interactions with students). From here and with a consideration of the literature in these areas, it was clear we were integrating a relational pedagogical approach with a culturally responsive pedagogy.

Figure 7.1 outlines a framework for an integrated approach to relational and culturally responsive pedagogy as used in our university setting at NIKERI Institute. Since the literature reviewed for this chapter acknowledges that culturally responsive pedagogy is a social practice, we have experienced firsthand that it can be integrated seamlessly with relational pedagogy at all levels. Writing in a Hawaiian context, Rishel and Zuercher (2016) agree that integrating the two pedagogies is an appropriate method to connect students to their

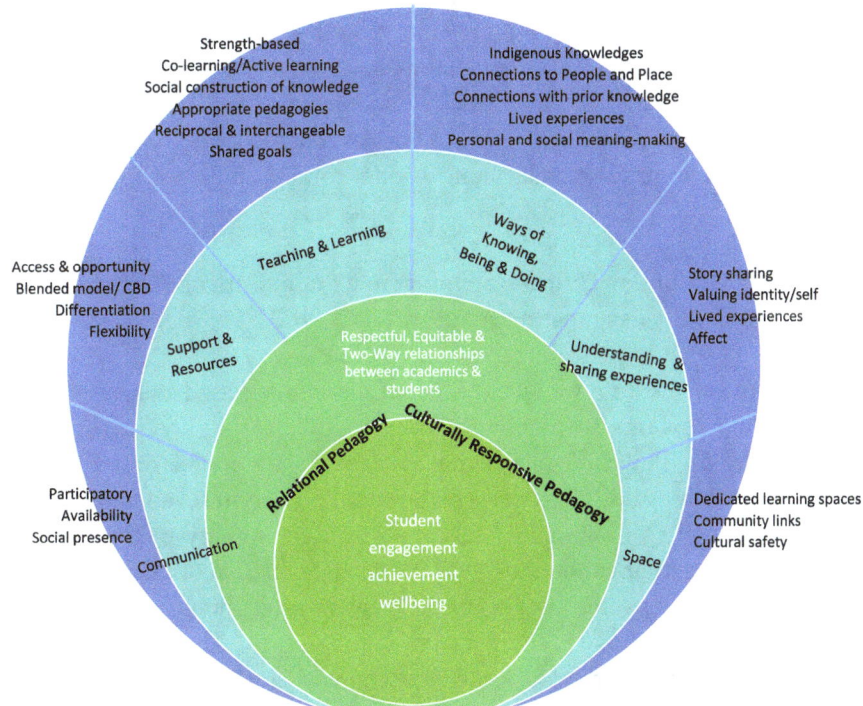

FIGURE 7.1   An integrated framework of relational and culturally responsive pedagogy

learning, in safe, caring environments. We agree that it is not only appropriate, but necessary in the context of Aboriginal and Torres Strait Islander learners in Australia. When teachers form positive caring relationships with learners and acknowledge that the prior knowledge and cultural experiences of those learners are valid and integral, then we can start to de-colonise the Australian education system and successful learning is likely to occur and lead to more positive learning experiences overall.

The remainder of this chapter will discuss the authors' reflections on the use of the integrated framework of relational and culturally responsive pedagogy (Figure 7.1) in the context of working with Aboriginal and Torres Strait Islander primary pre-service teachers at NIKERI Institute. It will outline the unique delivery mode used at NIKERI, as well as reflections on what we, the authors, have found to be best practice pedagogies to suit the needs of our student cohort, discipline areas, and the Bachelor of Education (primary) teaching degree.

The key outcomes and the central idea of the framework (Figure 7.1) is the focus on student engagement, achievement and wellbeing throughout students' study journeys. Our reflections on practice and pedagogy will continue to make reference to this central idea by challenging power imbalances and building respectful, equitable and two-way relationships between academics and students. We have identified six components that we use that make up the next layer of the framework and work towards our outcomes of relationship building to enhance the student experience. The final layer of the framework consists of examples that we have found facilitate working towards those outcomes.

6 Reflections on Utilising an Integrated Framework of Relational and Culturally Responsive Pedagogy

At the NIKERI Institute we teach using a Community-Based Delivery (CBD) model where students live at home but travel to the Institute and stay on campus in a purpose-built student accommodation for short periods of study. Each of these intensive study blocks lasts for one week and occur seven times a year, allowing students to maintain their family and community responsibilities without leaving their communities for the extended period of time it takes to get a degree. This enables students to 'bring their degrees home', get a local job and keep qualifications within their communities.

We, the authors, work with students in the Bachelor of Education degree, a four-year course consisting of 32 units (subjects) that qualifies graduates as primary school teachers. We teach the same accredited degree as offered in the 'main' Faculty of Education at Deakin University, but are a dedicated learning space for Aboriginal and Torres Strait Islander students.

We are focused on centralising our relationships with our students and are dedicated to nurturing student engagement, achievement and wellbeing in a higher education setting. Our use of the integrated framework of relational and culturally responsive pedagogy fosters reciprocal relationships between university academics and Aboriginal and Torres Strait Islander teacher education students, with cyclical engagement in teaching and learning (Rishel & Zuercher, 2016) through which academics learn as much as they teach. The small numbers of students in our classes enables rapport to be developed quickly between academics and students. Often student names are known even before they officially start classes (we will have previously met or talked with students at prospective student interviews and enrolment). Small student numbers also enable staff to teach using more appropriate pedagogies and more social interactions through discussion and sharing. This approach is distinct from traditional transmission modes of delivery common in university lectures and classes.

Also, unlike in more traditional university settings where staff tend to focus on one or two discipline units (such as literacy or science, for example), staff at the Institute are in the unique position of teaching units across discipline areas and across year levels within the degree. It is not uncommon for us to teach two or three year level cohorts and two or three discipline areas throughout a year. For example, Lisa teaches in first year (teacher pedagogy units); second year (literacy units) and fourth year (literacy, and assessment units); Kate teaches first year (teacher pedagogy units, and science content unit); third year (science education unit) and fourth year (design technology unit, science unit, and teacher pedagogy units). Teaching across the degree and across discipline area units enables academic staff to build positive, long-term relationships with students, and journey with students in their development and progression from first to fourth year. We are also strategic about building positive and caring relationships with students from the beginning of their higher education experience. Permanent staff in the Institute education team are allocated purposefully to teach in first year and fourth year of the degree, effectively 'bookending' students' experiences in the most important years: when they start university and as they prepare to graduate. This has been found to be effective in maintaining positive relations throughout the degree and recognised throughout our professional conversations as having a positive impact on student retention and success.

We agree with the aforementioned literature that relationships are the key to engaging learners in higher education. These relationships may mitigate some of the harm students have experienced previously in their education and allow students to appreciate having educational 'cheerleaders' in their corner. The pedagogical framework outlines the importance of respectful, equitable and two-way relationships between academics and students. This is in line with a relational pedagogy focus to enhance and nurture student engagement, achievement and wellbeing in a higher education setting (Shor, 1992).

It also supports a culturally responsive pedagogy that prioritises community relationships and social interactions that are two-way between academics and Aboriginal and Torres Strait Islander teacher education students, creating an exchange of knowledge where both sides can learn from each other (instead of knowledge only coming from the academic and usually associated with a western knowledge system) (Maher, 2012). According to Battiste and Youngblood Henderson (2000), academics who work in two-way interactions build a bridge of meaningfulness between the two cultural worlds, helping to break down the power relations inherent in both student-teacher and student-institution relationships (Pearce & Down, 2011).

The integrated framework of relational and culturally responsive pedagogy allows for six interrelated components that reciprocally feed into relationship building, as well as stem from positive relations and the integrated pedagogical practices used. These components are Teaching and Learning; Ways of Knowing, Being and Doing; Understanding and sharing experiences; Communication; Support and resources; and Space. Included in the framework in no particular order, these components are particularly common to our professional conversations, and how each allows for enhancing the learning experience for our students will now be discussed in further detail.

7 Effective Teaching and Learning

Our core business at the NIKERI Institute is teaching and learning so it stands to reason this is the first component from the framework to be elaborated on. An important aspect emerging from our professional conversations was that we must always advocate for a strength-based approach in our teaching and learning. This is often at odds with students' previous experiences in education settings; more than once we have heard of students working to and within 'deficit models' (Lawrence, 2000). A student deficit approach is unhelpful for Aboriginal and Torres Strait Islander students entering university if they are to succeed in their classes as pre-service teachers. Rather, our conversations have drawn on Lawrence's (2000) discussions of re-theorising students' cultural backgrounds as an important knowledge base and the importance of academics gaining familiarity with, engaging, negotiating and mastering the literacies of the culture to facilitate success in students' units.

The social construction of knowledge as discussed previously, is a key tenet of learning and teaching for both children and university students, and our pre-service teachers interact with this theory of learning through their degrees and into the teaching workforce. We try to model social construction of meaning throughout our discipline units and draw on appropriate pedagogies through collaboration, yarning circles, modelling, and hands-on activities, enabling students to construct their own understandings through interactions with peers and academics. Again, this facilitates active learning that is reciprocal and interchangeable.

The invited co-learning/active learning throughout our units is crucial to our pedagogical practices and the integration of relational and culturally responsive pedagogies. As Root, Augustine, Snow and Doucette (2019, p. 1) claim, co-learning is a way to "transform the university experience towards inclusivity and restore voice and vision of the community to equal standing". Active learning involves transforming theory into practice and can be enabled through group discussions, critical reflection, field experiences, and professional conversations (Acquah, Szelei, & Katz, 2019). As recognised by our professional conversation, other teaching approaches as suggested by Acquah and colleagues (2019) are utilised throughout units: group discussions, line-ups, gallery walks, critical reflection, immersion experiences, case studies, hands-on activities and explicit modelling all help to engage students in the construction of knowledge and reduce transmission of information.

The co-learning and active learning involved in storytelling and yarning with students, as we work through content, enables a two-way sharing of understandings and knowledges. We have learned a great many things from our students, who bring the knowledge of their communities into our classrooms. For example, students interacted with sustainability and the environment in science education and were able to integrate their local knowledge of plants and animals, as well as incorporate their own language to enable a two-way interaction of knowledge between the academic staff and the students, with both enhancing their understanding of sustainability practices in local contexts. This reciprocity enabled teachers and students to develop, negotiate and maintain their connection with each other and with cultural backgrounds and knowledges continuously (Ikpeze, 2018). And this shared meaning-making contrasts to the "default position of historically in-built deference [to western knowledge] which Aboriginal people have ingrained in them through contact with missionaries and other non-Indigenous people in positions of power" (Maher, 2012, p. 353).

Happily, the goals of our students are shared by us as their teachers. We want more Aboriginal and Torres Strait Islander educators because they are the key to improving education for Aboriginal and Torres Strait Islander children (Buckskin, 2016). Our degree enables the graduation of more teachers with diverse backgrounds by supporting students to achieve their goals of graduating, while maintaining their family commitments and community responsibilities. Our professional conversations between colleagues and students suggest that engaging with an integrated pedagogical approach such as in Figure 7.1 will help facilitate these outcomes.

8 Ways of Knowing, Ways of Being, and Ways of Doing

As well as teaching and learning, an area of equal importance in NIKERI's core business is that of consideration and links to Indigenous Knowledges and lived experiences of Aboriginal and Torres Strait Islander people. The integrated framework of relational and culturally responsive pedagogy in Figure 7.1, draws on Martin's (2003) work with Aboriginal and Torres Strait Islander research helping us consider student engagement in higher education in terms of Indigenous Knowledges and ways of Knowing, Being and Doing. These three components of relatedness in Indigenous ontologies position student experience and enable a holistic approach to teaching and learning. Martin (2003) defines ways of Knowing as one's own stories of relatedness, identity and place; ways of Being as relations with people that are respectful, responsible and accountable; and ways of Doing as the daily process and practices that are served by relatedness.

Indigenous Knowledges and the ways of Knowing, Being and Doing are valued and acknowledged in the Institute's education degree classes. Efforts to make connections to people and places and students are encouraged and students draw on their lived experiences throughout their degrees. In-class activities enable shared meaning-making and the drawing on of knowledge from all over Australia through collaborative discussion and storytelling. Nakata, Nakata, and Chin (2008) maintain that valuing what Aboriginal and Torres Strait Islander students bring to class is particularly important to maintaining and developing students' cultural identities and positions in relation to course content in higher education. Historically, experiences, historical understandings, and individual and community knowledge have been excluded, misrepresented and devalued in the Academy (Nakata et al., 2008). Recognising and acknowledging this is a good step toward breaking down barriers to success and enhancing student engagement, achievement and wellbeing.

9 Understanding and Sharing Experiences

The third component that our reflections recognised as impacting on relationship building and enhancing student study success is understanding and sharing experiences. As mentioned above, story sharing is widely used throughout the education degree as a way of understanding the experiences of others. Students share their stories with peers and academics, and academics share their own stories back, facilitating two-way reciprocal knowledge sharing. Students' negative previous formal education experiences have often been an impetus for enrolling in the degree (to provide better experiences for children in the future). These stories are referred to often (and often emotionally) during the first year of their degree. The teacher pedagogy units in first year have a focus on developing teacher identity and the social context within which modern schooling exists, as well as recognising the social context of disadvantage for children participating in this system. Assessment within these units tasks students with reflecting on their previous education, and classes will often consist of debriefing and validating prior experiences, enhancing self-esteem and confidence in learning abilities, and looking forward into a future as a reflective and inclusive practitioner. The first-year content and assessments are also purposefully geared towards positive relationship building and drawing on cultural capital and life experiences.

The 'Pecha Kucha' and 'Sociological narrative' as assessment in teacher pedagogy units engage students with reflecting explicitly on their previous education experiences. We have found these in particular to be quite emotional for students as they critically engage with their experiences and then share with us and their peers (if they want to). These reflections often acknowledge the racism, hidden curriculum and frighteningly low expectations some students were exposed to throughout their schooling. The academics also share their stories and experiences to continue to forge connections and enable the 'affective storytelling' as discussed by Skattebol and Hayes (2016). Again, this two-way reciprocal sharing process puts participants on a more even playing field with lecturers and can reduce the power imbalances that may exist between academics and students.

Valuing the lived experiences of students is also important when it comes to understanding why students engage or become disengaged, why they may not have submitted work by a deadline, or why they do not attend a class. One student tells of how he travels to our intensive study block – travelling by car from home to the airport, then on a plane from a Torres Strait Island to Cairns, then plane from Cairns to Melbourne, then bus from Melbourne to Geelong. This could take almost 12 hours of travel on a Sunday – no wonder he may not be ready to learn on a Monday morning! Continuing to take account of and value these lived experiences of attending university will only help support student success further.

10   Communication

Communication is another component stemming from our reflections and represented in the framework for relational and culturally responsive pedagogy. The education course team has an open-door policy when students are at the Institute for their intensive study blocks. We invite 'drop-in' visits and have tried to make our office a welcoming place, taking the time to 'be there' for students when needed. We encourage a variety of communication and contact methods when students are at home, which may mean texting, Skype, FaceTime, email, Zoom and Messenger. We have a social media presence, discussion boards and an online collaboration space. We recognise the importance of academics encouraging regular and unscheduled access outside of class (Pearce & Down, 2011), and feel successful in this regard as we often find students just 'hanging out' in our office during intensive study blocks, utilising resources (such as textbooks), or just catching up with us or each other.

Shor's work (1992) recognises that academics who utilise participative and affective communication to engage their students, have a profoundly positive impact on those students' learning. Participatory communication results in shared understandings and making those understandings common. For us it means we encourage discussion to break down ideas and reflect critically on understandings and differing perspectives. We do not claim to be knowledge keepers or the only ones with expertise in transferring knowledge. We utilise our students 'funds of knowledge' (Pearce & Down, 2011), draw on our students' experiences, and value their contributions to class discussion because that enables asocial construction of meaning. Participatory communication has an impact on hidden curriculum of higher education (Guywanga, 1991), providing an implicit message that students belong and are "both worthy of their place and able to succeed at university" (Pearce & Down, 2011, p. 492).

Participatory communication enhances relationships and may be particularly significant for students whose previous experiences in schooling led to feelings of marginalisation and isolation in education settings: "When academics do not recognise the potentially exclusionary impact of their pedagogies and thus fail to engage in a relationship that can provide support when it is needed, they may unconsciously perpetuate existing social inequalities" (Pearce & Down, 2011, p. 492).

11 Support and Resources

The fifth component of our integrated framework that we have found to enhance student engagement, achievement and wellbeing, is that of providing and enabling support and resources to students. There are many support mechanisms in place to enhance student achievement in our degree. Through our professional conversations we recognise that many of these supports began as deficit-based (Nakata et al., 2008). However, supports have now been put in place that are more culturally affirming and recognise the particular needs of our cohorts. These have been designed by or in conjunction with Aboriginal and Torres Strait Islander staff and students, and as Nakata and colleagues (2008) suggest, this provides a more positive framework for student support. Scholarships, learning advisors, and access to the internet, printing and textbooks all enable students to be successful whilst on intensive study blocks, and communication channels discussed previously help maintain engagement in between intensive study blocks.

Differentiation of assessment may also help some students be successful in their studies, particularly for our students who have English as second, third or even seventh language! We have developed effective partnerships with 'main' Faculty staff to enable flexibility in some areas of assessment to better suit the needs of our students. However, this is not always possible and there is a tension in focusing on differentiated and individualising student learning, whilst adhering to unit, university, and teacher accreditation and registration guidelines. This tension is felt by academics in almost all units taught, as we want students to be successful. Most 'main' Faculty education colleagues encourage flexibility of content and deadlines for assessment tasks to fit more appropriately with our intensive study block (CBD) model. But again, this may take time to negotiate and some academics are not open to this in units they curate. Our reflections noted that limiting factors such as lack of student relationships with Faculty staff, lack of flexibility or understandings of cultural needs (such as time away from study for Sorry Business) tend to result in higher rates of student attrition for those subjects. Providing a variety of support mechanisms whilst maintaining relationships is key to enabling Aboriginal and Torres Strait Islander students to experience success in their studies.

12 Space

The final component that was recognised in the integrated framework for relational and culturally responsive pedagogy was the provision of space for students' studies. Our degree is taught within the NIKERI Institute learning spaces. These spaces are dedicated to NIKERI students and are not open to other classes or cohorts of students and academics from the wider university. Although this 'separation' from the 'mainstream' teacher education cohort could be perceived as limiting and further marginalising NIKERI students, we do not believe this is the case. Our students report that having their 'own' space enables them to feel culturally safe. Displays and the physical layout of the rooms are more representative of their culture (Guywanga, 1991), they are working with people who they have relationships with, who understand them, their backgrounds and perspectives, and to whom they do not have to explain their culture. NIKERI students are often invited by other academics into the 'mainstream' classes, to share their culture with non-Indigenous students. While this would seem valuable for non-Indigenous students and academics, our professional reflections and conversations with NIKERI students recognise the ethical considerations needed here. We have needed to be protective of our students' rights to engage with their own degree and learn purely for their own purposes and goals, rather than being expected to be the cultural 'faces' of Aboriginal Australia to non-Indigenous people. Maintaining a dedicated space for learning plays an important role in recognising our students' own learning rights.

Space can also be interpreted through the need for and importance of supportive communities of learning. The notion of 'shame' in Aboriginal culture can be particularly debilitating in education where western perspectives celebrate individual achievements over those of the group (Ladson-Billings, 1995; Perso & Hayward, 2015). Space is needed for students to engage with learning without fear of judgment that might cause them to be 'shamed' (Perso & Hayward, 2015). Space is needed for students to put theory into practice without the 'shame' associated with being singled out, having to talk themselves up, expectations to complete work in front of large unknown class groups, or being expected to be the Aboriginal 'experts'. Providing both a physical culturally safe space and a figurative culturally safe learning space for students can effectively enhance student engagement, achievement and wellbeing throughout their studies.

13 Reflecting on Reflections

The reflections throughout this chapter have enabled us to integrate two pedagogical approaches that we have found to build effective relationships between academics and students at NIKERI Institute, and facilitate student engagement, achievement and wellbeing in our teacher education degree.

Although we can see the positive learning environment we have developed within the Institute and our degree, and see the difference in our student engagement, achievement and wellbeing, there are still many areas for improvement. For some, our hands are tied, we do not always have a chance to give input in unit/course development and content, or in the way Aboriginal and Torres Strait Islander people are represented within those units. And as Pearce and Down (2011) state, the role of the students themselves in initiating and maintaining relationships with academics needs to be acknowledged. As mentioned in a previous section, our methods of communication with students are varied and ongoing, however if students choose to forgo the relationship and 'go quiet' for whatever reason, there may be little we can do to re-engage them in their studies.

There is also tension between the need and desire to establish good relationships and enact an integrated relational and culturally responsive pedagogy, while being faced with the claim of 'over servicing' our students. We reject this claim, however, as building good relationships with students should never be seen as 'over-servicing', rather just good pedagogical practice. And we will continue what we see as our core business-supporting students to complete their degree to graduate as primary teachers.

Our professional conversations within this self-study are focused on improving our teaching and learning practice and the anecdotal evidence of our perceptions of student engagement and wellbeing within our degree. We acknowledge the limitations of self-study, and recognise the need to gather more information about student learning journeys to further enhance students' study experiences.

We believe the integration of a relational and culturally responsive pedagogical approach is effective for our NIKERI students within their teacher education degree. It centralises relationships as the key to nourishing student engagement, achievement and wellbeing, and utilises the components critical to this end-effective teaching and learning; recognising Ways of Knowing, Being and Doing; understanding and sharing experiences; communication; support and resources; and space. The framework utilises the best of both approaches to enable NIKERI students to reach their goals of becoming teachers.

Acknowledgement

We would like to gratefully acknowledge our students and the rich experiences and perspectives they bring to our classes. We are privileged to walk alongside them on their learning journeys.

References

Acquah E., Szelei, N., & Katz H. (2019). Using modelling to make culturally responsive pedagogy explicit in pre-service teacher education in Finland. *British Educational Research Journal, 46*(1), 122–139. Retrieved November 1, 2019, from https://onlinelibrary.wiley.com/doi/abs/10.1002/berj.3571

Aspelin, J. (2012). How do relationships influence student achievement? Understanding student performance from a general, social psychological standpoint. *International Studies in Sociology of Education, 22*(1), 41–56.

Australian Government Department of the Prime Minister and Cabinet. (2018). *Closing the gap: Prime Minister's report, 2018.* Author. Retrieved November 15, 2018, from https://www.pmc.gov.au/sites/default/files/reports/closing-the-gap-2018/sites/default/files/ctg-report-20183872.pdf?a=1

Batistte, M., & Youngblood Henderson, J. (2000). *Protecting Indigenous knowledge and heritage, a global challenge.* UBC Press, Purich Publishing.

Berryman, M. (2013). Culturally responsive pedagogies as transformative praxis. *Waikato Journal of Education, 18*(2), 3–10.

Biesta, G. (2004). Mind the gap: Communication and the educational relation. In C. Bingham & A. Sidorkin (Eds.), *No education without relation* (pp. 39–53). Peter Lang.

Boyd, R., Sullivan, G., & MacNeill, N. (2006). Relational pedagogy: Putting balance back into students' learning. *Curriculum and Leadership Journal, 4*(13). Retrieved November 1, 2019, from http://www.curriculum.edu.au/leader/default.asp?id=57&issueID=10277#art13944

Brownlee, J. (2004). Teacher education students' epistemological beliefs: Developing a relational model of teaching. *Research in Education, 72,* 1–17.

Buckskin, P. (2016). How to attract and retain Aboriginal or Torres Strait Islander teachers at your school. *Independent Education, 46*(3), 22–23.

Day, D., & Davidson, P. (2005). Career development for Indigenous students in Australian Universities: Personal and professional resilience for the future. *International Journal of Learning, 11,* 481–488.

East, K., Fitzgerald, L., & Heston, M. (2009). Talking teaching and learning: Using dialogue in self-study. In D. Tidwell, M. Heston, & L. Fitzgerald (Eds.), *Research methods for the self-study of practice* (pp. 55–72). Springer.

Gay, G. (2013). Teaching to and through cultural diversity. *Curriculum Inquiry, 43*(1), 48–70.

Gillan, K., Mellor, S., & Krakouer, J. (2017). *The case for urgency: Advocating for Indigenous voice in education.* Australian Council for Educational Research, ACER Press.

Guywanga, R. (1991). Hidden curriculum. *Ngoonjook, 5,* 26–34.

Hattie, J. (2008). *Visible learning: A synthesis of over 800 meta-analyses relating to achievement.* Routledge.

Ikpeze, C. (2018). Negotiating identity in a relational pedagogy: A cross cultural perspective. In E. Lyle (Ed.), *Fostering a relational pedagogy: Self-study as transformative praxis* (pp. 105–115). Brill | Sense.

Ladson-Billings, G. (1995). Toward a theory of culturally relevant pedagogy. *American Educational Research Association, 32*(3), 465–491.

Lampert, J., & Burnett, B. M. (2012, July). *Retention and graduation of Aboriginal and Torres Strait Islander students in initial teacher education: A review of the literature.* Paper presented at the Australian Teacher Education Association Annual Conference, Adelaide, South Australia.

Lawrence, J. (2000, July). *Re-thinking diversity: Re-theorising transition as a process of engaging, negotiating and mastering the discourses and multi-literacies of an unfamiliar culture rather than as a problem of deficit.* Paper presented at the 4th Pacific Rim First Year in Higher Education Conference, Queensland University of Technology, Brisbane, Australia.

Maher, M. (2012). Teacher education with Indigenous ways of knowing, being and doing as a key pillar. *AlterNative: An International Journal of Indigenous Peoples, 8*(3), 343–356.

Margonis, F. (2004). From student resistance to educative engagement: A case-study in building powerful teacher-student relationships. In C. Bingham & A. Sidorkin (Eds.), *No education without relation* (pp. 39–53). Peter Lang.

Martin, K. (2003). Ways of knowing, being and doing: A theoretical framework and methods for Indigenous and Indigenist research. *Journal of Australian Studies, 27*(76), 203–214.

Martin, F., & Pirbhai-Illich, F. (2016). Towards decolonising teacher education: Criticality, relationality and critical understanding. *Journal of Intercultural Studies, 37*(4), 355–372.

Nakata, M., Nakata, V., & Chin, M. (2008). Approaches to the academic preparation and support of Australian Indigenous students for tertiary studies. *The Australian Journal of Indigenous Education, 37*, 137–145.

Ortiz, P. (2009). Indigenous knowledge and language: Decolonising culturally relevant pedagogy in a Mapuche intercultural education program in Chile. *Canadian Journal of Native Education, 32*(1), 93–130.

Pearce, J., & Down, B. (2011). Relational pedagogy for student engagement and success at university. *Australian Education Research, 38*, 483–494.

Perso, T., & Hayward, C. (2015). *Teaching Indigenous students.* Allen & Unwin.

Quillinan, B., MacPhail, A., Dempsey, A., & McEvoy, E. (2019). Transformative teaching and learning through engaged practice: Lecturer and students' experiences in a university and underserved community partnership in Ireland. *Journal of Transformative Education, 17*(3), 228–250.

Ragoonaden, K., & Mueller, L. (2017). Culturally responsive pedagogy: Indigenizing curriculum. *Canadian Journal of Higher Education, 47*(2), 22–46.

Reeves, J., & Le Mare, L. (2017). Supporting teachers in relational pedagogy and social emotional education: A qualitative exploration. *The International Journal of Emotional Education, 9*(1), 85–98.

Rishel, T., & Zuercher, D. (2016). Reciprocal-relational teaching: Culturally-responsive pedagogy in the Pacific Islands. *International Schools Journal, 36*(1), 48–55.

Root, E., Augustine, S., Snow, K., & Doucette, M. (2019). Evidence of co-learning through a relational pedagogy: Indigenizing the curriculum through MIKM2701. *The Canadian Journal for the Scholarship of Teaching and Learning, 10*(1), 1–17.

Sabol, T. J., & Pianta, R. C. (2012). Recent trends in research teacher-child relationship. *Attachment and Human Development, 14*(3), 213–231.

Shor, I. (1992). *Empowering education: Critical teaching for social change.* The University of Chicago Press.

Sidorkin, A. (2002). *Learning relations. Impure education, de-schooled schools and dialogue with evil.* Peter Lang Press.

Skattebol, J., & Hayes, D. (2016). Cracking with affect: Relationality in young people's movements in and out of mainstream schooling. *Critical Studies in Education, 57*(1), 6–19.

Vygotsky, L. (1978). *Mind in society: The development of higher psychological processes.* Harvard University Press.

White, N. (2009). University-educated Indigenous women: Their struggles and triumphs in their leadership journeys. In J. Frawley, M. Nolan, & N. White (Eds.), *Indigenous issues in Australian universities: Research, teaching, support* (pp. 95–105). Charles Darwin University Press.

CHAPTER 8

A Meeting of Freshwater and Saltwater: Opening the Dialogue of Aboriginal Concepts of Culture within an Academic Space

Kelly Menzel and Liz Cameron

Abstract

This chapter will explore, interpret and examine aspects of culture within higher educational experiences of Aboriginal academics and their impact authority on cultural knowledge has on teaching and learning.

    The panel members who confirmed my PhD candidacy were non-Indigenous and particularly interested in how culture is interpreted as a set of culturally safe practices and represented in other settings. This confirmed to me that the complex concept of culture and that the contemporary definitions of cultural safety and cultural competence needed some deeper exploration from an Indigenous perspective. Particularly the language that is used in relation to culture and how that language can be interpreted, often incorrectly. Clarification of Aboriginal culture and language appears to lie in the sole responsibility of the Aboriginal person. Even when the onus of that fails to the non-Indigenous person to seek further understanding on Indigenous culture.

    When discussing this with Liz Cameron, venting frustration about how Indigenous people repeatedly need to frame and re-frame language and need to define our use of language to "set the scene" before discussing actual topic we want to discuss. I exclaimed "how far back do we need to go?" She said "200,000 years and then some more." Liz is wise. She has experienced exactly the same thing many times. From this we decided perhaps we needed to explore this further and write a chapter about this phenomenon.

Keywords

culture – indigenous – Aboriginal and Torres Strait Islander – colonialism – white bias – white privilege – language

1   The Connections of Two Rivers

This chapter presents the narrative life experiences of two Aboriginal academics and their progression towards undergoing PhD studies and associated research within higher educational institutions. Discussions surround the overwhelming additional workloads in white privileged institutions, combating racism and lateral violence, where cultural safety is often threatened. It is the intent of these personal narratives to highlight and expose how culture affects the daily lives of black women researchers in academia.

The notion of culture is multifaceted, dependent on interpretations through self and collective groups. From an Australian Aboriginal standpoint, culture and associated knowledges have led to misunderstandings from non-Aboriginal people who remain largely unaware, uneducated and demonstrate bias to other ways of knowing. There has been a long history of Aboriginal culture being collated, classified and haphazardly put together with little understanding of cultural and spiritual differences. This is evident in colonial practices such as Aboriginal missions, where various collective groups were placed into a centralised compartment with no consideration of individual or collective viewpoints. This collective imprisonment has been a major contributor to Aboriginal disharmonies. This chapter explores the contemporary experience of two Aboriginal academics and researchers, from two different nations, and reflects their narratives of the continued overwhelming experiences in educating others on cultural differences.

Aboriginal people have been denied access to the same educational opportunities as non-Indigenous Australians with the current system underpinned by western values. The cultural bias in higher education is of white privilege that continues to dominate Indigenous knowledge. Inequity, discrimination and marginalisation are all facets of oppression that continually impact upon Indigenous peoples. There is a present failure in recognising the enormous contributions of Indigenous peoples' in intellectual knowledge. From both our freshwater and saltwater perspectives and experiences, Indigenous Knowledge within higher education needs to be given greater attention where Indigenous intellectual rights and Indigenous Knowledges are represented. This requires a whole of university approach and commitment to address systemic issues in higher education institutions, coupled with collaboration and consultation. By exposing the challenges faced by Aboriginal academics in navigating the higher educational system our intent to provide lived experiences of the personal trials, confrontations and encounters to raise awareness of the need to establish university-wide responsibility to address issues of appropriate protocols that build cultural identity and Indigeneity.

2   Introductions, a Meeting of Freshwater and Saltwater Academics

I, Kelly, am a freshwater academic from South Australia. I have worked in universities in Australia, Hong Kong and the United Kingdom. I am a nurse by trade but a teacher in my heart. Working and walking in two worlds has presented its challenges and I have experienced bullying and marginalisation in all university settings, as both a student and staff member. My experiences of bullying have been perpetrated largely by white women in positions of power over me, or directed at me by white women colleagues. I find my professional knowledge and experience is regularly questioned and I often feel forced to defend the decisions I make. When I commenced as an academic I think I had a romantic view of academia. I thought I would have intellectual freedom. I wanted to argue with other scholars about philosophy and politics, maybe over a pint. I thought I would be able to engage in a civilised discourse. However, in reality I have been excluded from engaging in scholarly activity because my teaching and administrative load has been disproportionately high. I have witnessed this happen to other young women, particularly young black women. I have also seen young men fostered through the ranks. I witnessed them being supported by senior staff and invited to join research projects. This was shocking to me. I mean, I knew it happened because I read the textbooks, but to see it in real life truly opened my eyes. Because of my experiences, I feel it is my obligation to give back to my community, to share my knowledge and skills, and support black women particularly, into scholarly endeavours. I am also now in a position where I feel safe enough to write about my experiences and to connect with other black women who have shared similar stories with me.

I, Liz, am a saltwater Aboriginal academic. I hold a PhD and have worked at universities across various states. My work is argued to be extensive. I am seen as an expert now that I hold the 'white paper of privilege'. Yet I am questioned continually about all aspects of cultural understandings in all facets of knowing with the presumptive 'just because I am Aboriginal'. It is within these realms that I have become an advisor, knowledge conveyer, interpreter, informer and a source of acquiring a grant, 'just because I'm Aboriginal'. I have found myself being placed on grants without my knowledge or having my name on a grant with little to no input in the actual research project. This has resulted in me becoming overly cautious about who I choose to collaborate with and who I choose to trust. As a senior academic, I have been placed on various boards, consultative committees and advisory groups, 'just because I am Aboriginal'. I may not hold any knowledge of the associated disciplines, but I 'tick the box', 'just because I am Aboriginal'. From an artistic viewpoint, my images have been used without permission, as a tokenistic gesture with no recognition or acknowledgment as to who the artist is, again 'just because I'm Aboriginal'. I am deeply connected to my Dharug homelands in Sydney, New South Wales. This is my Country, the place where my spirit lies. Working in two worlds has been challenging and yet immensely rewarding. Now I sit in a more privileged position, it is my purpose to give back to community, support other Aboriginal colleagues and advance our cultural pride, because I am Aboriginal.

3 Sharing the Academic Journey of White Privileged Institutions along the River Way

In my freshwater experience, white, able-bodied, heterosexual men provide the human norm against which deviation is measured (Dyer, 1997). English is the language that sits alongside that norm, and English is the language that has colonised institutions. Douglas, Lewis, Douglas, Earl-Scott and Garrison-Wade (2008) argue that language, especially language used in institutions such as education, academia and health, is so profoundly colonised it is currently impossible for English to be used in a multicultural manner. Further to this, Higgins (2009) posits "[a]s English continues to spin ever outwards from its assumed centres, used in more and more contexts and in more and more diverse ways, there is a growing sense that we need new ways to investigate these new conditions of language" (p. 5). Investigation is timely indeed, because in reality not everyone uses, speaks, writes and understands standard English. This places many people at significant disadvantage and privileges others when entering and engaging with institutions.

From my saltwater experiences, other ways of learning have greatly affected advancing the low representation of Aboriginal participation. The bias and privilege within white institutions and embedded in curriculum excludes worldview knowledge frameworks that offer cultural responsiveness and holistic approaches to promote cross-cultural understanding. With a demand for access to online education, it can be argued that further concentration is needed to consider pedagogical development in multiple contexts, including visual literacies, to serve in embedding all knowledge systems.

Bearing this in mind, it is imperative that privileges are acknowledged and discussed. There are many privileges, such as the privilege of whiteness, class, race, heterosexuality and able-bodiedness. Privilege is not bestowed upon us, but rather it appears in the fabric of life (Wildman & Davis, 1994). Thus, it is time to stop privileging western modes of knowing, doing and understanding and interrogate western ontology, epistemology and axiology (Rigney, 1999) as white spaces are systemically and institutionally biased and racist (Tate & Bagguley, 2017). Institutional racism textures the experience of Aboriginal staff and students alike.

Staff in positions of power continue to be predominantly white men and curriculum is unashamedly whitewashed. Trudgett and Franklin (2011) state "the values, beliefs, customs and behaviours of the dominant Western culture are embedded in universities throughout Australia as well as other Western colonised nations" (p. 35). Therefore, universities are considered unsafe places by Aboriginal people, resulting in the continued low representation of Aboriginal students and staff. Yet there is a "critical need to improve enrolments of Aboriginal and Torres Strait Islander students in Australia if participation rates are to be equitable and key national social-justice goals are to be achieved" (Barney, 2016, p. 2). The under-representation of Aboriginal staff and students contributes to the higher levels of economic and social disadvantage that Aboriginal people experience. Not only does the low employment numbers of Indigenous staff need be taken seriously, best practice strategies need to be implemented to achieve better recruitment, retention, equity and parity. While Aboriginal professional and academic staff can support Indigenous students, a whole of university approach to advancing and incorporating Indigenous knowledges is required. The need to audit curriculum of Australian histories and eradicate incorrect historical facts of only white perspectives in one such starting point. Throughout my career I have come across either the silence of an Indigenous Australian past, misrepresentations of Indigenous people and racial slurs that demean all first nation peoples.

When Aboriginal students and staff do transition into higher education, we bring with us our values, beliefs and cultural understanding. Because there are significant differences between non-Aboriginal and Aboriginal cultural understandings, Aboriginal people can experience "serious, acute and sometimes chronic affective reaction" (Furnham, 2004, p. 88). This is a type of culture shock that in-turn increases the risk of Aboriginal students and staff experiencing stress, a sense of loss, fear of not fitting in and rejection, anxiety, helplessness, confusion and frustration (Trudgett & Franklin, 2011). Culture shock coupled with institutional racism makes engaging with the university sector challenging. This means that retention levels of Aboriginal staff and students are low and this must be addressed at a systemic level. It is our contention that if the marginalisation and discrimination of Aboriginal people is owned and reconciled in a meaningful way by white Australia, then other forms of marginalisation and discrimination may also be addressed.

4 There Is Not Enough of Us to Paddle in the Canoe

My saltwater experiences with academic involvement in addressing the low representations of both Aboriginal staff and students is noted by economic investment. It is this investment that has provided a gateway for Aboriginal people from low socioeconomic backgrounds to enter academic opportunities. Government funding has been injected into Academic institutions to increase the inclusion of Aboriginal people. Some institutions have taken admirable stances in their commitment to Indigenous participation while others have seen this as a 'financial benefit' rather than a deep obligation to enhancing low participation rates. Justifications can be noted through the high numbers of enrolments of Aboriginal students with little infrastructure to support progress. Over the years, I have witnessed high influxes of student enrolments that have resulted in high dropout rates due to the lack of concern over Aboriginal learning materials and processes. The clear dialogue of enrolment continues to result in poor continuing and completion outcomes. I have witnessed some institutions offering iPads, laptops, top-up scholarships, or deliberately undermine entry schemes, just to raise enrolments rates. I have also witnessed an increase in identified positions within academia for Aboriginal staff, but with little to no career planning or support. Clearly, the paucity of Aboriginal staff is an indicator of poor outcomes for student completions. There is also a lack of Aboriginal resources in white privilege libraries. The collections of whitewashed bias in libraries still captures negative Eurocentric theories surrounding Aboriginal people, including a noted void of Aboriginal authors.

My experiences within academia include a growing awareness of the many non-Aboriginal academics teaching Aboriginal studies; many of whom are unwilling to step down to hand over to an Aboriginal expert. I have witnessed this across varying institutions over the past 20 years. One would argue here who claims ownership and procession of Indigenous knowledge, or has it been simply recolonised. I have often witnessed white academics presenting knowledge concerning Aboriginal culture that is misconstrued, untruthful and exaggerated by early theories surrounding romanticism. In my experience a large percentage of white academics also have little to no knowledge of Aboriginal cultural awareness. This problem is reflected through Australian school where teachers with superficial knowledge (Clark, 2008) and lacking any opportunity to develop their cultural competency are expected to teach Aboriginal perspectives proficiently. Having sound cultural competence also provides the skills to successfully support Aboriginal students effectively. Recent reports, such as that of Universities Australia (2011), indicate an increasing emphasis on graduate outcomes in Indigenous cultural competency in Australian higher.

This should alleviate the many short online cultural awareness programs that attempt to explain over 250 years of knowledge and cultural perspectives.

As a freshwater academic, I was once asked to develop such an online course, simply because I was the only Indigenous person on staff. I was asked to develop a 'succinct history of Indigenous Australians' to be used as content for overseas nursing students coming to Australia. It is a freshwater opinion that this level of disrespect and lack of consideration lies deeply embedded with many institutions.

5   The Receiving of Gifts and Trinkets along the River's Edge

Critical Race Theory (CRT), whilst originally applied to an American context, is uniquely situated to examine the evolution of language framing inclusion in higher education in Australia (Harris, Barone, & Patton Davis, 2015). Ross (2013) states "Critical Race Theorists begin with the premise that racism is central, normal, and a routine feature of ... society and work to deconstruct racist ideologies, laws, and practices in support of social transformation" (p. 146). Harris et al. (2015) explain "[o]ne tenet of CRT that explicitly relates to this analysis is interest convergence, a concept that explores how advances for people of color are tolerated only when these advances benefit white society at similar or greater rates" (p. 22).

Interest convergence highlights that although there are initiatives established to increase inclusivity in higher education there have been no substantive outcomes, especially for Aboriginal and Torres Strait Islander people (Australian Government Department of the Prime Minister and Cabinet, 2019). Equity and diversity policies and principles employed by universities do not interrogate the institutional and systemic whiteness that exists within the structure, practices and assumptions perpetuated (Shepherd, Willis-Esqueda, Newton, Sivasubramaniam, & Paradies, 2019; Harris et al., 2015). "This means", argue Harris et al. (2015, p. 25), "that [universities] facilitate access on a procedural level, not on a substantive level". Just because a student has been granted access to university does not guarantee they will complete their course successfully. Although, the blame for the lack of success often lays at the feet of the individual student (and their race) rather than the system that set the student up for failure.

The discussion above highlights the pervasiveness of tokenism; we see it every day. Owen (2009, cited in Harris et al., 2015, p. 25) states "[i]nstitutional leaders, who are overwhelmingly white, may manipulate and construct a diverse student body to serve institutional needs ... because token incrementalism in terms of racial heterogeneity does not substantially threaten generations of institutionalized racial privilege". Tokenism can be described in a multitude of ways, however, Hughes' (1945) definition of the 'outsider' is fitting. It is "someone who meets all of the formal requirements for entrance into a group but does not possess the 'auxiliary characteristics' (especially race, sex and ethnicity) that are expected of persons in that position" (cited in Zimmer, 1988, p. 65). As a consequence, the 'outsider' is never permitted by the 'insiders' to participate fully and may even be rejected entirely if they stray too far from the constraints of what the 'insiders' define as appropriate. Tokenism allows an organisation to 'prove' that they are non-discriminatory without addressing any underlying structural or systemic issues.

My saltwater lived experiences within an academic space have been multi-shadowed by the lack of Indigenous voices and appropriate levels of cultural competencies by the 'other' within higher education. Perceived collaborations in gaining Indigenous viewpoints are witnessed as guided and managed by more senior non-Aboriginal staff and manipulated by their insights and understandings of Indigeneity, a gestured tokenism rather than a form of recognition. The receiving of gifts along the river ways of academia is witnessed as both tokenistic and racist, which continues to make universities unsafe spaces for Aboriginal staff and students. A government commissioned review of the Australian curriculum (Donnelly & Wiltshire, 2014) found too much emphasis on Aboriginal and Torres Strait Islander histories and cultures, and recommended embedding the cross-curriculum priority "only where educationally relevant ... where justified on epistemological grounds" (p. 247). The review expressed concern about potential tokenistic teaching of Indigenous content, as the current inclusion of Aboriginal and Torres Strait Islander content is weak, and unresponsive to historical and contemporary realities. Many non-Aboriginal teachers remain in the dark depths of unfamiliarity teaching about local Aboriginal culture or history. This lack of knowledge inhibits their teaching of Aboriginal perspectives and can lead to superficial, tokenistic, and potentially damaging outcomes for students. Hence, there is a direct need to replace forms of tokenism with true diversity. True diversity ensures that Aboriginal academics do not work in isolation and are not called upon to be the lone representative for their entire group.

Other forms of racism experienced by Aboriginal academics include passive and aggressive exchanges, with questioning over identity and knowledge rights. From our saltwater and freshwater experiences, encounters with the 'white Aboriginal experts' who claim they have learnt knowledge by just being with Aboriginal people are also confronting. These whitewashed fraudsters further exacerbate situations by 'claims of knowing', which are often incorrect, misinterpreted and lack extensive historical groundings. Yet they attempt to hold authority over us. This is belittling, arrogant and shaming.

To address such systemic issues, a real commitment from those in positions of authority in higher education institutions is essential to achieve substantive and institutional change. This must be coupled with collaboration and consultation with marginalised groups to develop strategic pathways towards equity (Garces, Ishimaru, & Takahashi, 2017). As we have indicated earlier in this piece, structures and curriculum in universities are overwhelmingly monocultural in Australia. Indeed, this is the case in most westernised institutions. Universities are white places that "can be understood as space where white individuals, whether culturally or physically, are overrepresented" (Rebollo-Gil & Moras, 2006, cited in Ross, 2013, p. 143). When a black person 'travels' through a white space, they can experience a sense of trespassing (Ross, 2013), a sense that they do not belong and they are not safe (hooks, 1992). Therefore, culturally acceptable spaces become an issue, especially in Australian institutions such as universities. In exploring aspects of culturally strong spaces require a set of higher expectations rather than a continued deficit model thinking Cultural space necessitates safe spaces from a place of strength approach that engages robust, challenging and critical dialogues surrounding an appreciation of worldviews and epistemologies. However, in no indigenous language does the concept of cultural safety exist (Yunkaporta, 2019). The nuances of cultural resilience exist, but not safety. To 'stay culturally safe' suggests the possibility of being 'culturally unsafe'. Prior to the invasion and colonisation of Australia, Indigenous people were culturally safe. Cultural safety is a modern phenomenon and has only existed since the invasion of Australia (Yunkaporta, 2019).

Further, Indigenous people are always going to be marginalised and disempowered, simply by engaging in a conversation in English. More than 350 Indigenous languages, including 800 dialectal varieties, were spoken on the continent at the time of European settlement in 1788. Only 13 traditional Indigenous languages are still acquired by children today. Approximately another 100 languages are spoken, to various degrees by older generations, with many of these languages at risk as Elders pass away (Australian Institute of Aboriginal and Torres Strait Islander Studies [AIATSIS], 2019). Some individuals speak up to six different languages prior to speaking English. Therefore, English is interpreted through a complex lens for those speakers of English as an additional language. Language is also gendered, but that is a topic for another paper.

Dolores Calderon (2014) and others have interpreted the use of settler colonial narratives and/or grammar. This exposes its use as a "function to simultaneously erase Indigenous claims to sovereignty and epistemological equality, whilst promoting a representation of Indigenous people that asserts the primacy of the settler colonial state" (Moodie & Patrick, 2017, p. 2). This further colonises Indigenous peoples and maintains "the myth of Indigenous homogeneity and subordinate position of Othered knowledges" (Moodie & Patrick, 2017, p. 3). Colonial settler narratives are founded by migrant groups, who assume the local Indigenous population are subordinate to them. This migrant group then go on to establish colonial states based upon their mother country (Weitzer, 1990). This is what occurred in Australia. It also ties into the manner in which the national identity of Australia and other colonial states has been shaped. In colonial narratives, national identity is seen as something that is born naturally and evolves over time, not an ideology shaped by power and dominance (Calderon, 2014). Power and dominance underpins the colonial nature of the structures, systems, language and education curriculum used in colonial states.

There is a much written about the English language relationship between parents and children and teachers and children, and any potential bias in the use of language (Brown, 1977; Crago, 1990; Delpit, 1988) but minimal about everyday language and potential bias in the language used in academia. Moreover, what is written is usually from an American or British perspective (Gillborn, 2005; Yosso, 2005). English is becoming a globalised language. English is now the common language for IT, science and academia (Hultgren & Erling, 2016). The bias held within the English language is concerning because the potential to re-colonise non-English speaking countries and marginalised, disenfranchised groups is even more profound. Gnutzmann and Intemann (2005) emphasise the globalisation of the English language, referring to:

> the increasing intrusion of the English language into the lives of town and city dwellers all over the world. This is a worrying phenomenon. Not only does it threaten to contaminate or wipe out local languages and cultures, but it also skews the socio-economic order in favour of those who are proficient in English. (p. 287)

We would add to the above quote, noting privileging English also serves to marginalise groups, such as Indigenous Australians from using their first languages and demands that they interpret and use English.

6   The Natives Are Restless along the River's Edge

It is important to highlight the conflict in inquiry methods between Indigenous and western perspectives. For example, western scepticism bases evidence within a scientific lens of acquirements, whilst Aboriginal knowledge is determined through experimental trans-generational history, as knowledge originates from ancestral truths. Within my saltwater PhD thesis, challenges bound in western research inquiries had further ramifications as I contemplated the strengths and weaknesses in outlining traditional healing practices. From a western lens I was challenged over interpretations of the 'placebo effect', as suggested by Nichter (1981), rather than forms of cultural sense-making (Jadhav, 1993). The placebo effect placed me in a position of debating cultural sense-making of collective inherited knowledges without current evidence to support my argument. If I was to write a thesis beneficial to all in order to address the need of cultural health processes, how was I going to get others on board? In creating documented evidence, I needed to become a historian and a white thinker to highlight my purpose in these investigations. I spent many hours seeking early western colonists' theories, including religious notions of 'the native'. It was emotionally challenging to re-enter the world of early missionaries who associated Aboriginal healing practices as shamanistic forms of primitivism, labelling complex processes as "extremely crude" (Wilber, 1981, p. 75). Reflecting on historical cultural ignorance and misconceptions based on flawed assumptions produced feelings of despair, as many of these notions remain prevalent today. I argue that cultural knowledges and practices continue to be ignored and/or undermined, "weakened to the extent that they fail in their capacity to imbue individual existence with meaning and value" (Halloran, 2004, p. 4). I wonder today who has read my thesis or does it sit on a dusty shelf.

7   Are We in the Same Canoe?

Post the invasion and colonisation of Australia and up until the 1970s, government policies banned Indigenous languages. Those who did speak in language were severely punished. This resulted in the loss of many Indigenous languages and although the English language was mandated across the country, many communities use Kriol or an abridged version of English.

However, post-colonial Australian history is dominated by monolingual and monocultural paradigms. Indigenous people have and still experience language suppression and oppression in achieving formalised education (Moodie & Patrick, 2017) and English has been used to exclude Indigenous people from educational institutions and the workplace. Due to this suppression and oppression, Indigenous people tend to 'code-switch'. Code-switching; the practice of interacting in different ways depending on the social context. It is not always limited to race. Most of us interact differently when with friends, than we do in a job interview. Technically, code-switching is "the use of more than one language in the course of a single communicative episode" (Heller, 1988, p. 1). However, it can be argued that Indigenous people code-switch even when only speaking English and this is my freshwater experience. As a consequence of colonisation, structural inequalities, different cultural norms and worldview, different ways of speaking have emerged among Indigenous and non-Indigenous lines. Because Australia's dominant culture is white and patriarchal, white patriarchy has become deeply embedded as normal, neutral and legitimate. Therefore, it is requisite for Indigenous people to code-switch, to adapt to the dominant culture to improve our prospects. This requires work on the part of the 'switcher' and places no onus on the listener. It is incredibly difficult, marginalising, disempowering and a form of assimilation. It takes away a person's agency and tells them their culture is less worthy than that of the white, patriarchal dominant way of doing things (Williams, 1988). White people rarely, if ever, feel this same pressure in their daily lives. Code-switching would not be necessary if white, patriarchal privilege were not so deeply rooted in the Australian society.

All Aboriginal nations are misleadingly categorised today as having the same characteristics, belief systems and social structures. The sense of romanticism has infiltrated all aspects of Aboriginal life and continues to devalue thousands of years of practice of cultural knowledge. Mendes, Major, McCoy, and Blascovich (2008) also argue that stereotypical assumptions ignore the importance of cultural reasonings. From a saltwater perspective, romanticism still thrives within Aboriginal cultures, pertaining to colonisation practices. Many Aboriginal nations remain lost and confused over cultural knowledges through the eradication of cultural practices. Sadly, today we witness some nations playing theatrical performances in 'Welcome to Country' ceremonies as a show piece rather than a traditional custom of acknowledgement. From a saltwater academic perspective, such interplay builds a sense of embarrassment between other Indigenous nations as we witness the whiteness infiltrating into cultural ceremonies. The populist fascination with the other sometimes boarders on a peak attraction, like a zoo animal or a circus act.

8 Studying the River Systems

From our experience and a research perspective, most Indigenous academics appreciate visual forms of expression as ways of interpreting data from a western perspective. Yet creativity is questioned and often disregarded, interpreted as a process that lacks refined statistical information and conclusive results. This is validated using traditional story telling that is often supported visual cues, along with sensory learning experiences. However, Aboriginal epistemologies are responsive to cultural knowledges and offer multiple ways of exploration rather than a singular pathway to findings that go beyond the parameters of stereotypical inquiries. From my saltwater experience within white academy, such inquiries are pushed aside as illogical reasonings, holding little purpose to meaningful contemporary practices. Creative Indigenous research incorporates complex visual and narrative knowledges that reflect psychological reasonings to produce a range of culturally based theories. Such knowledges are often rebuked within a western discourse, as spirituality is immeasurable. Yet spirituality is a fundamental part of Aboriginal social life and requires great consideration to illustrate effectively.

Rigney (2006) argues that lived experiences represent action based research that gives credence to cultural reflections of making and seeing. Reason (1994) also places value on lived experiences, by stating the importance of knowledge within verbal and visual form, imperative to expressing cultural validations. My argument as a saltwater Aboriginal researcher is that culturally appropriate decision-making is a necessity that goes beyond the bounds of white privilege. Repeatedly, I see non-Aboriginal researchers within an arts space disrupting issues surrounding sacredness. From an Aboriginal standpoint, I feel a continued obligation to be cautiously aware and distrustful of the public showcasing and investigations of sacred items within institutional settings. Many of these items are obtained without permission, stolen from the lands to which they belong, bought and sold like commodities and hung in private museums, university galleries and public spaces. Human remains of many ancestors have been removed, studied and scrutinised under the banner of advancing science, with no concern for the spiritual needs of the victim and their kinship groups. No attention is paid to their sorrow. As Aboriginal imagery continues to be violated, Aboriginal researchers are more cautious of exposing any sacred knowledges; personal obligation overrides a personal pursuit to investigate.

9   Riding the Tides

Hill (1999) poses "[w]hy, if nearly all scientists concur that human 'races' are imaginary, do so many highly educated, cosmopolitan, economically secure people continue to think and act as racists?" (p. 679). Through asking such questions, the questioner is partaking in a process of 'othering'. Barter-Godfrey and Taket (2009) state, "[o]thering is the social, linguistic and psychological mechanism that distinguishes 'us' from 'them', the normal from the deviant"

(p. 166). Othering is marginalising and disempowering and I often experience this as a freshwater academic.

In any critical discourse, it is imperative to wrestle with the notion of 'othering'. De Beauvoir (1949) introduced the concept of 'the other' as a construction opposing and thereby constructing 'the self'. Powell and Menendian (2016) argue that "[o]thering is a term that not only encompasses the many expressions of prejudice on the basis of group identities, but … that it provides a clarifying frame that reveals a set of common processes and conditions that propagate group-based inequality and marginality" (p. 17). Othering therefore separates us and divides us. It does not unite us. Othering creates anxiety and fear of difference, fear of the 'other' and whilst not only race based, creates marginality. This can occur at individual or group levels and underpins conflict on a global scale.

There are different dimensions of racism. Passive racism consists of "[b]eliefs, attitudes and actions that contribute to the maintenance of racism, without openly advocating violence or oppression. The conscious and unconscious maintenance of attitudes, beliefs and that support the system of racism, racial prejudice and racial dominance" (Wijeysinghe, Griffin, & Love, 1997, p. 89). Being unintentional does not reduce the significance of any act. It indeed makes the act of racism more significant, because of the insidious nature of the perpetration. Insidious racism is perpetrated every day, often with people unaware they are being racist. Mellor (2006) places emphasis on Essed's (1990) suggestion "that such everyday racism is often covert, subtle, and seemingly intangible" (p. 483). It is a "more powerful version of white supremacy; one that is normalized and taken for granted" (Gillborn, 2005). That is the power of every day racism in Australia, and it is a prevailing and common contemporary phenomenon. It is not insidious and, for those experiencing it, blatant at the same time. There is white bias, and it is embedded in language and behaviour. As Aboriginal people, we experience it every day.

10   Educating the Educated along the River

From a freshwater perspective, I became acutely aware of racial bias during my PhD confirmation of candidature (CoC) processes. The panel members who confirmed my PhD candidacy were five women, one of whom is Aboriginal. Neither of my supervisors were Indigenous. The non-Indigenous members of the panel were particularly interested in how culture is interpreted as a set of culturally safe practices and represented in other settings. Their lack of understanding of the Australian Aboriginal standpoint of culture confirmed that the concept of culture is complex.

Additionally, I was alerted to the need for contemporary definitions of cultural safety and cultural competence, to undergo some deeper exploration especially when considered from an Indigenous perspective. In particular, the language that is used in relation to culture and how that language can be interpreted in multiple ways is of interest to me. I believe that the academic non-Indigenous interpretation is often incorrect. Nakata (2007, cited in Morton-Robinson, 2013, p. 213) argues that:

> ... an Indigenous standpoint is not the 'aggregation of stories from lived experience' nor is it 'the endless production of subjective narrative to disrupt objective accounts. Rather people's lived experience is the point of entry for investigation of the Cultural Interface where western knowledge systems and Torres Strait Islander experiences are dialectically engaged. As such, an Indigenous standpoint is informed by family and collective consciousness, knowledges, politics and history It is not a social position but a discursive method of inquiry producing 'more objective knowledge'.

Thus, as an Aboriginal woman, my family, collective consciousness, knowledges, politics and history are the source of the authority of my knowledge. So, as an Aboriginal woman writing a PhD on culturally safe practices, I object to defining cultural safety, especially from a white man's starting point. My experience as an Aboriginal woman gives me insight in to this definition and means I have an in-depth understanding of culturally safe practices. However, clarification of the nature of the lived experience of Aboriginal culture and language appears to be the sole responsibility of the Aboriginal person, even when the onus of that falls to the non-Indigenous person to seek further understanding on Indigenous culture. Following my CoC panel meeting, I was asked to make some changes to my CoC document before it was to be submitted to the Graduate Research School. Thinking this would be a short process I dutifully went about making the recommended changes. This then turned into a 'to and fro' process that took five months! I felt the questions I was being asked to rationalise regarding my projects intention were unrelated to the CoC process and more about one of the panel members. She was more interested in Indigenous Knowledges and use of language from a very white, intellectual and traditionalist conformist perspective. By the end, I was frustrated, completely exhausted and ready to walk away from my whole PhD project.

Cultural knowledge is overshadowed by western imperial knowledge. As opposed to those who hold Indigenous Knowledge, the western knowledge holder is considered a certified expert in the field, despite often having little life experience, experimental practices or mentored validations. Justification of knowledge is also seen as a linear completion of work, rather than a holistic encounter. Working within an academic space in an identified Indigenous position is often an overwhelming experience that consists of educating the educated on Indigenous matters. Being seen as the expert in Indigenous issues leads to a confronting barrage of personal challenges due to the continued lack of knowledge associated with First Nation issues.

From a saltwater perspective, there is continued disruption within Indigenous academia on educating the other, explaining aspects of culture and verifying ones place in the academic world. My experiences include constant interruptions, 'just because I am Aboriginal', on many topics, that I may have no connection or knowledge in, 'just because I am Aboriginal'. I am often requested to be a 'go between', an asset for future partnerships with other Indigenous communities, even though I may not know of these communities, their ways of working and their customary laws. As indicated earlier, institutions feed off our connections as a way to advance Indigenous connections and 'tick the box' to position themselves as leaders in Indigenous related partnerships, research accomplishments and student numbers.

From a freshwater perspective, I also frequently receive requests to speak with students from other schools and faculties about Indigenous culture, cultural competency and working with Indigenous people. I get these requests 'just because I am Aboriginal'. This work is not included in my workload, but rather requested as a 'favour'. A favour that is never repaid. I was recently contacted by an academic I have never met. A friend had mentioned me in conversation. She invited me to speak with her students. She emailed me daily about the presentation, but gave me no intended learning outcomes. It was just about "having conversations with Indigenous people". I prepared my presentation, drove to another campus to delivered a 75 minute presentation to 80 students. As soon as she saw me, I knew we would have a problem. I am fair skinned and she was darker than me. She was really rude. I clearly did not fit the image of a little black Aborigine she had in her head. When I was finished, she simply said good-bye. I emailed her the following day to follow up and see if everything went well. I am still waiting for a reply. I think I will be waiting a while.

11 Getting the White Certification whilst Paddling Upstream

In my freshwater CoC document I have a section on culture and the complexities associated with defining it, especially from an Indigenous perspective. I started the section by describing culture from an Indigenous perspective, using the terminology: the concept of culture. One of the comments from a panel member about this was "But what about more broadly – you are making assumptions already about what culture means. How about making ref for e.g. to Raymond Williams Keywords and how 'culture' is approached there and compare?". It is natural that as I am an Aboriginal woman, I will always start from an Indigenous woman's standpoint. I begin my self-definition discussing my understanding of culture, my Aboriginal philosophies and spirituality and my connection to community and Country, and then go on to discuss western concepts. I am always going to be Aboriginal and my research is always going to be from my Indigenous perspective. I cannot stop being Aboriginal for the purposes of my PhD and I felt like that was what was being asked of me. Eades (2013, p. 57) states "[w]hile many Aboriginal people may speak English as their first language, the context of conversation has significant Aboriginal cultural and social aspects which lead to distinctively Aboriginal interpretations and meanings". Eades' statement is particularly relevant to my experience. I was being asked to defer to a western, dominant, white definition of culture because the panel members did not understand the complexity of my Indigenous standpoint. They did not accede to my way of knowing. I felt I was being asked to sanitise my own perspective of culture to a more acceptable, more powerful, white man's perspective. I was infuriated, confused and felt stupid and inferior. I do want to clarify, however, that I am not just wanting to whine about something 'not fair' (I use 'fair' on purpose). I am also not attributing blame to any individual. The CoC process is reductionist and the panel have to achieve a particular outcome within a limited framework. Panel members are also expected to have a vast array of knowledge and one cannot possibly know everything about everything.

My saltwater experience of undergoing a PhD is that it is daunting. For Aboriginal researchers this space is both threatening and personally exposing of cultural and spiritual beliefs that can have unpredictable outcomes. To further elaborate, many Indigenous PhD students feel isolated, given there are too few Indigenous supervisors or cultural mentors who have expertise in almost any chosen field. Exposing culture can also be challenging, particularly over areas of sacredness within language groups. Results can lead to dissatisfaction and threatening questioning over who has the right to disclose cultural knowledge. Indigenous students are also a source of inquiry to many non-Indigenous supervisors, who are either fascinated to hear cultural content and belief systems or may come with some embedded racist assumptions. This leaves the student open to be questioned continually about anything Aboriginal.

Additionally, the PhD process is difficult, unclear and isolating in general. Feelings of being stuck with no end in sight are common. The focus is primarily on the content of the project, while other issues, such as communication, teamwork and managing difficult situations, are often taken for granted (Gosling & Noordam, 2006). One can also be wracked with anxiety, lack of confidence and fear because one is wandering into uncharted territory. Further to this, navigating universities is difficult. Universities, like other institutions, perpetuate systemic racism, systemic sexism and systemic violence. In most institutions racism, sexism and other forms of violence are treated as idiosyncratic issues that are perpetrated by lone individuals with attitudinal problems (Ng, 1993). But, as previously stated, racism and sexism are embedded within the operation of the institution, creating power relations that have become normalised courses of action (Ng, 1993).

This power dynamic operates in everyday life and disempowers those from marginalised groups, such as women, racially diverse people, those with disabilities and so on. In my freshwater experience, along with me, the members of my CoC panel are all affected by power differentials. Irrespective of equity measures, such as anti-discrimination policies, people from marginalised groups enter and participate in the institution as unequal subjects (Harris et al., 2015; Ng, 1993). Gramsci (1971) argues racism and sexism have become hegemonic and 'common sense'. He asserts "[c]ommon-sense thinking is uncritical, episodic, and disjointed, but it is also powerful because it is taken for granted" (p. 321), and once something is considered 'common sense' it is no longer questioned or open to interrogation. Ng (1993, p. 195) argues, "[t]hese ways of doing things keep certain individuals groups in dominant and subordinate positions, producing the structural inequality we see both in the education system and in the workplace".

I have chosen to use only one of my freshwater PhD experiences, not a variety of examples, and I am not generalising. I am framing women's experiences and women's knowledge, as Dorothy Smith (1987) does in *The everyday world is problematic*. Luxton and Findlay (1989) explain, "Dorothy Smith's work has been important in revealing the ways in which women, women's experiences and women's knowledge have been systematically excluded from the realms of socially legitimated formal knowledge, particularly in the university" (p. 183). Smith's concept can be applied to many forms of power imbalance. My one example of an experience speaks to the many and varied ways the institution systemically perpetuates racial discrimination. My experience highlighted to me how powerful and all-consuming white, masculine, academic systems, language and pedagogy is. This non-Indigenous 'way of knowing' is considered the norm. Like white skin. It is seen as the starting point, the point of neutrality and all differences are deviations from the norm. Thus not normal. We are, however, gendered and racialised subjects (amongst other things). We are not equal. Our gender and racial background shapes who we are, how we are seen, how we interact with the world and, contents Ng (1993), affects and disables how we negotiate our way through higher education.

12   Sharing Stories over the Water Ways

There has been little documented about how the important traditional life of women within Aboriginal societies has been influenced by western interpretations. Colonisation has brought notions of women that deliberately devalue Aboriginal femininity, resulting in entrenched western ideals within Aboriginal societies. From being Aboriginal warriors, women have been reimagined within a spear of white domesticated subservience, no longer seen as an equal counterpart of men. As a saltwater academic I see this reflected by contemporary Indigenous dance, where women act out more nurturing simplified roles rather than being strong courageous hunters. Such performances contain no reference to resilience, valour, knowledge, skills and compassion.

As Aboriginal women scholars, we utilise our Indigenous ways of knowing, being and doing. We cannot be anything other than Aboriginal women, so to expect us to adhere to non-Indigenous ways of knowing is impossible, unrealistic and simply perpetuates systemic racism. Bhabha (1983) states:

> [t]he objective of colonial discourse is to construe the colonised as a population of degenerate types on the basis of racial origin, in order to justify conquest and to establish systems of administration and instruction ... discourse produces the colonised as a fixed reality which is at once an 'other' and yet entirely knowable and visible. (p. 23)

We are not degenerate, neither are our communities and we challenge the 'fixed reality' described above. We further challenge the dominant, white, patriarchal discourse. Our ways of knowing, being and doing include the way we learn and research and the way we process and translate information. This has been taught to us by our saltwater and freshwater Elders, to allow us the ability to navigate the space between two worlds and maintain our connection to Country and cultural practices.

13   How We View the River System

When conducting research, we use an Indigenous methodological (IM) approach, guided by an Indigenous Knowledge paradigm (Kovach, 2010). This paradigmatic approach is centred in an Indigenous belief system and this is, at its core a relational understanding and accountability to the world. Thus, our axiological, ontological and epistemological practices are seen and demonstrated from a different cultural and theoretical standpoint (Martin & Mirraboopa, 2003).

My saltwater experiences of developing Indigenous methodologic approaches was tidal as it was a time of a growth, exploration and validity. In exploring Aboriginal epistemologies, both narrative and visual content drove the direction of my PhD thesis. Having two Aboriginal supervisors assisted my own confidence in exploring inquiries through an Indigenous lens. Utilising visual making within an academic context provided me with a greater source of inquiry that resonated with illustrated knowledge through the exchange of the maker and the viewer. In accordance with Indigenous methodologies, the maker (the artist) became the narrator, whilst the viewer (the examiner) became the observer. The process was further enhanced by utilising Aboriginal ways of knowing that included cultural knowledges associated with deep seeing and deep sensory interplay. My artworks were created from guided processes that involved both intuitive and imaginative interaction, which I argue goes beyond the boundaries of obvious realities. My creative activities become an instrument for knowing and a powerful pedagogical tool within cultural processes. In pursuing my research, I recall clearly how my examiners responded to statements about spiritual guidance as a perceived subject matter, or how intuitive experiences as direct knowledge and alternatives to western notions conflicted with the examiners' personal assumptions. I took a risk, but a necessary risk to ensure I captured both creative practice and spiritual transference theories within a holistic framework.

An IM approach has certain characteristics, including:
- a de-colonising perspective
- a clear statement of personal and professional purpose of the research being conducted
- self-locating and locating self within the research community
- Indigenous specific ethical protocols
- methods of data collection that is congruent with Indigenous epistemology, such as storytelling and yarning circles
- Analysis and interpretation that reflects Indigenous sensibilities and congruency between epistemology, theory, method and interpretation (Kovach, 2011).

However, this is diametrically opposed to the structures I work, research, and study within and I, along with my Indigenous colleagues, face barriers that impede our development, success and advancement on a daily basis.

As a freshwater academic, I experienced subversive racism in my CoC and was responding to the western, white hegemony (Kivel, 2005). This was so subtle and I was oblivious to it. I responded to feedback I received from people I trust and respect. However, I was perpetually adapting my writing and my standpoint to fit into the strict parameters of the CoC document, while at the same time being asked to further develop certain 'cultural' concepts that the panel members seemed not to understand, although, I thought I was being very explicit and clear. As I mentioned earlier, I did this for five months following my confirmation. Each week my self-esteem and confidence waned. I felt as if I was not privy to some secret information that others were privy to, in order to successfully achieve full candidacy in a PhD. Therefore, I questioned myself. How was I going to complete the whole PhD if I could not even get past this milestone? I felt like I was being re-colonised.

As a PhD student, I was based within an Institute at a university. I specifically chose this Institute and fought very hard to become a PhD student in this space, because I thought it would be safe. And for the most part I *was* safe. I trusted and respected my supervisors and the other staff who have supported me in my PhD process. This is why the subtle form of racism I experienced came as such a shock and disappointment.

My saltwater experience as a researcher has been a challenging journey, as there is little recognition of the complexities and strengths of diverse Indigenous experiences. It has been a journey of struggle to capture cultural validations within a western space. I have also witnessed the increasing number of Indigenous scholars who undergo research and question their own authority, identity and personal confusion in walking in two worlds. Challenges encountered include individualised perspectives and seeking alternative methodologies to capture inquiries in a way that further transform and align with Indigenous ways of Knowing. The conscious evolving process is often confronting as it is not only a means of justifying an inquiry, but there are multiple times when it is necessary to justify oneself with supervisors in epistemological biases of Eurocentric thought.

Whilst discussions have been outlined on white privilege in institutions across Australia, our intent has also been to expose lateral violence in all levels of the academy and highlight the need for universities to raise their standards on black matters, because black academics matter. Higher education has been built on the colonial presumption that Aboriginal people were classified as not human, thus incapable of learning, knowing or having the ability to lead and achieve. This ideology has resulted in whitewashed academics seeing Aboriginal academics as victims who display a level of incompetence. Ober the years my saltwater experience has witnessed Indigenous students and academics being over-supported in various areas of university life. Perhaps a level of fear dominates the other as being seen as either a saviour of racist may deter the true hidden approaches to learning and personal development. Our presence has been predominantly an aesthetic one with career paths often limited because of such challenges. There appears no real commitment to increasing positive outcomes for Indigenous people, and thus we remain underrepresented in senior leadership positions. This demonstrates the inequality experienced as these challenges are intertwined with epistemological racism. The minimal participation in senior roles continues to disrupt advancement in Indigenous education within decision-making process that further disempowers meaningful progress. It is imperative that Indigenous people are more involved in university governance through inclusive processes that offers multiple voices in constructive timeframes.

Many white university staff and students continue to perpetuate ignorant and openly racist views about Indigenous peoples. As a saltwater academic, I clearly recall a time a lighter skinned Aboriginal student sat in an Indigenous unit behind two non-Indigenous students who commented on the Aboriginal lecturer in a racially derogative manner. The Indigenous student felt angry, embarrassed and culturally unsafe whilst the Aboriginal academic was left hurt and wounded. The incident was reported but nothing was addressed. There were no ramifications against any racial slurs from the student body, rather they were declared 'an Aboriginal thing' – to be followed up by Aboriginal senior staff.

The white academy perpetuates stereotypes, academics hold simplistic views on cultural differences in learning, and the system fails to address the issue of Indigenous under-employment. Indigenous peoples are employed in significantly low numbers by universities and when employed, are generally employed only within Indigenous-specific centres (Indigenous Higher Education Advisory Council [IHEAC], 2006; Moreton-Robinson, 1998a, 1998b). The system and staff within it fail to support Indigenous staff. An example of this is the failure of teaching workload policies to acknowledge the cultural and academic discipline knowledge of Indigenous staff and the time requirement and skill necessary to Indigenise curriculum, so it is meaningful for Indigenous students. This is tantamount to Indigenous existences not being valued at all. In addition to this lack of equity, there is no gender equity. It is our experience that Aboriginal women are consistently treated differently than Aboriginal men in the academy. Aboriginal men who successfully adopt white men's ways of Being and Doing can find some success. However, women are not viewed in the same way and often come up against significant barriers to career progression.

14 Back Paddling

Lateral violence within black academia is described as a form of overt and covert dissatisfaction and disruption amid members of oppressed groups (Native Counselling Services of Alberta [NCSA], 2008). Lateral violence within Indigenous academia includes bullying, harassment, backstabbing, gossiping, shaming, social exclusion, organisational conflict and sabotage, coupled with covert behaviours along with challenging other's Aboriginal identity (Clark, Augoustinos, & Malin, 2016). This is linked to intergenerational trauma that has its roots in colonialism. Lateral violence is described by Franklin and White (2010) as 'internalised colonialism' that results in harmful behaviours of intra-racial conflict rather than recognising and confronting the system that oppresses them. From a psychological standpoint, lateral violence occurs from an internal form of dissatisfaction, resulting in destructive behaviours, a blame mentality, jealousy and/or lack of control over one's own life.

In my freshwater experience of lateral violence, it is frequent and pervasive. I am fair skinned and live off Country. I have had my identity questioned and significant local Elders and other Aboriginal people often ignore me until someone Aboriginal introduces me as Aboriginal, as if they are vouching for me. I have always found this challenging. I am also frequently placed in a position where I feel I have to defend myself and my teaching ability in meetings with white colleagues. This makes me feel shame and discomfort, as if I am not a good enough teacher, that I am not trusted and that this is based on my Indigeneity. It is anxiety provoking. I try to prepare mentally for all scenarios before I go into meetings that invoke these feelings. This can be exhausting.

My saltwater experiences of lateral violence have been prolific, with individuals secretly directing their dissatisfaction with their work settings at co-workers within institutions. My first experiences of lateral violence began in my nursing career, with hierarchical bullying and criticism. I also noted other nurses experiencing the same violence that resulted in frequent absenteeism and thoughts about leaving nursing. Fifty percent of nurses surveyed in an ongoing American Nurses Association survey of nurses' health and safety said they had experienced verbal or non-verbal aggression from a peer (American Nurses Association [ANA], 2018).

Lateral violence within a black academic space is also sadly commonplace. My saltwater experiences have included subtle changes in communications, emails increasingly taking preference to direct conversations and conscious form of exclusion or avoidance. Other experiences included non-verbal innuendos including snide remarks, abrupt responses, malicious gossip, undermining activities, and withholding information that leads to broken confidences and organisational conflict.

Whilst it can be argued organisational conflict is generally easy to fix. From my saltwater experiences Indigenous organisational conflict is far more complex and challenging as it often involves multiple individuals. As most academic and professional staff working in some form of community engagement, when things go wrong, many are left on their own to defend themselves. I have witnessed their families being targeted along with any close associations. The advancement of social media has furthered this behaviour. I have witnessed some Aboriginal academics being challenged in public spaces over their identity, their right to knowledge and questioning if they have gained permission prior to holding cultural events. I have seen careers being jeopardised and nearly destroyed. This has created considerable difficulties working in two worlds and navigating institutional careers and community protocols. Many academics relocating to other geographical areas for employment opportunities often feel disconnected and marginalised from those residing in that community. The need to spend personal time being accepted within each new Aboriginal nation is not acknowledged within workplaces nor recognised as a part of cultural social and emotional health. Acknowledgement by universities that building these connections is vital to university community engagement work but also helps greatly in retention rates for students and academics needs further address.

15   Blocked Pathways

As discussed previously, Aboriginal people have been denied access to the same educational opportunities as non-Indigenous Australians. Since the 1967 referendum there have been increases in university enrolments, however, discrimination and racism have endured. Australia's current education system is underpinned by western values with Indigenous students residing within two worlds of knowing. To this date, there is a cultural bias in higher education of white privilege that continues to dominate western knowledge. White privilege offers a form of inequity, discrimination and marginalisation within learning that favours western knowledge. Klenowski (2009) asserts "teachers need to adopt culturally responsive pedagogy to open up the curriculum and assessment practice to allow for different ways of knowing and being" (p. 77). This sense of pervasive 'whiteness' involves the discrimination and oppression of non-white groups to privilege white individuals (Moreton-Robinson, 2004). In Australian universities, institutional practices of whiteness as neutral are prevalent and impact significantly upon Indigenous peoples, be they students, staff or community members. "Whiteness confers both dominance and privilege; it is embedded in Australia's institutions and in the social practices of everyday life" (Moreton-Robinson, 1998a, p. 11) and fails to recognise the enormous contributions of Indigenous peoples' intellectual knowledge. Indigenous Knowledge is also exploited, misappropriated, and patented without due recognition. For example, Indigenous cultural heritage and creative expressions are given little recognition as forms of cultural knowledge. This is because western system intellectual property rights do not provide adequate acknowledgment of, or protection for, cultural knowledge. The continued failure to recognise Indigenous Knowledge has also seen many Indigenous communities receive little or no recognition for their contribution, or their equitable share of benefits. To extend this further, little ethical concern is given to the collection of research or informed consent from Indigenous communities, and claims to product and knowledge rights result in few (if any) financial benefits being returned to Indigenous communities. From both our freshwater and saltwater perspectives and experiences, Indigenous Knowledge within higher education needs to be given greater attention. All students across multiple disciplines need to be informed of Indigenous intellectual rights and Indigenous Knowledges must be represented, particularly in the arts, environmental studies, sciences, educational practices and research fields.

16   Are All the Channels Open?

There is an ongoing dissatisfaction within western scientific philosophies and practices that has only recently encouraged Indigenous participation in western scholarship. Racialised research structures, philosophies and methods of investigation have taken away the voice of Indigenous students and researchers and little value has been placed on Indigenous contributions. There is a need to challenge racial superiority over the assumptions of Indigenous inferiority and irrationality within the scientific space. Currently, the patriarchal, male dominated, white scientific space challenges our theories on creation (Indigenous Dreaming) and has led to a destructive Australian historical consciousness. Langford (1983) asserts that Indigenous cultures can only be partially understood from within the inherited western scientific traditions.

All curriculum, whether in higher education or school, needs to include place-based contexts, Indigenous pedagogical theories and culturally responsive pedagogy concerning the nature of science and the relationship to Indigenous histories. Additionally, the implementation of Indigenous epistemologies and pedagogies within higher education, including research experiences, is necessary to build an effective, holistic scientific learning environment.

17   Final Destination

Exposing the challenges faced as saltwater and freshwater Aboriginal academics may assist other Indigenous people to navigate the higher educational system with a sense of heightened awareness and caution. It is our intent to provide lived experiences as storylines for the future in recognising the personal trials, confrontations and encounters with which most Indigenous academics will have to grapple. It is also our intent to raise awareness of the need to establish university-wide responsibility to address issues of cultural safety, cultural identity and Indigeneity.

References

American Nurses Association (ANA). (2015). *ANA panel aims to prevent violence bullying in health care facilities* [Press release]. Author.

Australian Government Department of the Prime Minister and Cabinet. (2016). *Closing the gap: Prime Minister's report 2016.* Commonwealth of Australia.

Australian Government Department of the Prime Minister and Cabinet. (2019). *Closing the gap: Prime Minister's report 2019* [Online]. Commonwealth of Australia.

Australian Institute of Aboriginal and Torres Strait Islander Studies (AIATSIS). (2019). *Indigenous Australian languages.*

Barney, K. (2016). Listening to and learning from the experiences of Aboriginal and Torres Strait Islander students to facilitate success. *Student Success, 7*(1), 1–11. doi:10.5204/ssj.v7i1.317

Barter-Godfrey, S., & Taket, A. (2009). Othering, marginalisation and pathways to exclusion in health. In A. Taket, B. Crisp, A. Nevill, G. Lamaro, M. Graham, & S. Barter-Godfrey (Eds.), *Theorising social exclusion* (pp. 166–172). Routledge.

Bell, D. A. (1980). Brown v. Board of education and the interest-convergence dilemma. *Harvard Law Review, 93*(3), 518–533.

Bhabha, H., K. (1983). The other question ... Homi K. Bhabha reconsiders the stereotype and colonial discourse. *Screen, 24*(6), 18–36.

Brown, R. (1977). Introduction. In C. Snow & C. Ferguson (Eds.), *Talking to children: Language input and acquisition* (pp. 1–27). Cambridge University Press.

Calderon, D. (2014). Uncovering settler grammars in curriculum. *Educational Studies, 50*(4), 313–338. doi:10.1080/00131946.2014.926904

Campbell, M. A., Finlay, S., Lucas, K., Neal, N., & Williams, R. (2014). Kick the habit: A social marketing campaign by Aboriginal communities in NSW. *Australian Journal of Primary Health, 20*(4), 327–333.

Clark, A. (2008). *History's children: History wars in the classroom.* New South Wales Press.

Clark, Y., Augoustinos, M., & Malin, M. (2016). Lateral violence within the Aboriginal community in Adelaide: It affects our identity and wellbeing. *Journal of Indigenous Wellbeing: Te Mauri – Pimatisiwin, 1*(1), 43–52.

Crago, M. (1990, April). Professional gatekeeping: The multicultural, multilingual challenge. *Communique,* 10–13.

De Beauvoir, S. (1949). *Le Deuxième Sexe.* Gallimard.

Delpit, L. (1988). The silenced dialogue: Power and pedagogy in educating other people's children. *Harvard Educational Review, 58*(2), 78–95.

Derrick, J. (2006). *Lateral violence* [Handout, 1 August]. Winds Wellness and Education Centre.

Donnelly, K., & Wiltshire, K. (2014). *Review of the Australian Curriculum: Final report.* Australian Government Department of Education.

Douglas, B., Lewis, C. W., Douglas, A., Scott, M. E., & Garrison-Wade, D. (2008). The impact of White teachers on the academic achievement of Black students: An exploratory qualitative analysis. *Educational Foundations, 22*(1–2), 47–62.

Dyer, R. (1997). *White: Essays on race and culture.* Routledge.

Eades, D. (2013). They don't speak an Aboriginal language, or do they? [Online]. In D. Eades (Ed.), *Aboriginal ways of using English* (pp. 56–75). Aboriginal Studies Press.

Essed, P. (1990). *Everyday racism: Reports from women of two cultures.* Brill.

Frankland, R., Lewis, P., & Trotter, R. (2010). *This is forever business: A framework for maintaining and restoring cultural safety in Aboriginal Victoria.* Victorian Aboriginal Child Care Agency (VACCA).

Franklin, M. A., & White, I. (1991). The history and politics of Aboriginal health. In J. Reid & P. Trompf (Eds.), *The health of Aboriginal Australia.* Harcourt Brace Jovanovich.

Furnham, A. (2004). Foreign students: Education and culture shock. *The Psychologist, 17*(1), 16–19.

Garces, L. M., Ishimaru, A. M., & Takahashi, S. (2017). Introduction to beyond interest convergence: Envisioning transformation for racial equity in education. *Peabody Journal of Education, 92*(3), 291–293. doi:10.1080/0161956X.2017.1324654

Gillborn, D. (2005). Education policy as an act of White supremacy: Whiteness, critical race theory and education reform. *Journal of Education Policy, 20*(4), 485–505. doi:10.1080/02680930500132346

Gnutzmann, C., & Intemann, F. (Eds.). (2005). *The globalization of English and the English language classroom.* Gunter Narr Verlag.

Gosling, P., & Noordam, B. (2006). *Mastering your PhD: Survival and success in the doctoral years and beyond.* Springer-Verlag.

Gramsci, A. (1971). *Selections from the prison notebooks* (Q. Hoare & G. Nowell Smith, Eds. & Trans.). International Publishers.

Halloran, M. (2004, July). *Cultural maintenance and trauma in Indigenous Australia.* Paper presented at the 23rd Annual Australian and New Zealand Law and Historical Society Conference, Perth.

Harris, J. C., Barone, R. P., & Patton Davis, L. (2015). Who benefits? A critical race analysis of the (d)evolving language of inclusion in higher education. *Thought and Action*, Winter, 21–38.

Hawkins, J. A. (1994). *A performance theory of order and constituency.* Cambridge University Press.

Heller, M. (Ed.). (1988). *Codeswitching: Anthropological and sociological perspectives* (Contributions to the Sociology of Language, Vol. 48). Mouton de Gruyter.

Higgins, C. (2009). *English as a local language. Post-colonial identities and multilingual practices* (Critical Language and Literacy Studies, Vol. 2). Multilingual Matters.

Hill, L. H. (1999). Language, race, and White public space. *American Anthropologist, 100*(3), 680–689.

hooks, b. (1992). *Black looks: Race and representation.* South End Press.

Hultgren, A. K., & Erling, E. J. (2016). English has taken over academia: But the real culprit is not linguistic. *The Conversation.*

Indigenous Higher Education Advisory Council (IHEAC). (2006). *Review of higher education access and outcomes for Aboriginal and Torres Strait Islander people.* Department of Education and Training, Canberra.

Jadhav, S. (1993). Anthropology and medicine: Bridging the link. *British Medical Anthropology Society Bulletin, 1,* 1–2.

Kivel, B. D. (2005). Examining racism, power, and White hegemony in Stodolska's conditioned attitude model of individual discriminatory behavior. *Leisure Sciences, 27*(1), 21–27. doi:10.1080/01490400590885926

Klenowski, V. (2009). Australian Indigenous students: Addressing equity issues in assessment. *Teaching Education, 20*(1), 77–93.

Kovach, M. (2011, July). *Indigenous methodologies and modified grounded theory method.* Paper presented at the Summer Institute in Program Evaluation, Winnipeg, Manitoba.

Langford, R. (1983). Our heritage, your playground. *Australian Archaeology, 16,* 1–10.

Luxton, M., & Findlay, S. (1989). Is the everyday world the problematic? Reflections on Smith's method of making sense of women's experience. *Studies in Political Economy, 30,* 182–196.

Malcolm, I. (1994, October). *Issues in the maintenance of Aboriginal languages and Aboriginal English.* Keynote address to the 10th National Conference of the Modern Language Teachers' Association, Edith Cowan University Perth.

Martin, K., & Mirraboopa, B. (2003). Ways of knowing, ways of being and ways of doing: A theoretical framework and methods for Indigenous research and Indigenist re-search. In K. McWilliam, P. Stephenson, & G. Thompson (Eds.), *Voicing dissent* (pp. 203–214) (Next Generation Australian Studies, Vol. 76). New Talents 21C.

Mathur, S., Moon, L., & Leigh, S. (2006). *Aboriginal and Torres Strait Islander people with coronary heart disease: Further perspectives on health status and treatment*. Cardiovascular disease series no. 25. Cat. No. CVD 33. Australian Institute of Health and Welfare.

Mellor, D (2003). Contemporary racism in Australia: The experiences of Aborigines. *Personality and Social Psychology Bulletin, 29*(4), 474–486.

Mendes, W. B., Major, B., McCoy, S., & Blascovich, J. (2008). How attributional ambiguity shapes physiological and emotional responses to social rejection and acceptance. *Journal of Personality and Social Psychology, 94*, 278–291.

Moodie, N., & Patrick, R. (2017). Settler grammars and the Australian professional standards for teachers. *Asia-Pacific Journal of Teacher Education, 45*(5), 439–454.

Moreton-Robinson, A. (1998a). White race privilege: Nullifying Native title. In Foundation for Aboriginal and Islander Research Action (Ed.), *Bringing Australia together: The structure and experience of racism in Australia* (pp. 39–44). Foundation for Aboriginal and Islander Research Action.

Moreton-Robinson, A. (1998b). Witnessing whiteness in the wake of Wik. *Social Alternatives, 17*(2), 11–14.

Moreton-Robinson, A. (2000). *Talkin' up to the White woman: Aboriginal women and feminism*. University of Queensland Press.

Morton-Robinson, A. (2004). The possessive logic of patriarchal White sovereignty: The high court and the Yorta Yorta decision. *Borderlands E-Journal, 3*(2).

Moreton-Robinson, A. (2013). Towards an Australian Indigenous women's standpoint theory. *Australian Feminist Studies, 28*(78), 331–347. doi:10.1080/08164649.2013.876664

Native Counselling Services of Alberta (NCSA). (2008, January 4). *Lateral violence*.

National Aboriginal Community Controlled Health Organisation (NACCHO). (2013). *Investing in healthy futures for generational change*. Author.

Ng, R. (1993). 'A woman out of control': Deconstructing sexism and racism in the university. *Canadian Journal of Education/Revue canadienne de l'éducation, 18*(3), 189–205.

Nichter, M. (1981). Negotiation of the illness experience: Ayurvedic therapy and the psychosocial dimension of illness. *Culture, Medicine and Psychiatry, 5*(1), 5–24.

Powell, J. A., & Menendian, S. (2016). The problem of othering. *Othering and Belonging: Expanding the Circle of Human Concern, 2*, 14–39.

Reason, P. (1994). *Three approaches to participative inquiry*. Sage.

Rigney, L. (1999). Internationalization of an Indigenous anti-colonial cultural critique of research methodologies: A guide to Indigenist research methodology and its principles. *WICAZO Sa Review, 14*(2), 109–121. doi:10.2307/1409555

Rigney, L. (2006). Indigenist research and Aboriginal Australia. In N. Goduka & J. Kunnie (Eds.), *Indigenous people's wisdom and power* (pp. 32–48). Ashgate.

Ross, S. N. (2013). The politics of politeness: Theorizing race, gender, and education in White southern space. In W. M. Reynolds (Ed.), *A curriculum of place: Understandings emerging through the southern mist* (pp. 143–159). Peter Lang.

Shepherd, S. M., Willis-Esqueda, C., Newton, D., Sivasubramaniam, D., & Paradies, Y. (2019). The challenge of cultural competence in the workplace: Perspectives of healthcare providers. *BMC Health Services Research, 19*(135).

Smith, D. (1987). *The everyday world is problematic.* University of Toronto Press.

Tate, S. A., & Bagguley, P. (2017). Building the anti-racist university: Next steps. *Race Ethnicity and Education, 20*(3), 289–299. doi:10.1080/13613324.2016.1260227

Trudgett, M., & Franklin, C. (2011, December). *Not in my backyard: The impact of culture shock on Indigenous Australians in higher education.* Paper presented at the 1st International Australasian Conference on Enabling Access to Higher Education, Adelaide, South Australia.

Wald, G. (2018) Foreword: Passing and "post-race". In M. Godfrey & V. Ashanti Young (Eds.), *Performing identity after Jim Crow.* University of Illinois Press.

Weitzer, R. J. (1990). *Transforming settler societies.* University of California Press.

Wilber, K. (1981). *Up from Eden: A transpersonal view of human evolution.* Doubleday.

Wildman, S. M., & Davis, D. A. (1994). *Language and silence: Making systems of privilege visible.* Law Faculty Publications, Santa Clara University.

Williams, M. (1988). Aboriginal English. In M. Williams (Ed.), *The Nunga code* (p. 10). Education Department of South Australia.

Wijeysinghe, C. L., Griffin, P, & Love, B. (1997). Racism curriculum design. In M. Adams, L. A. Bell, & P. Griffin (Eds.), *Teaching for diversity and social justice: A sourcebook* (pp. 82–109). Routledge.

Yosso, T. J. (2005). Whose culture has capital? A critical race theory discussion of community cultural wealth. *Race Ethnicity and Education, 8*(1), 69–91. doi:10.1080/1361332052000341006

Yunkaporta, T. (2019). *Forever Ltd: Indigenous knowledge and sustainability.*

Zimmer, L. (1988). Tokenism and women in the workplace: The limits of gender-neutral theory. *Social Problems, 35*(1), 64–77.

CHAPTER 9

Critical Social Work from Indigenous Perspectives

William Abur

Abstract

Social work has a critical role in supporting families, young people and others with complex needs, such as the elderly and those with disabilities. This chapter discusses critical social work from the perspective of Indigenous social workers who have experienced some forms of institutional marginlisation and also worked with marginalised community groups, using cultural knowledge to address a number of institutional injustice issues and practices. Social workers working with Indigenous community groups constantly experience and witness the challenges faced by those communities, including isolation within educational institutions. Social work as a profession is a growing area in Indigenous community groups because of social justice problems and historical marginalisation through colonial practices. Writing as a social work lecturer within an Indigenous educational institute, I recognise that social work has a significant role to play in Indigenous communities. It can empower people to speak up and speak the truth, supporting people through journeys of pain and healing, as well as acknowledging their experiences and cultural knowledge by validating those experiences. While walking alongside students and their families, social work lecturers bring their knowledge and their own experiences to enhance social work courses at university.

Keywords

Indigenous social workers – critical social work theory – discrimination – marginalisation – social work education – colonisation – community

1   Introduction

Social work has a critical role in supporting families, young people and others with complex needs, such as the elderly and those with disabilities. This chapter discusses critical social work from the perspective of Indigenous social workers who have experienced some forms of institutional marginalisation and also worked with marginalised community groups, using cultural knowledge to address a number of institutional injustice issues and practices. Social workers working with Indigenous community groups constantly experience and witness the challenges faced by those communities, including isolation within educational institutions. Social work as a profession is a growing area in Indigenous community groups because of social justice problems and historical marginalisation through colonial practices. Writing as a social work lecturer within an Indigenous educational institute, I recognise that social work has a significant role to play in Indigenous communities. It can empower people to speak up and speak the truth, supporting people through journeys of pain and healing, as well as acknowledging their experiences and cultural knowledge by validating those experiences. While walking alongside students and their families, social work lecturers bring their knowledge and their own experiences to enhance social work courses at university.

2   Positionality and Knowledge Area in Social Work

Positionality is a concept that is related to intersectionality, with power, culture, gender, ethnicity and other classes influencing us as human beings. People act and respond differently to different situations based on their positionality (Franks, 2002). My own position as a social worker is influenced by anti-oppressive and anti-discriminatory practices. I also identify myself as a social worker from a marginalised South Sudanese-Australian community with extensive experience in working with disadvantaged groups, young people and their families from different walks of life. I have witnessed marginalisation, stereotyping, direction and indirection discrimination and racism as a black social worker from South Sudanese Australian, and as someone who came to Australia as a refugee from Africa. My own personal experience of disadvantaged and marginalisation assist me to clearly see and understand intersectionality of social and political issues facing Indigenous community groups from critical social work perspective. My work with students and others is based on empathy and inter-personal relationships in order to help them with their problems such as social or educational issues. Therefore, Indigenous social workers have an ability to engage with people in an empathic manner and with an understanding of the fundamental issues facing individuals and community groups (Grant, 2014). As Trevithick (2005, p. 81) argues:

> [We] put ourselves in another person's place in the hope that we can feel and understand that person's emotions, thoughts, actions and motives.

Empathy involves trying to understand, as carefully and sensitively as possible, the nature of another person's experiences, their own unique points of view and what meaning this conveys to that individual.

Many social work students or social workers are motivated to join the social work profession either because of personal experience of being a victim or their families having been victims of traumatic events (Grant, 2014). Research suggests that Indigenous social workers bring community knowledge and experiences to their work and teaching roles. This includes a high level of support, empathy and caring for their clients and their community (Grant, 2014). As social work practitioners and human beings in general, empathy is very important for us to display when we are interacting with our clients and ourselves as professional practitioners. However, empathy is a hard call for some people. They have difficulties in applying empathy when engaging with other people or when working in welfare systems with vulnerable clients. Critical social work values empathy and is committed to ethical values in supporting vulnerable individuals and community groups (Healy, 2001). The following are examples of empathy theory and reflective process when working with clients (Grant, 2014):

- *Empathy*
    1. Compassion and warmth
    2. Ability to take perspectives of others
- *Reflective ability*
    1. Processing the effect of interaction
    2. Self/other awareness
    3. Control emotion
- *The ending results of empathy and reflective ability can be*:
    1. Accurate empathy
    2. Empathic distress

The importance of social work for both generally and for Indigenous communities (including discussions of oppression, marginalisation, advocacy, empowerment as a way of bringing changes in society and in life of clients).

Doing social work is about one's commitment to serve vulnerable families and individuals who are facing social, health and political issues. There is often a gap between mainstream social workers and social workers from Indigenous community groups in the way they interact with their clients because of cultural understanding and lack of cultural understanding. In our critical social work teaching, we encourage a critical reflection of what we are doing and how we do it. Social workers must remind themselves, as critical social workers and practitioners working with vulnerable people in society that their role is about supporting people when discussing issues such as racism, discrimination, families and individuals. For instance, when talking about anti-racist theory as a social worker or a practitioner working with Indigenous community groups, it is essential to start questioning your own values and how you stand in relation to anti-racism discourse. As such, Indigenous social workers encourage and promote the idea of critical reflection by asking simple questions such as, "Where do I stand in the anti-racism and anti-oppressive discourses?" There is deeper understanding when anti-racist social workers start with themselves/ us. Indigenous social workers are more likely to understand about critical issues facing people who are underprivileged positions. In other words, they understand social issues from their own experiences of underprivileged/privileges. This is hard for those who never experience issues that are experienced by underprivileged population. Some people in privilege positions continue playing racism and discrimination cards as they hold on the powerful (Jeffery, 2005). The author believes that Indigenous social workers are more likely to respond appropriately to our clients and community groups when we work in a sensitive way.

As Indigenous social workers with experience and knowledge in and of the community, we are aware that we may not know everything from the perspectives of Indigenous experiences and knowledge, but we are placed in the position of knowing the systematic problems within institutions such as higher education. We are informed about the impact of colonisation on communities and individuals, and understand trauma, racism and discrimination at the institutional level and in practice. Some of these issues are well-documented in social research, indicating that people from Indigenous community groups face systematic racism in education, the criminal justice system, the welfare system, and in public and private housing areas (Herring, Spangaro, Lauw, & McNamara, 2013; Jeffery, 2005). As a result of such institutional problems, there is a growing need for Indigenous researchers to engage in discourses of de-colonisation to shift oppressive thinking and empower Indigenous communities (Bennett, Zubrzycki, & Bacon, 2011). Indigenous social workers bring their own experiences and knowledge to teaching and promote a better critical social work practice to social work students. Similarly, social work students bring their own experiences, cultural knowledge and practical knowledge to critical issues in the community.

Our experiences in teaching social work, interacting with students and listening to community members' concerns in area of ongoing racism and marginalisation, often aid our cultural knowledge and deeper understanding of the levels of trauma left in the community as a consequence of colonisation and the ongoing denial of justice to Indigenous community groups. Our teaching values are based on a high level of support services, working with students and community members who have experienced some level of disadvantages and vulnerability. We strongly value the philosophy and sense of community, walking side by side with our students to achieve their education outcomes. The main goal of our work in this academic area is to empower students with the knowledge and skills that they will use to address social justice issues in community.

We teach our students how to address social justice issues, and human rights in general, through the lens of critical social work. Social workers in Indigenous community groups have a critical role to play in addressing health and inequality issues with clients and community groups in general (Green & Baldry, 2008). Based on some of the social and justice issues mentioned above, we value community-based education that is driven by Indigenous Knowledge and experiences rather than by colonisers' philosophies and knowledge. Community-based education always values experiences and knowledge from within that community. The community-based education model is often driven by a community's knowledge, expertise, and cultural practice as a core principle of understanding cultural issues. Therefore, it is more relevant to Indigenous community groups who experienced some form of colonisation and marginalisation (Gair, Miles, & Thomson, 2005). The current practice appears to be driven from business and hierarchical order which does not consider community views or a bottom-up approach.

> Many present-day politicians, and the intellectuals who advise them, tend to believe that for governments to succeed, the whole world is best viewed as a business and best interpreted in business terms. (Corson, 1998, p. 238)

The challenge here is that the business thinking and approach does not acknowledge or recognise the Indigenous ways of education and thinking. We know that Indigenous community groups are still facing many challenges in the contemporary world because of colonisation. Many people working in the institutions that are supposed to be the leaders for change are failing Indigenous community groups by protecting institutional racism and discrimination. There is no doubt that some critical issues of isolation and marginalisation practices can be seen in many institutions such as universities, hospital, government bodies and other private bodies cross Australia. This kind of institutional isolation of Indigenous community services requires attention and critical thinking (Green & Baldry, 2008). I have used the terminology Indigenous community to highlight the collective experiences of different Indigenous community groups within and beyond Australia (Green & Baldry, 2008). I have also deliberately used the term 'critical social work' which is explained in next section to describe different views of inside and outside cultural knowledge as a persistent way of seeking to improve services.

3   Critical Social Work Theory

The term critical social work emerged in literature in 1996 in Canada and 1997 in Australia (Fook, 2003; Ife, 1997). The term critical social work here is referred to debates around social injustice issues and as an empowerment for marginalised community groups and disadvantaged individuals. In other word, critical social work refers to different theories and practices that recognise issues in social, cultural and economic processes in society, such as inequality for Indigenous people, as well as gender and race (Abrams & Moio, 2009; Green & Baldry, 2008). Critical social work also describes different approaches in social work that are diverse, but which share a common commitment to structural and personal change (Pease, Goldingay, Hosken, & Nipperess, 2016).

Thus, critical social work explained different forms of oppression and injustice in different societies across the world. This challenges historical and existing negative perceptions about community, vulnerable individuals and families. Indigenous social workers know through history and research that families, individuals and community groups are struggling with the consequences of colonisation at many levels (Abrams & Moio, 2009; Gair, Miles, Savage, & Zuchowski, 2015). History also tells us that institutions have played and are still playing a significant role in these struggles by continually pushing Indigenous communities to the edge of government services and other private community services because of the discrimination and racism experiences(Abrams & Moio, 2009; Green & Baldry, 2008). This causes those communities to be viewed as fringe-dwellers. At the same time, these institutions have viewed Indigenous peoples as having an "extreme need of social services, education, and housing and child protection services" (Green & Baldry, 2008, p. 390). Indigenous communities have been victims of brutal government policies since the beginning of colonisation and that victimisation is continuing in some organisations and institutions today, including hospitals, community health centres, education and police departments. These continual inequitable practices also create problems in higher education fields. As a social work and a lecturer in social work, I'm committed to critical social work theory as a way of highlighting intersectionality issues such as impact discrimination and racism, gender, domestic violence issues in community, voice of diversity, youth issues and social change. I strongly believe that social work and education in generally can bring changes in marginalised and disadvantaged societies.

Critical social work is a distinct paradigm that promotes a structural approach to address social problems in a diverse society (Ortiz & Jani, 2010). It emerged from critical postmodern theories that aims to understand issues in society, such as oppression and transformation at an individual level. Therefore, critical social work researchers often attempt to develop theoretical methods that trace the voice of the marginalised individuals and community groups by understanding the culture and values of specific locations/community groups (Kleinman & Benson, 2006; Ortiz & Jani, 2010). Postmodern theory in social work is about understanding differences, criticism and emphasis on essential characteristics (Ortiz & Jani, 2010). There are three functions or levels of postmodern theory presented below. These three functions demonstrate different lens and techniques use in critical social work:

1. *Functions of postmodernism*
   - Refusal of positivism
   - Recognition of intersectionality
   - Deconstruction of social constructions
   - Understanding of categorisation
   - Rejection of totalising categories
2. *The lens through which the functions operate*
   - Critical race theory (focus on social racial segregation)
   - Neo-Marxism (focus on class segregation)
   - Neo-feminism (focus on gender segregation)
   - Queer theory (focus on sexual orientation segregation)
3. *Informs your technique*
   - Ask the right questions
   - Focus on transformation
   - Be contextually competent
   - Refuse assumptions

Critical social work theory assumes that oppressive practices against different races are social constructs (Ortiz & Jani, 2010). Therefore, it promotes a framework of emancipation and holistic approaches to address injustice issues such as institutional racism and discrimination in society. The holistic framework of postmodern above is based on supporting individuals and families who are struggling with wellbeing issues, including but not limited to: mental health and physical problems, child abuse or neglect, domestic violence, family breakdown, cultural isolation or dislocation, low socio-economic or disadvantaged groups.

4   Critical Social Work from Indigenous Perspectives

Critical social work is very important from an Indigenous community groups' perspective, because critical social work speaks to injustice issues and encourage marginalised community groups to speak up on the issues that concern their people. Critical social work theory and social work education as applied in Australia and other parts of the world, supported the voices of indigenous social work globally to speak up on colonisation matters. In research, Indigenous social work and knowledge is a growing area in both internationally and nationally, with particular interest in education and innovation (Battiste, 2005). The definition of critical social work within the Indigenous context is a combined practice of cultural knowledge, experiences and relevant social work training in both theoretical and practical knowledge. This includes ways of Knowing that draw liberally on western social work theory and practice (Green & Baldry, 2008, p. 329). Indigenous researchers and social workers know that Indigenous people have developed and will continue to develop experiences, knowledge-sharing with Elders, adaptation to local culture, and local knowledge on issues such as the environment. This knowledge is used to sustain the community and its culture. As Barnhardt and Oscar Kawagley (2005, p. 19) write:

> The ways of constructing, organizing, using, and communicating knowledge that have been practiced by indigenous peoples for centuries have come to be recognized as constituting a form of science with its own integrity and validity, as indicated by a day-long.

Indigenous Knowledge has always been there and exists in different forms. As Battiste (2005, p. 1) notes, "the recognition and intellectual activation of indigenous knowledge today is an act of empowerment by indigenous people". The manifestation of Indigenous Knowledge can be traced back to the origins of humankind, and Indigenous people have kept building from there into today's modern world (Horsthemke, 2008).

Indigenous social work approaches are drawn from critical, anti-oppressive and anti-discriminatory social work. Therefore, Indigenous social work approaches applied critical reflection to challenge underlying prejudices and stereotyping. This critical reflection is about critiquing the assumption of inclusivity based on social justice and other issues that Indigenous community groups have faced for many years since the beginning of colonisation (Green & Baldry, 2008). Indigenous social workers bring a wealth of knowledge and experiences to de-colonise some of the assumptions and policies that are designed, whether intentionally or unintentionally, against community ways of doing things, their philosophies and knowledges. Indigenous social workers have deeper knowledge and understanding of the social justice issues that are affecting community groups, individuals and families than their mainstream colleagues. Indigenous social workers bring a high level of empowerment and advocacy using a human rights approach to challenge policies and assumptions when it comes to social justice issues in the community. Green and Baldry (2008, p. 329) write:

> The Indigenous Rights Movement has provided concepts that resonate with indigenous peoples in Canada, the US, Aotearoa New Zealand and Australia, and these concepts have begun to be incorporated into an informal body of indigenous social work thinking and practice driven by indigenous social workers.

I believe that Indigenous social workers bring a high level of resilience in challenging policies and the resistance of institutions to adapt and change policies to meet the needs of community groups. Johnson (2008, p. 386) argues that "Resilience is a dynamic process involving shifting balances of protective and vulnerable forces in different risk contexts and at different developmental stages". The level of resilience and commitment to create change exists in many Indigenous community groups. Indigenous social workers also teach skills that support existing levels of resilience to social work (and other) students, allowing them to take back those skills to their different community groups. Indigenous people are resilient and have resisted different forms of racism and discrimination, including institutional racism. According to historical records, there are serious social justice and human rights issues facing Indigenous community groups, including educational issues (Altman & Fogarty, 2010). Indeed, research suggests that,

> Students in indigenous societies around the world have, for the most part, demonstrated a distinct lack of enthusiasm for the experience of schooling in its conventional form – an aversion that is most often attributable to an alien institutional racism and discrimination. (Barnhardt & Oscar Kawagley, 2005, p. 10)

Therefore, it is critical that social work presents a platform for challenging and disrupting historical biases and practices such as institutional racism in higher education. Institutional racism and a lack of cultural sensitivity remain prevalent in many Australian higher education facilities (Abrams & Moio, 2009).

One of the critical social work practices that is used to examine social, economic and political issues facing Indigenous people is anti-racist social work. For instance, in our social work teaching and practice, we are mindful of marginalisation and the trauma caused by racism and discrimination in society. We are also conscious and mindful of how social work is largely dominated by mainstream practices of Eurocentric deficit-oriented views regarding Indigenous peoples (Abrams & Moio, 2009). For example, Eurocentric history and contemporary discourses tell of Indigenous peoples' culture, knowledge and experiences from a coloniser's positional gaze of whiteness, privilege and supremacy (Gair et al., 2015). From the lens of critical social work teaching and experiences, we see that these stories are captured as truth, with little or no recourse directly from Indigenous peoples themselves. This has often led to ongoing colonial practices such as pushing Indigenous people to the fringes of society. This is sometimes evident in the location of Indigenous facilities in higher education institutions.

Critical social work has a mission to engage and enlighten social workers to think critically on different social and political issues impacting on people (Healy, 2001). Critical social work theories emerged in the 1960s from radical critiques of traditional social work with the new perspective of challenging dominant cultures and practices that are oppressive to other people (Fook, 2003; Healy, 2001). The literature around the idea of critical social work argued that the voices of minority groups and Indigenous groups must be included in any discourses. This could then lead to better understanding, changes of policies and practices (Fook, 2003; Ife, 1997, 1999). Healy (2001, p. 2) has stated:

> ... [A] commitment to co-participatory rather than authoritarian practice relations. This involves workers and service users, as well as academics, practitioners and service users as co-participants engaged with, but still distinct from, one another; working with and for oppressed populations to achieve social transformation.

Indigenous social workers are concerned about and strive for changes and encourage change to happen at the institutional and hierarchical levels of practice. Indigenous social workers know that domination is something that individuals have achieved through exploitation, ruling and internal self-deception (Fook, 2003). The presence of Indigenous social workers' voices is critical in any form of discourse that challenges oppressive practices at structural, personal and interpersonal levels (Abrams & Moio, 2009; Jeffery, 2005). I believe it is crucial that social workers or researchers in the critical social work space should take the lead in challenging colonial practices and the domination of marginal groups and individuals (Fook, 2003). Therefore, the author comes from a critical social work perspective when working with clients, community groups and institutions. Indigenous social workers believe that it is fundamentally important to understand the experiences of people and to think of better ways to address issues that are affecting them and their community in a way that relates to their culture and experiences. Healy (2001, p. 3) argues,

> the recognition of the many influences shaping human action, including institutional pressures and individual irrationalities, can open the critical practice tradition to new understandings of the relationship between theory and practice.

5 Remaining Issues

There are still many issues remaining in social work education and beyond for Indigenous community groups that required Indigenous social workers to continue voicing their concerns. Once would think that issues of discrimination and racism are addressed in Australia? My answer is that we still have a long way to go. Marginalisation is still practice in prison systems, in employment system, education system, in housing system, in hospital system and so forth. Thus, Indigenous social workers are aware of direct and indirect racism that comes with power and privileges over Indigenous and other minority community groups. Therefore, it is fundamentally important for Indigenous critical social workers to raise awareness about institutional racism and privilege issues in our discourses. The concept of white privilege is not new in academic discourse and highlights the disparity between whites and non-whites within the same social, economic and political circumstances (Collins, 2018; Kendall, 2012; Myers, 2003). Part of problems with the institutions, marginalisation and push out minority groups is that white privilege exists in places with structural power, such as businesses, government institutions and schools (Collins, 2018; Kendall, 2012).

In these institutions, inequality is less likely to flourish if leaders are well-informed about the cultural differences between Indigenous people and non-Indigenous people. It is to be responsive and recognising the strengths of different cultures and diversity. Privilege also relates to the level of trust established between Indigenous peoples and the mainstream white population. It is not difficult for a white person to position himself/herself as an expert in different fields, including the very field of Indigenous studies. On the other hand, recognition is not given to an Indigenous person's level of expertise. There are issues of privilege in the health service, the housing service, education and employment services (Kendall, 2012; Myers, 2003). In the education system, there is a considerable amount of literature designed to promote white privilege (Jeyasingham, 2011).

6   Understanding Cultural Related Issues

Understanding cultural background often assist social worker to conceptualise how individual clients were raised, and this includes understanding their personal priorities, religious beliefs, and family structures. Culture dictate some communications and define family structure of how family members interact with one another at home and with those outside of home. Cultural competence is one of the great ways of acknowledging Indigenous cultures and practices. The intention of cultural competence is to raise awareness, create a platform of communication, and to interact effectively with people from different cultures. The concept of cultural competence practice primarily refers to ethnic and racial minority groups. Cultural competence is disrupted by anti-oppressive and critical social work discourses and challenges the multiple oppressive practices by paying close attention to understanding individuals' interests (Clarke & Wan, 2011). The concept has been used broadly in higher education and community service sectors as a recognition and acknowledgement of minority, non-white groups. It has specific guiding principles such as being aware of attitude, knowledge and competent skills to be displayed by non-Indigenous practitioners when working with clients from different cultural backgrounds (Van Den Bergh & Crisp, 2004). This form of recognition is crucial because of cultural-sensitivities. Acknowledging cultural issues and acting sensitively is fundamental to critical social work (Weaver, 1999).

However, cultural competence is often acknowledged in the contemporary world in tokenistic ways, in order to 'tick the boxes'. From the lens of critical social work, Indigenous social workers believe there is a great need for embedding cultural competency lessons in higher education teaching with consistency. Indigenous social workers know that the current cultural competence practice model has been a practice from experience but has been never evaluated in a systematic way (Gair, Miles, & Thomson, 2005). Critical social work, with historically supported values, knowledge and skills in the area of cultural competency or cultural knowledge, is one of best ways to support Indigenous community groups (Gair et al., 2005).

Critical social workers value integrated frameworks when working with clients and community groups, allowing then to look at issues holistically. Therefore, understanding cultural competency is a very important part of critical social work. It is all about developing positive relationships and being aware of one's own biases and worldviews when working with cultural community groups. Cultural competency promotes skills that facilitate the recognition and deconstruct issues such as racism and oppressive practices (Van Den Bergh & Crisp, 2004). However, a cultural competence framework does not solve the critical issues facing people from Indigenous communities. Sometimes, it is very tokenistic and fails to recognise the racism problem within the dominant group. It does not take away the negative experiences and white privileges. For instance, in Australia, systemic and casual racism is still one of the problems facing Indigenous people and can remain debilitating as it causes trauma and low self-esteem (Herring et al., 2013).

7 Conclusion

Social work is a profession that aim to assist individuals and families who are struggling with social issues, mental health or health issues by providing resources and relevant information they need to their social issues and to live comfortable and healthy lives. Social workers do these by supporting vulnerable children at schools, assisting sick clients to understand their conditions and mange changes to their daily routines. Social workers also advocate for better services on behalf of their clients and community groups they are working with. Therefore, this chapter addressed critical social issues facing Indigenous community groups from Indigenous social workers' perspectives. The chapter presented exclusion and voice of the Indigenous social workers on racism and discrimination issues that have been facing different generations of Indigenous people because of brutal colonisation. Regardless of many years of advocacy on critical issues facing Indigenous people, there is still a long way ahead. Indigenous social workers are constantly hearing difficult stories and experiences of their clients facing social issues of exclusion and marginalisation in 21st century. In other words, there are many issues that are very concerning for Indigenous people across the world and in Australia that needs social work education to continue voicing on behalf of the marginalised individuals and community groups.

References

Abrams, L., & Moio, J. (2009). Critical race theory and the cultural competence dilemma in social work education. *Journal of Social Work Education, 45*(2), 245–261. doi:10.5175/jswe.2009.200700109

Altman, J., & Fogarty, W. (2010). Indigenous Australians as 'no gaps' subjects: Education and development in remote Indigenous Australia. In I. Snyder & J. Nieuwenhuysen (Eds.), *Closing the gap in education: Improving outcomes in southern world societies* (pp. 109–128). Monash University Publishing.

Barnhardt, R., & Oscar Kawagley, A. (2005). Indigenous knowledge systems and Alaska Native ways of knowing. *Anthropology and Education Quarterly, 36*(1), 8–23.

Battiste, M. (2005). Indigenous knowledge: Foundations for first nations. *World Indigenous Nations Higher Education Consortium (WINHEC) Journal*, 1–12.

Bennett, B., & Green, S. (2012). *Our voices*. Macmillan International Higher Education.

Bennett, B., Zubrzycki, J., & Bacon, V. (2011). What do we know? The experiences of social workers working alongside Aboriginal people. *Australian Social Work, 64*(1), 20–37.

Clarke, J., & Wan, E. (2011). Transforming settlement work: From a traditional to a critical anti-oppression approach with newcomer youth in secondary schools. *Critical Social Work, 12*(1), 13–26.

Collins, C. (2018). What is White privilege, really? Recognising White privilege begins with truly understanding the term itself. *Teaching Tolerance*. Retrieved September 2019, from https://www.tolerance.org/magazine/fall-2018/what-is-white-privilege-really

Corson, D, (1998). Community-based education for Indigenous cultures. *Language Culture and Curriculum, 11*(3), 238–249.

Fook, J. (2003). Critical social work: The current issues. *Qualitative Social Work, 2*(2), 123–130.

Franks, M. (2002). Feminisms and cross-ideological feminist social research: Standpoint, situatedness and positionality – Developing cross-ideological feminist research. *Journal of International Women's Studies, 3*(2), 38–50.

Gair, S., Miles, D., Savage, D., & Zuchowski, I. (2015). Racism unmasked: The experiences of Aboriginal and Torres Strait Islander students in social work field placements. *Australian Social Work, 68*(1), 32–48.

Gair, S., Miles, D., & Thomson, J. (2005). Reconciling Indigenous and non-Indigenous knowledges in social work education: Action and legitimacy. *Journal of Social Work Education, 41*(2), 179–190.

Grant, L. (2014). Hearts and minds: Aspects of empathy and wellbeing in social work students. *Social Work Education, 33*(3), 338–352.

Green, S., & Baldry, E. (2008). Building Indigenous Australian social work. *Australian Social Work, 61*(4), 389–402.

Healy, K. (2001). Reinventing critical social work: Challenges from practice, context and postmodernism. *Critical Social Work, 2*(1), 1–13.

Herring, S., Spangaro, J., Lauw, M., & McNamara, L. (2013). The intersection of trauma, racism, and cultural competence in effective work with Aboriginal people: Waiting for trust. *Australian Social Work, 66*(1), 104–117.

Horsthemke, K. (2008). The idea of Indigenous knowledge. *Archaeologies, 4*(1), 129–143.
Ife, J. (1997). *Rethinking social work: Towards critical practice.* Addison Longman Wesley.
Ife, J. (1999). Postmodernism, critical theory and social work. In B. Pease & J. Fook (Eds.), *Transforming social work practice: Postmodern critical perspectives* (pp. 211–223). Routledge.
Jeffery, D. (2005). What good is anti-racist social work if you can't master it? Exploring a paradox in anti-racist social work education. *Race Ethnicity and Education, 8*(4), 409–425. doi:10.1080/13613320500324011
Jeyasingham, D. (2011). White noise: A critical evaluation of social work education's engagement with whiteness studies. *British Journal of Social Work, 42*(4), 669–686.
Johnson, B. (2008). Teacher–student relationships which promote resilience at school: A micro-level analysis of students' views. *British Journal of Guidance and Counselling, 36*(4), 385–398. doi:10.1080/03069880802364528
Kendall, F. (2012). *Understanding White privilege: Creating pathways to authentic relationships across race.* Routledge.
Kleinman, A., & Benson, P. (2006). Anthropology in the clinic: The problem of cultural competency and how to fix it. *PLoS Medicine, 3*(10), 1673–1676.
Martin, K. (2003). Ways of knowing, being and doing: A theoretical framework and methods for Indigenous and Indigenist research. *Journal of Australian Studies, 27*(76), 203–214.
Myers, L. (2003). If not reconciliation, then what? Race and the 'stolen generation' in Australia. In W. Darity & A. Deshpande (Eds.), *Boundaries of clan and colour* (pp. 82–104). Routledge.
Ortiz, L., & Jani, J. (2010). Critical race theory: A transformational model for teaching diversity. *Journal of Social Work Education, 46*(2), 175–193.
Pease, B., Goldingay, S., Hosken, N., & Nipperess, S. (2016). *Doing critical social work: Transformative practices for social justice.* Allen & Unwin.
Simpson, L. (2001). Aboriginal peoples and knowledge: Decolonizing our processes. *The Canadian Journal of Native Studies, 21*(1), 137–148.
Trevithick, P. (2005). *Social work skills: A practice handbook.* McGraw-Hill International.
Van Den Bergh, N., & Crisp, C. (2004). Defining culturally competent practice with sexual minorities: Implications for social work education and practice. *Journal of Social Work Education, 40*(2), 221–238.
Weaver, H. (1999). Indigenous people and the social work profession: Defining culturally competent services. *Social Work, 44*(3), 217–225.
Williams, C. (1999). Connecting anti-racist and anti-oppressive theory and practice: retrenchment or reappraisal? *The British Journal of Social Work, 29*(2), 21.

CHAPTER 10

Conclusion

Tarquam McKenna

The narrative structures of the preceding chapters are, in my estimation, akin to the Indigenous practice and methodology of yarning (Yunkaporta & Kirby, 2011), as taken up progressively and used within both Indigenous and non-Indigenous research paradigms (Geia, Hayes, & Usher, 2013). Tarquam McKenna and Davina Woods (2012) link artful autoethnography with yarning to create a restorative and inherently political Indigenous research methodology they name as 're-claimative' – a practice of reclaiming identity, community and knowledge. In the context of the preceding chapters, we have yarned with each other and with others in a widening circle, telling stories. These stories do not warrant being seen as reduced to mere psychological themes or literary forms and norms. They do however reclaim identity, community and knowledge. We weave the strands of emerging Indigenous knowledge and experience back and forth, threading broader reflections on colonisation through accounts of local encounters with these academics' life experiences; weaving stories together with information around our continuously moving, ever-changing identity.

As more First Nation Australian People enter Australian universities as academics, they join this predominantly white profession. We are now seeing a push for recognition (Thorpe, 2014) of First Nation Australians' ways of knowing (McKenna, Cacciattolo, & Mahon, 2011), and through the Universities Australia (UA) strategy, the 39 member universities are committed to making further gains in Aboriginal and Torres Strait Islander participation, retention and success in universities. This initiative was formalised only three years ago. The formal adoption of a strategy to recognise, amongst other things, the 'cultural competency' of the First Nations People by the UA Plenary in February 2017 was the vehicle for this express commitment by each university and its Aboriginal staff and leaders. The actions pledged under the scheme seek to:

1. improve enrolments and performance in students, academics/researchers and staff;
2. increase the engagement of non-Indigenous people with Indigenous knowledge, culture and educational approaches; and
3. improve the university environment for Aboriginal and Torres Strait Islander people.

A culturally competent workspace should ensure universities are consciously aware of the backgrounds and the different experiences and perspectives of people who are First Nation Australians and engaging with and in a non-Indigenous Australian university. An overlooked area is that of Indigenous cultural safety, including consideration of how Indigenous people are either made to feel safe or unsafe in the university context. This chapter, as a summary of the book, discusses the importance of Indigenous voice and representation of First Nation Australians in the academic professions across two years at Deakin University (2019–2020). "As well as the need for Indigenous people to be taking a leading role in determining priorities around access, management and content of cultural materials", there is a need to work alongside and walk alongside the non-Indigenous Australian team members (Thorpe, 2014, pp. 211–214).

The stories delivered in this book are personal and collective. The concept of cultural competency is, however, the one key emerging theme. This is an area of imperative interest in Australian universities and brings voice more so to the First Nation Australians who were hitherto invisible.

John McPhee coined the phrase 'deep time' (Griffiths, 2018, p. 5) to describe the course of geological events, the formation of glaciers and the movements of tectonic plates: the rifting, crushing, carving forces that slowly sculpt the earth's surface, creating mountains, canyons, seas and continent. Like its twin, 'deep space', the phrase demands that we leave behind the world we thought we knew to confront the limits of our understanding. The deep listening – and looking – that the book requires comes through 'dadirri', which is offered and explored in many moments of engagement and relational belonging.

Dadirri is threaded through the narratives we authors have collected here, allowing all readers to consider our pursuits in universities so that we could come to understand Country. These writings explore the emerging complexity of each of our unique cultural identities and how we belong in Community. Notably, a person cannot be judged on genetic grounds to be Indigenous, non-Indigenous or 'a little bit Aboriginal' as this replicates the divisive and even genocidal colonial practices of categorising First Nation Australians Peoples as 'full-blood', 'half-blood', 'quadroons', 'octoroons', etc. (Tomlinson, 2008) and then removing children of 'mixed heritage' from their First Nation families and communities and 'making them White'. Rather, contemporary definitions of Australian Indigeneity rest on the three criteria of descent, identification and community acceptance. Membership of the First Nation Australian Peoples depends on biological descent from the Indigenous people and on mutual recognition of a particular person's membership by that person and by the elders or other persons enjoying traditional authority among those people.

For example, for someone working in the space of First Nation Australians knowledge and practices – the balance is a delicate one between prematurely claiming to be Indigenous and acknowledging that for many identities this has been hidden by practices of colonisation, displacement and stealing of First Nations' children.

The following poem, offered unsolicited for the conclusion, underscores the terrible injustice inflicted when Country was declared by the invaders to be *terra nullius* – the Latin expression translating as 'nobody's land'. The invaders were met by traditional custodians, but the colonising invader settlers dismissed these people as 'nobody'.

> *Indigenous knowledge, a distinct way of knowing Kin and Country and being*
>
> Knowing place heightens our belonging, identity and connectedness,
> Being and aligning within a landscape of cultural traditions.
> Changing landscapes of Eurocentric ideologies,
> designed to preserve and maintain harmful colonial inheritance.
> Surrounded by colonised education as symbolised colour,
> another racist status quo of enslavement.
> Lost in the oppressions of a possessed landscape we became the forgotten,
> but we have endured.
> Hidden secrets, false claims, collective amnesia,
> Inequality, injustice with a longing of (delete before) language and land (before).
> New warriors transformed to write to intellectually testify our domains of knowing and being,
> we challenge privilege, rights, sovereignty, we contest nationhood.
> The keepers of the knowledge, the link to the past,
> of messages, stories and ritual embedded within knowledge.
> Together we centre our stories to weave our voice,
> our concerns for the future, our sacredness we embrace.
> Marginalised, disempowered but resilient People at heart,
> for we are the true custodians of the past, present and future.
> (Belanjee Guwaali)

In International Law *terra nullius* describes territory that nobody occupies or owns; the first nation to 'discover' it is entitled to take it over – 'finder's keepers' – so the colonising British treated Australia as unowned land. Under their colonial law, the First Nations People in Australia had no rights in and to the land and colonisation accordingly vested ownership of the entire continent to the British government. The doctrine of *terra nullius* remained the law in Australia throughout the colonial period and beyond, until the landmark, 'land rights' decision of Mabo v Queensland in 1992 (Banner, 2005).

Australia remains the only country in the world that is without a formal treaty with, or recognition of, its First People. The deep listening – and looking – that this book brings offers many moments for pedagogical and andrological engagement and recognition of the ultimacy of relational belonging. These collected writings, presented at a time when 'Black Lives Matter' echoes as the catch-cry of a global network for justice and healing, bring together our encompassing knowledge systems beyond our singularity.

Acknowledgement

This chapter draws strongly on a publication jointly edited and published as Gilroy, A., Linnell, S., McKenna, T., & Westwood, J. (Eds.). (2019). *Art therapy in Australia: Taking a postcolonial, aesthetic turn*. Brill | Sense.

References

Banner, S. (2005). Why Terra Nullius? Anthropology and property law in early Australia. *Law and History Review, 23*(1), 95–131.

Gilroy, A., Linnell, S., McKenna, T., & Westwood, J. (2019). An introduction of sorts, or all kinds of introductions. In A. Gilroy, S. Linnell, T. McKenna, & J. Westwood (Eds.), *Art therapy in Australia: Taking a postcolonial; aesthetic turn* (pp. 2–42). Brill | Sense.

Griffiths, B. (2018). *Deep time dreaming: Uncovering ancient Australia*. Schwartz Publishing.

McKenna, T., & Woods, D. B. (2012). Using psychotherapeutic arts to decolonise counselling for Indigenous peoples. *Asia Pacific Journal of Counselling and Psychotherapy, 3*(1), 29–40. doi:10.1080/21507686.2011.631145

McKenna, T. J., Cacciattolo, M., & Mahon, L. (2011). Indigenous literacies: 'White Fella engagements'. *International Journal of Learning, 18*(1), 631–644.

Thorpe, K. (2014). Indigenous records: Connecting, critiquing and diversifying collections. *Archives and Manuscripts, 42*, 211–214. doi:10.1080/01576895.2014.911692

Tomlinson, D. (2008). *Too White to be regarded as Aborigines: An historical analysis of policies for the protection of Aborigines and the assimilation of Aborigines of mixed descent, and the role of Chief Protectors of Aborigines in the formulation and implementation of those policies, in Western Australia from 1898 to 1940* (PhD thesis). University of Notre Dame Australia. http://researchonline.nd.edu.au/theses/7

Universities Australia's Indigenous Strategy 2017–2020. (2020, February 27). Retrieved October 9, 2020, from https://www.universitiesaustralia.edu.au/policy-submissions/diversity-equity/universities-australias-indigenous-strategy-2017-2020/

Yunkaporta, T., & Kirby, S. (2011). Yarning up Aboriginal pedagogies: A dialogue about eight Aboriginal ways of learning. In N. Purdie, G. Milgate, & H. R. Bell (Eds.), *Two way teaching and learning: Toward culturally reflective and relevant education* (pp. 209–215). ACER Press.